To dear

Wishing eternal

of <u>HAPPINESS</u>! :)

SEVEN WONDERS
OF THE SELF

ACCESS YOUR
HEALING POWERS

Maria

15.11.23

SEVEN WONDERS OF THE SELF

ACCESS YOUR HEALING POWERS

MARIA ZHURAVLEVA

Matador
Unit E2 Airfield Business Park,
Harrison Road, Market Harborough,
Leicestershire. LE16 7UL
Tel: 0116 2792299
Email: books@troubador.co.uk
Web: www.troubador.co.uk/matador
Twitter: @matadorbooks

ISBN 978 1803134 789

British Library Cataloguing in Publication Data.
A catalogue record for this book is available from the British Library.

Printed and bound in Great Britain by 4edge Limited
Typeset in 11pt Adobe Caslon Pro by Troubador Publishing Ltd, Leicester, UK

Matador is an imprint of Troubador Publishing Ltd

Contents

CONTENTS

CONTENTS

Foreword

I would like to introduce you to your friend. It is in your hands now. This book loves you very much and wants to connect with you. It has told me to write it and put it into your hands, so you can read it and nourish yourself with this energy.

I have put something special in this book. I have put your own essence in this book. This book is a mirror of who you are and when you hold it in your hands, it is talking to you. Do not doubt your mirror; it has got something very special to tell you today.

Each word that I put in this book is you. It wants to see you and connect with you. Each word is alive and it would like to dance with you and have a great time together. The words have asked me if I can show them to you and introduce their wonderful energy. And then they came.

This book is alive and it has its own consciousness. It talks to you not only when you are reading it and holding it in your hands, but also when you are asleep, when you are having a good time with your friends, when you are walking in the park and looking at nature. This book is everywhere. And so are you.

I can see you in the leaves of the trees that are standing in the park. I can see you in the smiles of the children who are running by.

I can see you in the bright shining of the morning sun as it greets the world into a new day. I can see you in everything.

When you are holding this book, you connect to its energy. Sometimes just this magical touch is enough. Feel it with your heart, feel it with your soul. Don't try to explain or understand it, let the book explain itself. Let it connect you to your essence effortlessly, purely, with a lot of love in the heart. Let you enjoy every moment of the book and fly together, like two angels in the sky. I can see you there right now.

You are perfect as you are. You were born into this world to create beautiful energy and heal yourself. You were born to share your light with the others and serve them by being yourself. I truly love you.

Let this book be your guide and your friend. If there is something that you don't find in this book, don't worry. It is still there. Place your hand on one of the pages and ask for the information to come through. Then feel it in your heart and it will come to you that very moment. This is the magic of energy.

Walk step by step and savour every moment of the book. Let it explore you, love you, guide you, help you, make you feel good. Let it be your dear friend who cares about you and wants you to feel love all the time. I will be with you every moment of your journey.

It is such a joy to share this energy with you.

With a lot of love and magic,

Maria Zhuravleva

Introduction

This book came to me in a dream. I saw it spiraling down from the sky as I was lying on the green grass on a sunny day. The title of the book said: "Seven Wonders of the Self". At the time I didn't know what the book would be about, but I felt a strong inspiration to write it. It was almost like a message from above that I had to follow. So, I began.

It took me several years to solidify the material for the book, based on my experiences and healing work. Some parts of the book I received in meditations by focusing my energy to channel important knowledge for my healing practice. Some parts of it came from my actual work with people, such as Healing Energy Sessions and Quantum Healing Hypnosis Technique. My vision was to make the book simple and friendly and, at the same time, provide a chance for a deeper exploration of our own healing self.

My interest in spirituality began many years ago when I first came to the United Kingdom. It felt like a higher power invited me to explore the spiritual world and this is why it brought me to this beautiful country. I arrived here in 2010 to take a Master's Degree in Tourism, taking a break from work, unsure of what career I wanted to pursue afterwards. After trying several jobs in the past, from being a language teacher to a tourism manager, I still felt that I hadn't found my life purpose. It was almost like a sense of a void inside of me that needed to be filled in.

Just before I came to the United Kingdom, I received a very strong feeling that gave me the words 'intuition' and 'extrasensory'. Something inside of me said that I needed to look into these subjects and explore them properly. The inner voice was so strong that I listened to it and began to look for clues in the world around me. I started by searching the internet for more information and, to my astonishment, I found that there was so much happening in that area. There appeared to be an abundance of places where one could discover the spiritual world and meet like-minded people who share the same interests. Meditation, energy healing, yoga, healthy eating – it was all out there and waiting to be explored.

I felt irresistibly drawn to this fascinating subject. Everything around me began to manifest in a different way. People, who were interested in spirituality, would appear on my path in the most unusual circumstances. I joined many groups that taught about the Universe, energy healing, law of attraction and astral travelling. My reality started to change on many levels, as I opened to this new, or maybe long-forgotten, world inside of me.

I remember one particular instant when I was going through the homework assignment with a fellow student at Bournemouth University. All of a sudden, changing the subject, he began to talk about meditation and chakras and share information about his spiritual journey. He explained how to focus on the blue light in the third eye chakra and how to use it to connect to your inner self. I was listening spellbound to his story as it seemed so fascinating and magnetic. As he spoke, I could feel a change in the air around me, as though the time slowed down and magic appeared in the space. It felt like a different reality.

The Universe seemed to be giving me more and more opportunities to explore the world of spirituality. I could hear an inner "yes" to almost everything that I encountered on the spiritual path. I went to meditation classes, experienced yoga, joined several meet-up groups in London and attended practically every spiritual event that appeared in my reality. It was like remembering once again who I was and finding, to my delight, that there were so many like-minded souls on this path, too.

One day when I was in my studio room in Bournemouth looking through some YouTube videos, an interview with Dolores Cannon suddenly came up. I didn't know about Dolores at the time, but something inside of me strongly said: "Open the link." That voice was so powerful that I simply couldn't ignore it. As soon as I pressed it, I realised that I was right. Something unusual had happened. I heard the voice of Dolores, which was strong, profound and captivating at the same time. It was like an instant connection that echoed somewhere deep in my spirit. Immediately I was magnetised to the screen, feeling that an important shift was about to occur in me.

Dolores spoke about other dimensions, reincarnation, life after death, extraterrestrials, healing miracles and spirit guides. All these subjects had always intrigued me and deep inside I wanted to believe that they were true; however, I had never had a chance to hear about them in the outside world. Dolores confirmed all of it in her lecture. She spoke with such confidence and magnetism that I realised that my internal feelings were right. What struck me the most was that she explained that the Subconscious was the source of infinite knowledge within us and that it had the power to heal and transform an individual. I felt instantly connected to this information, as though I had always known it in my heart.

Dolores said that the Subconscious was the loving and all-knowing power that existed in each person. This power can be accessed at any time and it is possible to ask it for healing and guidance; this is what Dolores used in her Quantum Healing Hypnosis Technique (QHHT) sessions. Somehow, hearing that we all have a power that looks after us and knows everything about us made me very feel very emotional and touched. I almost remembered that this was my path to follow.

I have to say that I have always felt quite different from other people. As a young child, I used to feel very lonely and abandoned, as though I didn't belong to this planet and was sent here temporarily for some unknown reason. I did not feel comfortable in my own body and I had a hard time adjusting to my family and social surroundings. I was convinced that there was another life somewhere outside of this reality and I was missing that home dimension very much.

My only consolation was my inner world, where I would constantly imagine different fantasy beings, like fairies, gnomes and wizards, who would come and visit me in daydreams. I pleaded for them to manifest in my real life so we could talk on the physical level and exchange love and understanding, but that simply wouldn't happen. No matter how much I tried to imagine them appearing in my physical reality, it didn't work. It often left me feeling sad and disillusioned, because I knew that these beings existed but I just couldn't get in touch with them.

It wasn't until I discovered the work of Dolores Cannon that I realised that my being on this planet had a purpose and I was here to help other people. All of a sudden, my life started to have a meaning and I felt encouraged and loved by the Universe. I learnt in my QHHT sessions that many people came to Earth to help the planet raise its vibration and elevate the group consciousness. It is time for Earth to ascend to a new level now and many of us have incarnated here with this mission. It turned out that I was one of these people and I had an important job to complete. This realisation was soothing and exciting. Finally, I had found my purpose...

At the same time, by a fortunate coincidence or synchronicity, I met Miguel Chavez, who is a Reiki Master from Mexico. My first meeting with Miguel was an immediate eye-opener. As we sat in a vibrant café in Camden, he shared his passion about energy healing and said that Reiki had changed his life, opening his healing abilities. *Hand healing?* These two words ran through my heart like a lightning and, once again, I remembered who I was. I had to learn Reiki.

Within the same month, I booked the Reiki Level 1 course with Miguel, eager to explore the new world of energy healing. I felt completely confident that I was on the right path. I believe that this feeling comes when you finally connect to your true life purpose. My soul was happy and singing. I could feel the vibration changing in me already.

As soon as I did the Reiki attunement, I felt an immediate shift in my hands. It was as though I began to feel the energy of my hands with an increased power. Everything I touched and connected to responded with a vibration that I felt I could read and understand. It was like an old knowledge came back to me. I remember going to Regent's Park one day and stopping in awe in the middle of the glade, as I realised that I could sense the trees talking to me. I was amazed and deeply touched. Everything had energy and was vibrating with a frequency that I could understand! That discovery opened a new world for me and gifted me with an ability to feel energy and communicate with it through my hands.

On another occasion, while I was visiting a friend in Russia, we sat down one evening to talk about our life journeys. She asked me for some advice and I suddenly felt that I needed to take her hand and connect to the right answer there, instead of looking for a reply in my head. I felt that by touching her energy, I could give her a more truthful message. And indeed, as soon as I took her hand and closed my eyes, the words just started coming to me. My friend told me that the messages were truthful and helped her to see the situation in a better way. This was how I discovered that the energy of the hands contained important messages and we could read them just by touch.

Soon after I learnt Reiki, my healing energy practice started. I had a feeling that I needed to practise as much as possible to learn more about the technique, so I remember asking all my friends and relatives if they would like to have a free Reiki session. Many people were delighted to have this experience. And indeed, magic was happening during the sessions. I could feel the energy lifting up in the room and enveloping each person in the healing glow. It brought a peaceful sensation of relaxation and light to both of us.

One of my first volunteers was my grandmother, who wasn't feeling well at the time as her legs were constantly twitching and aching. To my surprise, she was open to having a Reiki session with me and received some benefits from it. She said that it had made her feel calmer and more comfortable, and her pain had subsided. I must say, it was quite challenging for me in the beginning to give healing to her, as her body was moving all the time, but this experience brought us closer together and gave me more trust in the healing process.

In about a year, I received an email from a friend saying that Dolores Cannon was coming to England to teach QHHT in September 2011. By that time, I had already read many of her books and even attended one of her lectures in London. I became a real admirer of Dolores Cannon, captivated by the depth and purity of her teachings and character. So, I decided to take this chance and learn the technique, even though the idea of practicing hypnosis seemed a bit daunting to me at the time.

The technique represents a profound session, in which a person experiences one or several of their past lives and receives contact with their Subconscious. This unique method helps to get important messages for the person's life path and bring physical and emotional healing through their own Subconscious. I feel very fortunate to have been able to learn the technique directly with the founder, Dolores Cannon, as, sadly, she passed away several years later.

The learning experience turned out to be precious and life-changing. The class took place in the small village of Farringdon in Oxfordshire, where we drove early in the morning. The night before, I had the most wonderful vision of some magical beings blowing green light into my hair and making me laugh and feel good at the same time. I felt that this was the preparation for the class.

We were a large group of about one hundred people in the class, all very friendly and eager to learn the fascinating technique. Dolores had a powerful magnetic presence, delivering the lecture in her loving and direct manner. During several days, we were taught how to conduct QHHT sessions and how to communicate with the Subconscious to bring the healing for the person. Needless to say, we were all mesmerised by the presence of Dolores, by the inspiration in her words and the power of the technique itself. We couldn't wait to start. The special vibration of light and healing was already in the air.

Upon returning to London, I started gaining practice in QHHT immediately, as Dolores had said, "Get as many people as you can to practise on in the start." I was excited to learn more about the technique and once again asked all my friends and acquaintances if they wanted to have a free session. The exploration started.

My first ever QHHT session was quite a funny one. I did not know exactly what to expect but I knew that I had to trust the Subconscious to do the healing work. My brave first 'client' was my partner at the time, called Mark. I was a bit worried, because it was my first attempt to connect to the person's Subconscious, and I didn't want Mark to experience anything strange or outside of his comfort zone. It turned out to be quite the opposite.

As soon as we started, Mark drifted into a very relaxed state and started to describe a beautiful walk in the forest. He began to give so many vivid details and was cooperating with me so much, that, in my naivety, I thought that he was just pretending to please me.

I remained suspicious throughout the session only to find out later that he couldn't remember anything about the session at all! He was one of those people who go into deep trance instantly and forget about what happens in a session. It was a lucky start for me. I was truly impressed with how this technique worked and it helped me to believe in the power of the Subconscious. Gradually, I learnt to trust that the Subconscious always does the best for each person.

We did a lot of healing with Mark in subsequent sessions and received important advice for his life path. I remember clearly one session when I asked the Subconscious about my QHHT work and learning progress. They said: "You are doing very well. You are doing better than anybody could have imagined. You **must** continue the work that we have chosen for you. There will be darker times, but you must always see the light. You must continue." These words have stayed with me till today.

Quantum Healing Hypnosis is a unique technique. With the help of deep relaxation and guided imagery, a person achieves a state where they can access memories of their past life and connect to their Subconscious. In the first part of the session, we explore one or several of their past lives and find out the story of that incarnation. That includes going through the main events in their life and following it up until the last day. We are mostly focused on finding out the lessons of that life and discovering how they are linked to their current life, as this is the essence of healing. It is interesting that whatever past life is shown to a person, of any time period or subject line, there is always an important message in it.

For example, a past life regression can help people to find reasons for the patterns in their behavior; explain feelings like fear, guilt, abandonment or mistrust; and determine the underlying causes for some physical and emotional ailments. It can also provide explanation for spiritual connections with other people and, on many occasions, share positive inspiration from the past into the future.

A very common type of a positive message from a past life is a person achieving success through self-belief and trust in their talents. Many past lives show great examples of people following their hearts and doing what they were called to do – for instance, writing, public speaking, healing. In these lives people usually feel very happy and content, because they follow their dreams and are not afraid to express their gifts. In this way the Subconscious prompts the person to find the courage to fulfil their dreams in this life. "If you did it in the past, you can do it again now," often says the Subconscious.

In the second part of the session, we access the Subconscious, the omnipotent source of love and knowledge that exists within each person and can give them healing and guidance. The Subconscious is capable of instantaneous healing during the session, if it decides that it is the right time to do it. It can also give advice to the person about how to be happy and fulfil their life purpose.

For example, the Subconscious can recommend the person to change their habits and focus more on themselves. They may explain that, in order to heal, the person needs to do more of what they love doing, like writing, dancing or painting. The Subconscious can also provide advice on lifestyle and general wellbeing. They always recommend to spend more time in nature and meditate regularly. "You have to listen to yourself and your feelings. Do what you enjoy the most." These precious words come from higher powers nearly in every session.

When the Subconscious does the healing, magic happens in the room. You can feel how the energy elevates and becomes very strong and transformative. The Subconscious scans the body of the person and finds the areas that need healing. Then they use the white light or a very high frequency energy to release the old pain from the body and replace it with healing and harmony. This is a powerful process that is fascinating to watch. It is even more astounding to observe how the person's life changes after the session, as the healing helps them to find their path.

I am very grateful to this technique as it has given me incredible knowledge throughout the years. The stories of people, who have had lives in many different historical periods, from ancient to modern times, share beautiful, timeless wisdom that we can apply in our life now. The sessions taught me that we come to Planet Earth in order to experience life in a physical form and learn how to deal with emotions in a human body. We incarnate because our soul wants to grow and evolve, and Earth is an advanced school where we can learn lessons such as love, patience, courage and more. This is why meditation and connection with our Subconscious is very important – it helps us to remember who we are and what our higher purpose is.

Meanwhile, I continued to work with Reiki and my energy powers began to open up. I felt that the energy was communicating with me through my hands and guiding me in a certain direction. I experienced a new type of energy, which told me to move my hands and create colours and shapes in order to reach a higher healing state. I listened to my hands and began to interact with this energy and create beautiful motions with my palms. This practice gave birth to my technique, Energy Creation, which I now teach in my classes.

Energy Creation is a playful technique that is based entirely on intuition and the energy of the hands. It allows the person to channel their own power and create high healing vibrations in their body and aura. The beauty of this practice is that, by listening to your hands, you become your inner creator and you choose what frequency you would like to invite into your life. It can be the energy of love, joy, miracles, freedom or any uplifting vibration that you need the most now. Then, within seconds, the healing energy begins to appear and transform your whole being, on the level of frequency. Like magic wands, your hands become your teachers and they guide you to heal your body and receive answers to your questions.

I feel that it is time now for people to start channeling their own healing gifts, without referring too much to the outside source. We are all healers by nature and we can create any energy that we like in our life. This is a gift that has been forgotten, but it is coming back now to Planet Earth. Energy Creation is one of the techniques that will help humanity to discover once again their powerful abilities to heal the body and manifest their reality. Most importantly, this technique will help us to feel creative and playful again, something that every person is looking for in their life.

For many years I have been running Healing Energy Workshops in London, which have become quite popular and attracted a wonderful group of people. We meditate, play with energy and experiment with directing the flow of light with our hands. The participants often describe a blissful sensation when they work with energy because they feel that they can perform magic with their hands and heal themselves and other people. I am grateful to these precious classes as they became the inspiration for my Energy Creation practice.

Sometimes I feel like an explorer of energy who arrived to this world to translate the information from the energy dimension into the physical realm. It is often challenging to live in both worlds, shifting between the energetic and the physical and adjusting to various types of frequencies, but I feel that it is important to bring the messages to people and connect the two worlds together. This way we can reach a level of awareness where we receive information naturally from the subtle energy realm and help each other to transform our lives.

I believe that the main thing that I learnt during this time is that magic is possible. This is the question that had always touched me as a child: why don't people on Earth believe in magic and use it in their lives? Why do we have to follow the limitations of the physical world without opening up to our greater gifts? I felt that I wanted to bring this energy here, but I didn't know how. Now I feel that I am getting closer to the answer. Magic is in our hands, our hearts and our own energy. We can heal and transform the energy just like magic.

I must say that I have been blessed to have had so many wonderful people on my journey and to have explored the world of energy together. With every practice, more light is coming into our lives and more kindness is being spread into the world. I believe that, if we continue to explore our own gifts of healing and empowerment, we will be able to conquer many diseases and emotional imbalances that we currently experience. And then we can allow peace and loving energy to be our guides in a beautiful life on Earth.

Just like the famous Seven Wonders of the World, we, as human beings, have our own Seven Wonders. But our wonders are not written in books or studied in historical lectures. Our wonders are **here and now**, in our own body, ready to be tapped into by us and used for the greatest healing power.

I invite you to look within your body to find the Seven Wonders of the Self inside of you. These wonders are here to serve you and to bring the most precious changes into your life. These wonders are simple and yet deep, and they will transform your life in miraculous ways.

This book will take you on a magical journey of your gifts and will provide practical exercises to explore each one of them. Your wonders deserve your loving time, so it is recommended to go through the practices slowly, savouring every moment of meditation. Each time you repeat an exercise, you will learn something new about your wonderful self, so keep exploring and learning.

Enjoy being your own healer!

ONE

EVERYTHING IS ENERGY

Let's imagine for a moment that everything is made of energy.

Take a deep breath and connect to the world around you through energy. Imagine the trees, the people, the houses, the earth, the water, the air – all that there is. Feel that our entire world is vibrating at a certain frequency with the energy flowing constantly between its various forms.

Let's relax and feel it for a moment.

Now imagine that things that we cannot see, like sounds, thoughts, emotions, intentions and even dreams, also have energy. Recreate them in your space now. Feel them vibrating all around you.

Now visualise that your body is also made of energy and imagine that it is vibrating at a certain frequency. Feel your entire being: your head, your heart, your solar plexus, your hands – all connected and alive now.

This is our world. This is our being. This is our entire Universe.

The energy of the world is moving around in a constant flow: creating, joining, shaping, manifesting.

The energy flows through every vein of the world, like the breath of the Universe. Everything is created from energy and everything transforms into energy. The essence of every being on the planet is energy, including the planet itself.

In this constant flow of energy, we find ourselves having an experience in a physical form and learning more about who we are.

We begin this journey as little babies who are unaware of the physical world but have a beautiful inner spirit. Then we grow and we learn how to live in a physical body. We grow into who we are now, at this very moment, being in your space and feeling the energy.

What do you feel about yourself? Who are you? What is your place in the Universe? What do you perceive from your own energy?

You can connect with yourself now and feel your inner essence. The energy of your spirit will tell you more about you, if you just ask. This is the best way to find answers to your questions – through energy.

We are like colourful fishes that swim in the currents of life and flow from one experience to another. On our journey, we are joining other fish, exploring the corals, swimming near the surface or diving more in deep waters. Following the currents of the sea, we create our experiences and move through different elements of our life.

We are the fish and yet we are the currents ourselves, representing the big energy that forms our reality. We are the currents in the sea and yet we are the sea itself, being part of the source and having an effect on all that there is around us. We are the little fishes and the eternal ocean at the same time.

We are part of all and all is part of us. Everything we do, think and feel has an effect on the reality around us. We are all intrinsically connected through the energy of life, which is the breath of the Universe.

For example, when we have a thought, it is born in our mind and it flows into the space around us. It is real, it is alive. Another person can pick up our thought and feel it; the same way it happens with emotions, feelings, intentions and other energies that we share with each other, even when we are keeping them inside. We feel every vibration around us. Everything is connected.

All that happens has a cause and an effect. We have an effect on everybody around us, on the places that we go to and on our own physical bodies. In the same way, we are influenced by the people we meet, the places we spend time in and the objects that we interact with. It is a constant exchange of energy. Everything is linked. We are all part of the One.

When we are aware of our energy and the power to create every moment of our life, we are capable of changing our experiences in a positive way. We begin to realise that everything that we think and do has an effect on our reality and we can start using this energy in a healthier way, choosing the right frequencies for ourselves. We become our own Masters of Energy, planting beautiful seeds for our future life.

ENERGY FEELS DIFFERENTLY

All energy around us and inside of us has a vibration. It is a certain frequency that is emitted into the world like a radio station. In this broadcasting there are millions and millions of various frequencies that all feel differently and play various types of energy in our life.

We may or we may not like a particular radio station when we are listening to it. Some music may be too loud or too slow, while other tunes may feel wonderful and be just perfect for our ears. In the same way, we react to different energies around us.

It is through our feeling that we perceive what type of energy we come into contact with.

In general, we can view energy as having a higher or a lower frequency. Within it, there are many subtypes – for example, more neutral energies, stronger or softer energies, energies with various flavours, like peace, love and joy. But, on the whole, energy can make us feel in two different ways: it can either uplift us or bring us down.

We know very well our reaction when we come into contact with a certain energy. We have an inner feeling that tells us exactly how the frequency of our body responds to this energy. This feeling may be subtle, but it is always there, serving to discern between different types of energy. With practice, our ability to understand and feel energy increases as we are becoming more aware of the abundant range of frequencies around us.

Energy can take different forms in our life. For example, energy can be represented in the people that we meet every day. You notice that some people make you feel very uplifted and joyful, while others may evoke less pleasant feelings in you. This is because your vibration responds differently to the various vibrations of people who come into contact with you.

Similarly, you may have different reactions to the places that you go to. There will be spaces where you feel cosy and comfortable and you want to stay there longer, and at the same time, there may be others that make you feel uneasy and even ill. It is all about the energy.

There is not one rule about what kind of energy is right for us – it all depends on our own frequency and how we feel about it.

Energy talks differently to different people as it has its own way to connect through the vibration. You can ask yourself: "How do I feel now?" to understand more about the frequency that you encounter.

If you ask yourself questions about how you feel, you can determine whether a certain energy is comfortable for you or not. For example, you can ask: "What happens inside of me when I am in contact with this energy? Does it make me feel good or not?"

High-vibrational energy will make you feel good and uplift you. Low-vibrational energy will bring you down and evoke unpleasant sensations in you.

High-vibrational energy can be represented in feelings, thoughts, nature, music and different objects in our life. This frequency incorporates everything that makes us feel good, happy and energised. The origins of this energy are all the beautiful feelings that we experience in life, such as love, joy, happiness, laughter, peace, acceptance and unity. These energies elevate our being, bring the connection to our true selves and help us to heal internally.

High-frequency energy can be encountered in the wonderful people around us who give us love and joy. We feel good when we are with people like that and we want to stay longer in their company. These people carry a high vibration and help us to remember this frequency in ourselves. Our interaction becomes healing and we usually feel energised and happy after meeting these people.

The works of art that are intended to bring positive emotions and make people feel good are also carriers of high frequency. When we go to a theatre play that is full of love and kindness, we feel joyful from within and our spirits rise. Similarly, a painting with bright shiny colours, which emits the energy of harmony, can bring a smile to our face. This is the high vibration working its magic.

When we encounter a high-vibrational energy, it begins to work with us through its frequency. We don't have to do anything; just receive it and enjoy.

All that there is in nature: trees, plants, flowers, rivers, seas, the sun, the moon and the earth – are made of high-vibrational energy. There is a certain lightness and tranquility that we experience when we come in touch with nature. We often notice that we feel a lot calmer and happier surrounded by trees or water. If we could see the energy with our eyes, we would notice a powerful light emanating from nature – this is the healing manifestation of high energy in the physical realm.

Healing is the natural quality of high energy.

Creations that are produced by people with love and positive emotions are naturally filled with high frequencies. These are the books that make our heart feel good, the music that is delightful to our ears, the clothes that feel special for the body, the food that is cooked with joy. We can find a high-vibrational energy practically everywhere, if we look closely.

When we experience a positive emotion, we add a special ingredient into the space around us. It is like a wave of light that is emanating from us and lifting up the vibration of all that there is around. Magic happens in the air and for a moment we step into a different dimension of being. Have you noticed how wonderful it feels when you are in love?

The manifestations of high-vibrational energy elevate our being and make us feel happy. When we come in contact with high frequencies, we forget our sorrows, release the weight of heavy emotions, open to the light and begin to smile. Healing happens naturally when we encounter higher energies.

There is an abundance of natural high-frequency energy around us, which we come in contact with every day. Some of us are aware of it consciously and look for it; others just connect to it unconsciously. However, this energy is free and available and, what is most important, can be created and reproduced by us.

High-frequency energy is a reminder of positive aspects within us. Every time we come in contact with high frequency, we activate our own positive energy.

6

On the opposite side, there is a low and dense frequency. These are the energies that carry a lower vibration, like anger, frustration, fear, worry, stress and so on. When we experience these feelings or find them in the outside world, we can feel sad, confused, scared and less able to express ourselves freely.

Lower frequencies affect our energy field and bring us down.

When we regularly come in touch with these frequencies, the world may start to seem unhappy, making us see the reality through the prism of darkness. Everything begins to appear wrong and one upsetting thing attracts another one, giving us an illusion that we are trapped.

Denser frequencies have a tendency to become sticky and habitual. Once we believe in the low frequency and give in to it, this illusionary power can begin to take over our thoughts and actions. It may seem that we are surrounded by these energies and they are in everything that we see. This is why it is helpful to focus on the light and maintain our own frequency.

Low energies can creep into spaces like old houses, historical buildings and places with a lot of saturated energy from the past. They can also be found in the places where people activate lower vibrations – for example, through arguments, violence, control or fear. You will always sense a lower energy place when you step into it – something will feel uncomfortable and not right for you.

People around us can sometimes carry dense vibrations, too. This energy can be a result of being upset, annoyed, angry or holding on to the past. When we encounter such frequencies, we intuitively feel the heaviness and lower energy in the person's aura. This situation can be tricky for sensitive people as they may feel uncomfortable meeting such dense vibrations and being in their presence for a long time. If we approach it with understanding, this could be seen as an opportunity to learn more about energy and perhaps even to help the other person by saying a kind word. There is no place for judgement when we see somebody carrying a lower energy – we all go through complicated emotional lessons in our life. At the same time, we have a choice of what kind of vibrations we want to surround ourselves with when we meet new people.

Artificial foods, chemicals, some modern technology, loud distorted sounds, hurtful rude words – all these have a lower frequency and some are even harmful for our environment. Many of these creations appear from the space of a limited awareness, because some people may not realise what they are bringing into the outer world and how it affects other people and the space. Not everybody is aware yet of how energy works.

Our own destructive and unloving thoughts and feelings of hurt, mistrust, shame, anger or jealousy can also produce a lower vibrational effect on ourselves and the world around. Sometimes we can't do anything about it and these feelings just take us over. This is part of learning the emotions on Earth and, fortunately, there are many practices that can help us to grow spiritually and transcend lower feelings. We are learning to balance our emotions and create a more harmonic relationship with ourselves and the world.

While there is a space in our reality for both high and low energies, we can make a conscious choice of which energies to interact with on our life path. Every second of our life, we are choosing what kind of energy to accept into our frequency and what to leave behind. Our inner guidance will help us to understand which energies are our friends and which energies it may be time for us to release.

We choose which energies we come in touch with and what we would like to learn from them. We have the power to surround ourselves with higher frequencies and let them heal our body and soul. It is a choice.

Imagine a child sitting at a white table, holding pieces of modelling clay in his hands. The child is looking at the variety of colours – green, yellow, red, blue, white – and choosing how to put them together in order to create something beautiful. This is us manifesting our life experiences through choosing different energies and shaping them together with our feelings, thoughts and actions.

The energy just is. We may call it differently and assign various labels to it but, ultimately, the energy is just energy. It is our purpose to find our way in life and choose the right vibrations for us.

In the current time, the Earth is experiencing a rise in vibration and is shifting from lower frequencies to higher frequencies. Together with the Earth, many people are experiencing an awakening and starting to feel new energies of a lighter character in their life. They are getting more in touch with themselves and the spiritual world. Our divine wisdom is coming back to us; the pearl that has been kept deep inside of our spirit for centuries is ready to shine again.

As a result of this shift, many people are becoming aware of energies and are starting to look for their true life purpose. People are beginning to realise the power in their hands and the ability to create their own reality. We are becoming increasingly interested in looking after nature, treating ourselves with alternative healing, finding ways to connect to our bodies, and helping each other. It is a beautiful time to live in now. We are blessed.

ENERGY INTERACTS

Energy is like water – it is constantly moving, flowing, joining and separating. Energy carries a frequency and comes in touch with other frequencies, often attracted to the ones that carry the same vibration. It is like people who get drawn to each other because of similar interests.

Energy is in a constant flow and activity. It is influencing and being influenced by other energies around and experiencing continuous interaction on the vibrational level. A leaf on a tree sends out a vibrational frequency to the air; the people who walk by are breathing the air into their body, as a result of which their body elevates and releases the stress. It is a constant process of energy exchange that we don't always realise on the physical level.

We have to feel the energy in order to understand the world in a deeper way.

Energy has a very important quality – it can transform itself and other energies. As soon as a certain kind of frequency appears in the space, it begins to affect everything in it. Every drop of energy has the power to change the vibration and it influences the space instantly. As such, energy can be transformed to a very high frequency with the power of our intention and a directed inner flow. This is where the magic of healing happens.

When we focus on high energy, we create a very concentrated solution of goodness where lower energies can naturally dissolve. High energy is a natural healer.

In this manner, the energy of love and laughter transmutes pain and misery, peace and relaxation relieve stress, joy and happiness disperse grief and discontent. High energy is like a very good loyal friend who takes lower frequencies by the hand and helps them to see the light and change in a positive way.

Lower frequencies can also have an effect on higher frequencies. When lower energy comes into the space of high frequencies, the space can become cloudy and the tone of energy can go down. This can affect the mood of the participants and the atmosphere in that space.

The cunning nature of lower energies is such that they often take our attention away from higher frequencies and temporarily make us forget about the light inside of us. When we are overwhelmed by pain and sadness, it is hard to focus on the light and see hope in front of us. This is why humanity has been given so many tools to work with lower energies and help us step into the higher dimensions. We can learn to work with our feelings and uplift our energy from within with the help of meditation and energy healing practice.

When lower energies are brought into the light of awareness, they can dissolve like darkness in the rays of the morning sun. Then they begin to lose their relevance for us, and our energy field starts to cleanse and uplift. And we are the ones who can make it happen.

People are the great magicians who have the power to transform energy with their minds and their hands. This is the power that is yet to fully come to humanity in the near future.

ENERGY AND THE BODY

Just like the Universe is a cosmos of energy that emanates different frequencies, our body is a Universe of energy with a myriad of vibrations in it.

Every thought, every emotion, every feeling, every sound brings a particular energy to our body and aura.

Imagine if we had magical glasses through which we could perceive energy; we would see a fascinating picture. All our organs would shine with energy and light. Some light would be brighter, some may be dimmer. This energy inside of us would be constantly vibrating and interchanging. We would notice that we can be affected by the way we feel and by the experiences that we go through in life.

Throughout our body there would be energy centres, which are the vortices of energy and are connected to important parts of our body, such as the head, eyes, throat, heart, stomach, sacral, hands, feet and so on. These are the chakras that are responsible for the energy flow in the corresponding organs and represent the powers that we have in this life, such as the connection to the divine, intuition, expression, love, willpower, creativity, survival, grounding and others. Each energy centre is equally important and carries a significant role for our happiness and wellbeing.

From the top of our head, we would see a ray of light that connects us to the sky above. From our feet, we would see a flow of energy that goes down into the earth. This is our connection on this planet. We are constantly interacting with the cosmos and the earth and exchanging energy with it, which is naturally healing.

Around our body we would see a shiny ball of light that we carry with us all the time. It is our energy field. There we can find the imprints of our thoughts, emotions, intentions, experiences, memories and many other frequencies that are created in our life. These imprints are like radio frequencies and can be perceived by other people energetically, sometimes through awareness and sometimes unconsciously.

Whatever we go through in our life has an effect on our body and energy. A word said by another person, a film watched on TV, a deep emotion felt in the heart, the food eaten at dinner – every particular vibration has its special effect on us and these changes often happen without us even realising it.

In an ideal world, people want to remember their power to create a happy, balanced and abundant life. We want to cherish the fact that our body has cells that can renovate and replenish on a regular basis. We want to acknowledge that the healing energies are available around us all the time, in the shape of nature, water, earth, cosmos, the sun. The truth is that we can create healing energy and direct it into our body at any time, just with our own hands and imagination.

Once we learn how to use the healing energy kindly provided to us by the Universe, we can significantly advance in our spiritual development and wellbeing. We will understand that any situation can be explained and transformed with the help of energy, and we can just ask the higher power for guidance and healing. There is abundant free energy on the planet; all we need to do is to become aware of this gift and use it with love.

It takes some awareness and belief to begin to use the energy in a healing way. At the moment, the majority of people are still following the mind and scientific findings as the main route to receive information. People need to connect more to their own feeling and intuition, so more pathways for healing can be open. This will come with an open mind and complete trust in our powers, something that we are beginning to learn about now.

Sensing energy is crucial for our development and the expansion of our healing gifts.

When we learn how to feel energy, we become capable of discerning between higher and lower frequencies. We realise that lower frequencies can affect our health and create illnesses. We also notice that stress weakens our immune system and breaks the natural flow of energy in the body. This awareness gives us an opportunity to choose the experiences that are beneficial for our energy. With the help of higher frequencies, we can gradually restore the balance in the body and bring the healing energy to our system.

The experiences that we have, the places that we go to, the people that we interact with, even the music that we listen to – all the smallest details of our everyday life affect our energy and the way that we feel.

Everything affects everything and it all happens on the level of energy. There is not a single experience that our body cannot hear or feel – it perceives it all. Our body is constantly listening, interacting and communicating with us. When we become aware of energy, we can then choose which frequency to cooperate with and how to channel the healing energy with our own hands.

We need to realise our power to heal and look after ourselves. For a long time, we have been giving our power away and relying on outside help. It is time now to bring our gifts back and help to transform our lives with our own energy.

THE ELEMENTS OF HEALTHY ENERGY

Energy can manifest itself in different ways. It can be happy and balanced or low and distorted, depending on what frequency it carries, just like people can have different moods and feelings.

If we look carefully at energy and observe it in its natural state, we will notice that energy enjoys a free movement. We see it in water, in the breath, in the air, in music. Energy likes a **flow**.

Just like the oceans, which contain eternal drops of water that unite and merge and dance together in a free motion, the energy in our body also likes free movement. Our cells are like water – deep within they are interconnected and communicating with each other. They have memory and consciousness and can feel everything that is happening. Like water in the ocean, our body enjoys a free flow of energy.

Free flow in the body is a natural healthy state of energy. The more we allow the energy to move in the body, the better we will feel.

The cells in the body can also hear and receive messages. They are constantly listening to all that we are thinking, feeling, saying and experiencing. We are the most important voice for our cells, which tells them what to do. We are interacting with our body all the time.

Our cells are aware and, like any other being on Earth, they want to be loved and to radiate love. Being an integral part of our body, our cells look for appreciation and kindness coming from us. **Love** is the frequency that makes the energy heal and transform.

When we experience love, we heal from within and come back to our natural state of being. The energy enjoys the feeling of love just like we do. As soon as love enters our space, the molecules of energy transform instantly and turn into a beautiful balanced structure.

Love is the highest healing energy.

Energy has a lot in common with music as they both produce different frequencies. They can travel, they can move, they can be created by us and brought out into the world. Just like musical notes, energy consists of different elements connected together, which constitute an energy flow.

If we want to create a beautiful orchestra, all the instruments in the band have to be in tune and play together as a team. The energy needs to be in **harmony**. The same pattern works for our body – all the organs need to be in harmony so they can create healing energy for us.

Everywhere around us we see harmony: in trees, in flowers, in the sea, in perfect geometric shapes. Looking at harmony makes our hearts feel warm and happy. When we recreate the natural harmony inside of us, we are bringing healing for our body and mind.

Flow, love and harmony are the elements of healthy energy.

In this book we will journey together to create the special musical notes that are needed for the healing of our body. We will join in the flow, love and harmony so our energy can go back to its most natural way and smile again.

TWO

THE 1ST WONDER OF THE SELF: WE CAN HEAR

The Universe is made of sounds, voices, whispers – all kinds of frequencies that reach our ears daily. The Universe also creates silence, which, on another level, also comes to our awareness.

All the sounds in the Universe have an effect on how we feel and help us to receive information from the world around us. Some sounds make us feel uplifted and happy – for example, kind words, harmonic music, joyful laughter and the whisper of the leaves in the trees. Other sounds can make us feel less balanced and bring our energy down, such as the roaring of cars, the noise of heavy machinery, loud music, angry words and shouting.

These various frequencies enter our ears and influence our energy. This interaction happens all the time. We constantly perceive information from the world around us and, consciously or unconsciously, become aware of the subtle messages from the Universe.

Our ears are a gift. They give us the power to communicate with the outer world and receive information about it. With the help of the ears, we understand the speech of other people, the spirit of nature, the language of the animals. Without the ears, we wouldn't be able to perceive the full glory of our life on Earth. The sounds of the sea, the rumbling of the thunderstorm, the purring of the cat, the laughter of our loved ones – this is what makes our experience on Earth so special.

Close your eyes and just listen to the sounds around you for a moment. What do you hear?

Interestingly, our ears operate in two dimensions at the same time: the physical and the psychic. While we can hear the sounds of the Universe with our physical ears, we can also perceive intuitive information from the energy world with our inner ears.

Our non-physical ears are receiving messages and guidance from all the sources around us. We get unconscious messages about people when we meet them: what they are like and what they are thinking. We receive information about the characteristics of objects when we touch them and feel their energy. Nature, in the shape of the trees and the earth, communicates with us constantly through its vibration. Even houses and buildings interact with us as we pass by, sharing information about their history. In reality, we hear much more than we can ever imagine.

There is a power within us that helps us to hear all these messages. And this power is called intuition.

Our intuition is the main guide on our path that provides direction for our life journey.

Intuition is a wonderful gift that we receive at birth. Everybody has a very strong intuition, even if they don't realise it. Intuition is the most important source of guidance in our life and it goes beyond the conscious mind, connecting us to the divine realm of knowledge.

It is our intuition that helps us to understand and heal our own body. We are constantly receiving messages about our health, our needs, our wishes and our energy flow. Our inner ears connect to our intuition and tell us exactly what is happening in our body. If we stay tuned in to this channel of information, we can find out how to help our body in the best way.

Every moment we have a chance to perceive higher guidance from our intuition.

We were blessed with the gift of the sacred connection to our body, and this is the source of information that we need to turn to in the first place when we want to heal. Who, if not our body, will know the reason why it hurts? Who, if not our body, will find the best way to heal and replenish it?

The wisdom is always within us and it is our responsibility to listen to our inner guidance and act upon it.

THE BODY SPEAKS

Imagine that our body is a living being that has its own thoughts, emotions, desires and visions. Every day the body is going through many experiences and it has a necessity to communicate its feelings to us.

The body finds its way of reaching out to us by giving us a sensation. It may be a feeling of joy, a feeling of happiness, or it may be an expression of anger, sadness or frustration. The body will communicate everything that is going on inside of us. When some of our emotions are out of balance, the body will try to show it through an evident sensation so we can get the message. For example, we may feel low, tired, hazy in the head or lacking inner power.

When we don't understand the message, the body may create a symptom to bring it across in a stronger way. Every symptom, whether it is big or small, is a message from the body that something important needs to be addressed in our lives. We may be in a wrong relationship or perhaps we spend too much time at work, creating a lack of balance in our life. Symptoms that have been there for a long time may be connected to our experiences from the past. These messages need to be looked into on a deeper level so they can be understood and healed.

The body is asking us to pay attention to it by creating a symptom.

Sometimes the body finds it difficult to process certain emotions, for example, excessive fear or worry. It may be overwhelmed by the amount of stress that we experience every day, which leaves the body little chance to release the emotion on its own. The body cannot cope with too much unbalanced energy and, after some time, it may decide to manifest it in a physical symptom to show us that something is wrong in our lives. This is where illness begins to show.

The body stores the emotions that we go through and can manifest them in the physical form.

It is important to remember that our body is like a treasure box of wisdom that is communicating with us on a daily basis. It knows exactly what is happening to us physically, emotionally, mentally and spiritually. It wants to make sure that we are balanced and healthy on all levels. The body will let us know if we need to change our lifestyle and thinking, so it can function in a better way.

We are the power that our body believes and follows. The body is constantly listening to our thoughts and feelings. The body may or may not agree with the choices that we make in life, but its internal wisdom will always guide us on the path of healing. We can maintain the connection with our body by listening to its voice and trusting our instincts.

The body is acting in our best interest and wants us to live in happiness and harmony.

In the contemporary world, the connection with our body is not as strong as it used to be. Nowadays too much attention is given to pharmaceutical products, media and unnatural ways of healing the body. Our loving attention to ourselves is taken away by the illusion that the outside world is the only source of help. People don't always listen to their bodies as they are afraid that they won't be able to heal themselves. So, they put the responsibility on other people instead.

This way of thinking starts when we are small and we are taught to develop our analytical skills at school. A lot of attention is given to understanding and memorising the external information, instead of helping people to learn to trust themselves and channel their inner knowledge. This limits the development of our intuition, which is so vital for being happy and reaching our goals in life. If we were to learn meditation and intuitive healing from a young age, this could prevent so much sadness in our society.

INTUITION AND THE CONSCIOUS MIND

Our intuition is the bridge that connects us to our higher consciousness and brings important information for our wellbeing. It always acts in our best interest as it knows what is really good for us. Intuition is a subtle voice that guides us in life, like a compass. It is more of a feeling than a conscious thought and is often represented by a 'first sensation' that we get about a certain situation. "Something tells me that I should…" – these are the words that our intuition usually whispers to us.

Intuition is similar to an inner calling that comes from deep within. For example, if we repeatedly feel that our body needs some exercise and a healthier diet, this is probably our intuition trying to tell us something. We just **know** that we have to do it.

Then our analytical mind can find millions of reasons not to do it, but the underlying feeling is always there.

The mind resembles a restless kid who is trying to get our attention and distract us from our true connection with ourselves. It is shouting, screaming, making comments and trying to explain everything that we see. An overactive conscious mind can cloud our intuitive perception and suggest only limited solutions based on past experiences and the reasoning of the head.

The purpose of our thinking mind is analysis, comparison, strategy and basic functioning in our reality. While it is good for many everyday activities like planning and learning new things, when we listen to the conscious mind too much, it can become very loud and overwhelming and take our attention away from our true wisdom.

"Don't listen to your feeling!" the mind says. "Listen to me! Give me proof. Explain. Help me to understand. Give me a reason!"

This loud voice represents only a tiny fraction of ourselves. In essence, our higher consciousness is much bigger and wiser than our daily thoughts. The conscious mind just enjoys our attention and is in a constant search for reasons, doubts and questions. It is far from the real deep knowledge that we have. Listening to the mind, we can sometimes forget that we have access to natural guidance from within and can receive precious advice at any time.

As a result, we rely more on what we hear from other people and the information that we get from the outside world. We try to fit into the picture that the mind has created for us and we don't always notice that it is a very small box for us to live and play in. The moment that we connect to our intuition during meditation, we feel free and powerful again.

Then the real truth starts to come out. We realise that we are the creators of our life and we can expand to eternity, manifesting in any shape that we like. We understand that we are the holders of a unique energy that can be directed for healing our body and empowering our life.

The real source of wisdom is kept in our hearts and our intuitive connection. It is like a beautiful river of light that is given to us from birth and it brings us truthful messages every day. This power knows how to help us and we can learn to communicate with it just by listening to it.

Awareness, inner work and meditation are the pathways that will open our connection to the intuitive realm of knowledge. Enjoy this exercise to connect to your higher power and balance your heart and mind.

PRACTICE TIME
MEETING YOUR HEART, MIND AND INTUITION

◊ Find a comfortable position and close your eyes. Take several deep breaths until you feel that your body is calm and relaxed.

◊ In your inner world, imagine a beautiful room of your choice. It is a delightful, wonderful space. Let it come to you naturally as your first impression. What does your room look like? See it with all the details: the colours, the lights, the furniture, the textures, the atmosphere. Explore the room as much as you can.

◊ Now imagine that there is a door in this room. The door opens and you can see somebody coming in. It is your Heart. See your Heart coming into the room and sitting at the table. What does your Heart look like? Imagine it in a way that comes first to you. It can take the shape of a person, a colourful energy or just a feeling. What do you feel from your Heart? How does it act when it comes into the room? Ask your Heart if it has a message for you today. Listen to the first impressions that come to you.

◊ Now the door opens again and your Intuition comes in. See what your Intuition looks like. How does it act? What does it do? Explore everything in detail as you watch it entering the room. Let your Intuition sit down at the table and interact with your Heart. How do they speak with each other? Observe your Intuition and your Heart and spend some time with them. You can ask your Intuition for a message for you.

◊ The door is opening again and now you can see your Mind coming in. Observe it. What does your Mind look like? Picture it coming into the room and finding its place at the table. How does your Mind act? What impression does it give to you? Does it say anything or make any gestures? Invite your Mind to sit at the table and join the other participants.

◊ Watch the Heart, the Intuition and the Mind interact with each other. How do they communicate? How do they feel about each other? Are any of them louder than the others? Are they helping each other in any way? Ask your Mind for a message if you like.

◊ Now let all the guests hold hands together and connect. Slow down and feel the unity of these three aspects of yourself. Imagine how the healing energy is spreading through them and enriching each one of them. What is happening now? How do you feel?

◊ Now that all your three aspects are united, see if you want to ask them a question. It can be something important about your life or yourself. Just direct this question to the three participants at the table and see how they respond. You may find that each of them responds differently. Feel the answers intuitively and listen to your first impressions.

◊ When you are finished, thank all the participants for their help and encouragement. Thank them for being in your life and for assisting you. Leave the scene with much love and gratitude. Take several deep breaths and slowly come back to the current moment. Take your time to orientate yourself completely in your space.

HOW DOES THE BODY SPEAK?

The body gives messages. Whatever it wants to say, it does so in the form of inner awareness, sensations or physical symptoms.

The body can communicate to us through a feeling or a sense of knowing, for example, when we feel we need to relax more in order to feel better. This is the body asking us to pay attention to it and step on the right path. The mind might find a reason to stop this intuitive message and say something like "I need to finish my work first", "There is no time to relax", "Not today" and so on. But the body always knows the truth and will keep giving us helpful guidance.

If we get an inner calling that sounds like "Pay attention to me", "Have some rest", "Drink more water", "We don't need so much sugar", it is our body trying to communicate with us. We need to listen to it and act upon it even if our conscious mind is protesting. The voice of the body is always right.

If we receive a symptom, this is a powerful message from our body. It usually means that something is not working on an energetic, physical or emotional level in our life and the body is trying to reach out to us in order to fix it. The body knows how to be in harmony and peace, so it creates a symptom to notify us of the lack of balance. If we don't listen to the first intuitive sensation, the symptom can become stronger, as the body will keep drawing our attention to it.

The body may create an itch, a pain, a discomfort, a burning sensation or any other signal for us to notice. It will find the most obvious way to communicate to us so we can look at the symptom and face it. Ignoring a symptom is like ignoring a phone call from a friend who wants to give us some important information for our wellbeing.

Every symptom contains a message; the way to understand it is to connect it to the underlying feeling that comes with it.

It may be a good idea to write down a list of all your symptoms, whether they are strong or subtle, to get a clear picture of how the body is trying to talk to you. You can create one column for the symptom and its description and another column for the intuitive feeling that you get from it. You can then meditate, connecting with your body and asking the following questions about your symptoms so you can get more intuitive messages from your Higher Self.

For example, if you receive a pain in a particular part of your body, notice what this pain means to you. How does it feel? What kind of a physical sensation is it? Strong or soft, pinching or throbbing? How often does it come? What aspect of your life does this pain remind you of? How long have you had this pain for? When did it first appear? What was happening in your life at that time? You can explore it and understand what the body is trying to tell you just by closing your eyes and asking yourself these questions.

All the body wants for you is to be well. It wants you to live happily and be in harmony at all times, so if you are doing something that disrupts the balance, the body will notify you immediately. Creating a physical symptom or speaking through our intuition are the best ways for the body to reach out to us.

In this book you will find the exercises that have proved helpful in my practice to connect to the body and begin the healing process from within. Looking after yourself may take some time and diligence, but the fruit of your self-care will be the most delightful.

IT IS BETTER TO LISTEN EARLIER THAN LATER

The body is an incredibly clever being that is constantly trying to help us. It is deeply connected with all our emotions and experiences and it gives us a red signal if something goes wrong.

It always starts with a little prompt, in the form of inner awareness or a sensation. We may get a feeling that something is wrong or receive a lower vibration in a certain part of the body. We may also feel intuitively that something in our lives is not working and it is causing us emotional pain; we may just 'know' it intuitively.

The body has no wish to make us suffer or have pain. It is only trying to communicate a message. If we receive the message, understand it and act upon it, the body will probably remove its signal. If we don't, the body might have to persist and show us more of the same message for our highest good. It will say, "Listen to me, please!"

The physical symptom is the message from the body telling us that we need to look at a certain aspect of our lives.

The body creates a physical symptom to draw our attention to it. By this time, the energy of the problem has probably accumulated so much that it has manifested in the physical realm. This is when we start getting pains, discomforts and unwelcome changes in the body. It becomes so obvious that we start looking for help. This is why it is always easier to work with the problem on the energy level when it first appears, rather than later when it gets physical.

The symptoms manifest first on an energy level.

For example, let's say that a person experienced an emotionally traumatic relationship and is feeling very hurt. They may have a subtle pain in their heart or a feeling of being shut down and upset. They may feel that they don't want to trust anybody again. Maybe they become lonely and refuse to let anybody into their life. These are the lower feelings that appear first as a sensation and probably bring a message to the person that they need to forgive and let go of these emotions.

What can a person do to help themselves? First of all, they can become aware that there are untreated emotions in the body. Awareness is an important step in healing. We can't always control our emotions at the time of the experience, but we can start treating them when we accept that they are there. We can begin to observe them from a distance and perceive them as separate from our body. Once we realise that we don't need these emotions anymore, we can decide to let them go.

Then we can turn to meditation, self-love, forgiveness practices and other types of alternative healing. The emotions, which have been stuck in the body for a while, need a way to come out and practices like yoga, breathing, visualisation, hypnotherapy and positive affirmations can help to release the emotions from the body for good. This may be accompanied by herbal remedies, healthy diet and healing therapies that work for the person. They will start noticing the improvement on the emotional level and in some time on a physical level too.

It is always better to treat the energetic cause of the ailment.

Sometimes we choose not to work with ourselves or simply don't realise that the problem is there. We may take pills and try to subside the symptoms on the surface, but deep inside that energy may be still disturbing us. This is the reason why some illnesses persist. The energy of that emotion is still there. "You still haven't solved your problem," the body is telling us.

For example, imagine that we are not giving ourselves enough love. Maybe we daily criticise ourselves and we think that we are not good enough, and punish ourselves all the time. This can create tension in the body and a state of feeling down and depressed. Perhaps it could even give us fatigue and a foggy mind. If we begin to treat it on the physical level, without realising the reason, we are only scratching the surface. It may help for some time, but the main reason will still be there. We still haven't learnt to love and look after ourselves. So, the body may get upset again and will try to guide us in the right direction.

We need to respect the advice of our body and listen to it.

The problem always lies underneath, deep beyond the physical symptom. We need to make the connection with the body and listen to its messages when they are given. This will maintain our loving communication and prevent suffering and unnecessary harm in the future.

Of course, sometimes physical help for the body is still necessary. We might have left it for so long that the body needs to be assisted by other people in the healing process. We do not disregard the outside help. The knowledge of professional people can save lives and move us in the right direction. Our intuition will guide us to the right person and choose the type of healing that can help us.

When learning to communicate with the body, it is good to imagine that it is a very good friend of ours. Think about it: your body has been with you all your life, like a loyal friend, and has been serving you in every situation. Wouldn't you find time to listen to your faithful friend? You probably would be delighted to do so.

◊

Tssshhh… The Body speaks… You can hear it now… What does it say? How does it feel? Is it okay? Breathe deeply… Don't think… Feel.

Can you feel something? What is it? Is it a pain? Is it a discomfort? What is it? Ask the body…

How is it feeling now? What would it like to tell you? Give yourself a moment to connect to your body, to listen to it… It is here to help. The body is your friend. Ask it…

Receive the first message that you get and trust it. It is true what you feel and what you hear. The more you are going to listen to your body, the clearer the messages will become. You will know, you will understand. Just do it…

Feel it. Don't ignore the body… Don't look away. Would you ignore somebody you love? No, you wouldn't.

Connect to your body. Allow it to speak. Listen to it. It has got something to tell you. Trust it and the body will trust you. Do it right now, this very moment. Give this gift to yourself.

◊

LISTENING TO THE BODY

We already know that the body is constantly communicating with us. The very awareness of this process strengthens the connection with our body and delivers its messages in a better way.

In order to bring this connection, it is important to set a time to meet with your body and give it a chance to talk and express how it is feeling. This resembles giving time to your partner or a very good friend when you decide to meet for an important conversation.

When you want to share your secrets and recent news with a dear friend, you choose a relaxing, comfortable place to talk. In the same way, when you meet with your body, you can choose a cosy, pleasant environment that will bring you more intimacy and trust. You can induce this process by bringing relaxing elements to it, like lighting a candle or playing some soft music.

Relaxation in a comfortable setting is a wonderful way to connect to your body.

Meeting your body can take many different forms. For example, it can be a light meditation, when you relax your mind and give quality time to yourself. In this peaceful state you will be able to bring your awareness inwards and hear the messages from your body in a clear way. It will become more obvious to you what is happening inside of your body, as you will tune in to the voice of your intuition. Meditation can give messages in the form of images, feelings and sensations, and it is a great chance to allow the body to speak. It is also great for calming your mind and expanding your consciousness in general.

Energy healing is another beautiful way of communicating with your body. Energy naturally connects you to the processes inside of your body and helps you to understand your physical self better. When you place your hands on your body, your own energy starts to circulate harmoniously inside and helps to balance your body in a most loving and caring way. Then the body opens up and begins to heal, responding to the kind intention of your hands. You can get a lot of inspiration and awareness of your body through energy healing.

Sometimes a light form of communication with the body is also helpful. It can take the shape of a simple walk in the park, relaxing in the garden or sitting down by the river. A natural setting will provide a calming energy for your body and help it to relax quickly. It will take away your thoughts and give you a chance to listen to yourself better.

The trees, the plants, the sun, the earth and the water are the helpers who are here to connect us to our inner self. If you direct your attention inwards while being in nature, you will get the messages needed for this time of your life. Your body will communicate to you the most important information for your health and wellbeing. Just simply listen.

There are many different types of healing practices, like massage, aromatherapy, sound healing and others; all of them are very good for maintaining the connection with our body. Whichever way you choose will show love and respect to yourself, and your friendship with your body will blossom. Every little thing counts, and sometimes it is your positive intention and regular dedicated practice that will do the magic.

Simply ask your body, "What message do you have for me today?" And listen. The body will tell you everything through the feeling and inner awareness.

It is important to trust your body when you communicate with it and believe everything that you receive or feel. Your mind might be telling you that you are making this up, but don't listen to its distracting voice. Instead, focus on the inner feeling and the love that you have for yourself. It will give you so much more freedom to heal your body holistically.

With practice, you will find your own special way of communicating with your body. You may choose walking in nature, meditation or self-massage as your preferred way of inner connection. At some point, it may become enough for you to just close your eyes, tune in and receive the messages immediately. You will make an agreement with your body to stay in touch with each other and keep helping each other. You will know what works for you the best and savour these precious moments with your very good friend.

The body needs your time.

HOW CAN WE QUIET THE MIND?

Our intuition is like a beautiful ocean floor with colourful fish, picturesque corals and vast sandy landscapes. The treasure of our inner knowing is always there, on the deep level of our consciousness, where we keep the messages for our intuitive guidance.

The water in the ocean represents our daily experiences and thoughts. When it is calm, we can clearly perceive our intuition and enjoy looking at beauty of the ocean floor. When our mind is busy, the water in the ocean can become so stormy that all the debris comes up to the top and we cannot see the depth through our clouded mind.

Thoughts and worries occupy the space in our mind, which otherwise could be a clear channel for receiving information from the higher realms. If we want to listen to our inner guidance, we need to relax and clear our mind first; in other words, calm down the waves of the ocean.

Meditation is one of the best remedies to soothe the constant thinking in our heads. In the beginning it may seem difficult to relax, as the mind appears active and dominating. But, with time and more practice, the mind will get used to finding peace and allow itself to let go.

We can learn to calm down the mind through practice and trust.

There is an exercise called 'Clear Head', which you can practice to develop the ability to quiet the mind. During the day, for short periods of time, imagine that you clean the area inside of your head with an invisible brush and hold the space of emptiness, like a white room that hasn't been decorated yet. Imagine that your head becomes hollow, and stay in the space of nothingness for as long as you can.

This feeling of 'nothingness' will increase your ability to calm down the mind. You just need to get used to the feeling of a peaceful mind. The pace of the outside world doesn't always allow us to do so, as it is constantly inviting us for different sorts of explorations. If you feel that the mind activity is returning, simply bring the attention back to the empty space inside.

You can gradually increase the time that you spend with a clear head and enjoy these moments of relaxation. Even little step of practice will greatly increase your ability to let go and will help you to free the mind from incessant thinking.

Another way to clear the mind is to spend more time in nature.

Trees and plants have a very high peaceful vibration that will automatically tune us to a positive frequency. We feel more flow in our bodies and less stress in our heads when we are in nature. Just looking at water can increase our power to connect to ourselves and develop our intuition.

When you are surrounded by natural energies in a calm setting, you can hear your inner self more clearly.

You can also connect to your inner self when you bring the attention to your body. This includes various physical activities, like dancing, yoga, stretching, massaging – all of this will help you to release the tension from the head. When we focus on the body, we give a chance for the mind to relax. This way we create an empty space and the intuitive information can come through more easily. Let us enjoy this powerful exercise of connecting to the wisdom of your body.

PRACTICE TIME
LISTENING TO THE BODY

◊   Take a comfortable position, lying down or sitting in a quiet space. Close your eyes, take several deep breaths and relax. For several moments, focus on your breath and allow it to release the thoughts and the worries from the body.

◊   Bring all your awareness inside. Feel your body and imagine that you are scanning it. Notice any sensations that come to you first. How is your body feeling now? Do you notice any tensions or stress in the body? Ask your body to show you what you need to pay attention to the most now. Let the first sensations or images come to you. Trust what you feel.

◊   Now ask the body what you can do to help it. What would make your body feel good? What would your body like the most now? Let it talk and express itself completely. Let it guide you in the right direction. You can even say aloud the words that come to you; it will help you to channel this information more. What kind of food would your body like? What would help it to relax? Would it like to spend more time in nature? Receive your own personal messages and trust the wisdom of your body. Tune in to your own natural frequency.

◊ Become aware of what your body is telling you through sensations and images. Make a mental note of these messages. Imagine yourself implementing these changes and feeling wonderful. Enjoy the strong connection with your body.

◊ Now let's send love and gratitude to your body for being such a helpful friend. Feel the joy of being in touch with your higher wisdom. Spend some moments bathing in this kind energy.

◊ Start taking deep breaths to gently wake up your body and begin to move slowly. Take your time to come back to your full awareness and open your eyes. If you want to, you can write down the messages that you received from your body so they can stay in your memory. It is helpful to come back to these messages from time to time.

KEEPING THE CONNECTION WITH YOUR BODY

The connection with your body is like a flower that needs constant nourishing and care. It will blossom from the attention and the loving energy that you give to it. It is important to maintain this sacred connection and keep communicating with your body. We can't water our favourite flower just once; we have to nourish it regularly.

It is a good idea to write a plan of how you would like to stay in touch with your body. You may decide on the days that you would like to spend together and the activities that you would like to do. A diary will help you to form a clear intention and stay friendly with your physical self for a longer time. Whatever you choose to put in your diary, whether it is a relaxing bath or a meditation with colours, it will bring magic into your body.

When you receive the messages from the body, write them down as well. By doing that, you will show to the body that you have acknowledged what it has suggested. Explore the advice that your body has given to you and turn it into a plan of action.

For example, on Monday you can do healing energy exercises and allow your body to relax. On Tuesday you can take a walk in the park and enjoy the view of the beautiful trees and plants. The day after you can focus on meditation and self-practice to clear your thoughts. The list goes on and on. Responding to your body is a wonderful gesture that shows that you care, listen and respect what it says. The body will see that the messages are being reciprocated and will gladly give you even more help.

You may want to place this plan of action somewhere in the visible space so you can see it regularly. For example, you can stick it to your wall or the inside of your wardrobe; this way you can see it every time you open it. The visual reminder will give you an inclination to follow the plan and will also spread a positive healing energy in your house.

Of course, looking after the body doesn't limit itself to meditation practices, it goes far beyond that. The body is talking to us all the time! You may find it whispering in your ear during the day: "I would like a stretch!", "Let's go for a walk", "I feel I need some rest". It is important to listen to the small messages in the moment and act upon them. It is rewarding to follow the wishes of the body as this way you show love and respect to yourself.

PRACTICE TIME
LISTENING TO YOUR BODY THROUGH TOUCH

This exercise will help you to receive the messages from your body through touch. It is a powerful way to connect to your body and feel the emotions and energies that are stored in various parts of the body. I recommend using the tips of your fingers for this practice, as it will help you to connect more precisely to the energy of each organ that you explore.

◊ Sit or lie down comfortably, surrendering completely to the energy of your body. Take several nice deep breaths and relax your body from your head to your feet.

◊ Think of a place in your body that gives you concern. It may be a place where you feel pain or discomfort or perhaps a part of you that you want to learn more about. Maybe you would like to connect more to this aspect of yourself and understand it better. Follow your intuition to find the place that needs your attention now.

◊ Place your fingers on that part of the body (it may be your heart, your stomach, your knees, etc.), close your eyes and breathe deeply. Spend some time just touching it and opening the connection. Start feeling the energy of that part of your body. Imagine that it is flowing through your fingers and your hands into you. Become aware of it and connect to this energy. What kind of a vibration is it giving to you? What do you feel? Is it happy or sad? Is it light or dense? Are there any particular emotions coming from that part of your body? Feel it. It may help to say aloud what you feel as this will strengthen your self-trust.

◊ Ask this energy what you could do to make it feel better. What can benefit this organ the most now? Listen to what comes first and allow the messages to flow in without limitation. It may be images, feelings, words or just a sense of knowing. Trust it. Maybe your body wants you to release the heaviness and breathe it out slowly. Perhaps it asks you to imagine a beautiful light inside of you. Just connect to your intuition and feel it for yourself. The first impression that you get is right. Remember that just holding your hands on your body is already healing.

◊ Repeat the same exercise with each organ that you want to speak to. You will notice that they all feel differently. Stay patient and loving to your body when you do this practice; give some time for your energy to express itself. You are creating a wonderful bridge between you and your body. Let the inner wisdom come to you in a natural way.

◊ At the end of the exercise send gratitude to your body and embrace it in your loving energy. Spend a moment in the blissful state of being present. Remember the messages that the body has given to you and bring them with you to the physical reality.

◊ When you are ready, start taking deep breaths and orientate yourself back to the present moment. Begin to gently move your body and feel your physical self. Allow the full awareness to come to you. Take your time to return to the current moment. When you are ready, open your eyes. How are you feeling? It would be helpful to write down the messages from the body, as you may use them later in your healing practice.

THE CONNECTION OF THE SYMPTOM TO THE EMOTIONAL SIDE

Every message brought to us by the body contains important information. The symptom doesn't come on its own; it carries an energy that helps us to understand what is happening inside of us. If we tune into the message, we will be able to perceive why we feel out of balance and what course of action can help us to improve it.

The messages of the body can come in a myriad of different ways, depending on what the body is trying to tell us. The body can talk through pain or discomfort when it is feeling upset about something. It can speak through visual signals, like itching or marks, when it wants us to pay attention to something. Sometimes it heightens our awareness through repeated sensations, like heaviness, bloating, inflammation and so on.

Each symptom is unique and carries its own message for us to decode.

There is a reason why a certain symptom appears in a particular part of the body. Our body is like a mirror, a kind of a projection of the energy states that we experience in our life. The location of the symptom is the clue to where the problem begins and what area of our life we need to look into.

Every part of our body is responsible for a certain aspect of our life. These connections are very easy to make, if we just ask ourselves, "What does this organ represent in my body?" Then we can look for the mirroring function of this organ in our life. For example, if our eyes help us to see the physical reality, the corresponding spiritual function of this organ may be to be open to the full vision of life and not being afraid to look at ourselves. If our lungs help us to breathe, energetically they may be related to the ability to feel free and not restricted in life. The stomach, which is responsible for digesting food on the physical level, serves us emotionally by digesting life situations.

Each of the functions are both physical and spiritual. Thus, if somebody is experiencing a problem related to a certain organ, they first need to see what this organ represents metaphorically in their life.

Very often a discomfort is associated with a strong emotion that has been kept in the body for some time. Perhaps it was a difficult situation in life, for example, a loss or a hurtful relationship, that has brought a person a feeling of anger and sadness. Without a chance of being released, the energy of lower emotions can build up in the body and start to show itself physically after a while. This is the so-called entrapment of emotions and it can sometimes happen even without the person realising it.

As human beings, we are often subject to fear, which is a reaction to something that is outside of our comfort zone or reminds us of a dangerous episode in the past. While useful in some situations, fear can be overwhelming in everyday life and become a challenging energy to deal with. When accumulated in the body, fear can lead to imbalance and even create illness. It happens because the vibration of fear is very low and disturbing for the body. It brings the energy of the organs down and creates a discomfort in the energy flow of the body, similar to a freezing sensation. When we are working with healing, it is important to release the fear and turn it into positive energy by inviting trust and love into the heart. This will help to bring the body back to the natural state of balance.

Another common factor that can lead to ailments in the body is stress. Nowadays the pace of life is so fast and demanding that people tend to fall into stress very easily. They put pressure on themselves and, as a result, the body tightens up and feels contracted. Such tension doesn't allow the energy to flow freely in the body and can lead to imbalances on the physical level. This is why relaxation often becomes a number one treatment in healing sessions – the body just needs to come back to its natural state of peace in order to start the healing process.

Many of these imbalances develop with time and it is not always immediately obvious where the symptom comes from. Hence it is important to talk to the body and give it time to gradually discover what has happened and how it can be reversed back to the balanced state. We need to sit down with the body and understand the reason why it is feeling this way. There are certain questions we can ask our body in a meditation in order to understand more about the source of the issue.

Where does the symptom show? What is it trying to tell me? Why is it appearing in this part of the body? What does this part of the body represent in my life? How do I feel about this organ? Is there anything that I need to change in my life? Is my body happy and in harmony with my emotions?

Each symptom is unique and carries a special message. Maybe the headache is telling us to stop thinking too much? Maybe the joints are stiff because they would like us to move forward in life? Perhaps the aching back is telling us to release the weight of responsibilities and to take better care of ourselves?

The answers will be personal to you. No one knows your body better than you.

You are in your body. There is a reason why you are there and why you are having this experience. There is a reason for every little thing that happens in your body and in your emotional world.

In QHHT sessions, we get a lot of information about the connection between the physical body and the emotional side. Sometimes we hear the Subconscious explaining an ailment this way: "She needs to stop worrying and look after herself properly. This is where her symptoms come from. It is a reminder that she needs to relax." Another common reason for a discomfort in the body, according to the Subconscious, is stored anger. "He is angry with himself. This is where his stomach pain comes from. He needs to let go of his anger and then the pain will disappear." In one such session, the Subconscious explained the person's problems with the digestive system this way: "He is carrying guilt in his intestines. He feels guilty about the things he has done and things he wanted to do but didn't. This produces the pain and the bloating. The guilt has to be released." After the person realises the cause of the ailment, it becomes easier to heal it and let it go.

These are some examples of explanations of illnesses that come during the sessions. They are very individual and depend on the person's life story and emotional background. However, this general knowledge can help many other people to heal because it will prompt them to understand the link between the emotions and the body.

The Subconscious can be asked to work on the body and do healing during the session, if the person is ready. It is usually done with the help of a beautiful white light that spreads healing energy in the body. The white light has the power to clear the organs energetically, release the old emotions and restore the balance where it is needed. The Subconscious works on the physical organs and heals them with high-frequency energy, sometimes instantly. "We have removed the pain," they often say. "He will feel better now." The person usually experiences a pleasant warm sensation in the body after receiving the healing.

There are cases when the Subconscious wants the person to make changes in their lives, so the illness doesn't repeat. In this case, they will recommend the person to do some self-work, according to what is needed at the time. "He needs to spend more time looking after himself and meditating. The symptom is a reminder for him to find inner balance," the Subconscious may say, and their words always have a very strong power. Sometimes they may explain that the person is in a toxic relationship or that a certain work environment is not serving them. The Subconscious always leaves the decision to the person as they have free will in this life, but may give recommendation to what is right for their highest good.

We can connect to our Subconscious in a meditation and ask it for some advice in our life. This is the higher power that loves us and looks after us all the time; it really appreciates when we get in touch with it and listen to its messages. You can ask your Subconscious to work on your body and remove the causes of the symptoms, explaining where they came from. This practice will strengthen your intuitive powers and help you to heal your body in a natural way.

Your own Subconscious is the best healer and guide for you.

There are plenty of literature sources that explore the connection between the symptoms and the emotional causes. Some of these connections are also explained at the end of this chapter. This knowledge can help us to become aware of this connection and receive inspiration to work on ourselves. However, one needs to remember that the most powerful and truthful way of gaining information is turning inwards and asking our own body.

There is a higher wisdom that exists in our consciousness from centuries before, from our past lives. Many of us have been healers in the past, and this knowledge is still imprinted somewhere in our souls. We subconsciously remember that our body has the power to regenerate naturally and heal itself from within. It is now time to connect to this knowledge and trust it. We will be much stronger if we learn to listen to our body and act upon its messages.

We have been healers in the past and we still remember this knowledge on the soul level.

In my QHHT practice, many people experienced past lives of healers who worked with plants, crystals and energy healing. These people knew the truth about the healing powers of our body. They usually lived in natural surroundings and assisted others with healing. For example, they collected plants and made remedies to balance the body and emotions of other people. This knowledge was passed to them through generations and also travelled in soul memory through time. People with such past lives naturally remember how to heal and are usually drawn to learn more about plants and natural healing. You may be one of them.

Unfortunately, in the past many talented and knowledgeable souls like these have been suppressed in their life because they seemed dangerous to the system at the time. Many natural healers were prosecuted for practising witchcraft, even when they had the purest intentions to heal others. People have been punished and taken away from home, so they wouldn't compromise the authority. This is the reason why nowadays many people are afraid to show their wonderful healing gifts again; they don't want the past to be repeated.

The Subconscious always says to people with such past lives: "It is okay to show your gifts now. Times have changed. You will not be punished anymore. It is time to share your knowledge openly." These words offer beautiful support to people who feel a calling to become healers in this life.

To achieve a healing result, the body needs to remember what it is like to be in balance and harmony. Having an illness can become habitual when people forget that it is possible to live without it. We need to remember that we deserve to be healthy and happy. We can allow the joy of healing to take place in the body. It is a very good idea to ask your body from time to time: *What would it be like to have complete balance and harmony? Show me what balance is.* You will be amazed how quickly the body responds to this request and starts to rearrange the energy inside to show you what balance feels like.

There are plenty of various techniques to connect to your body and understand its messages. In this book you will find some useful practices that will help you to communicate with your body and your soul. As you progress on your healing journey, you will discover your own techniques and begin to receive powerful insights about yourself.

THE POSITIVE IMPACT OF MEDITATION

The deepest and most direct way to connect to our body is through meditation. When we are in a meditative state, our conscious mind calms down and gives way to the world of the Subconscious. On that level it is much easier to connect to the wisdom of our inner self and hear the messages from the body.

Our Subconscious has information about everything that is happening in our body, including all the organs and systems. It can detect when something is out of balance and direct our attention to the right part of ourselves. It can also understand the emotional connections in our body and suggest pathways for healing. The beauty of the Subconscious is that it knows us very well and always works in our best interest, like an old friend.

The Subconscious communicates with us every day by giving us signals, dreams, visions and feelings. The main channel for receiving the information from the Subconscious is our intuition. We constantly get messages of guidance, which are designed to nudge us in the right direction. Some of these messages reach our daily awareness; some stay in the deeper level of our consciousness, waiting to be accessed in meditative practices.

Then, as we go deeper in a meditation, the Subconscious becomes active and begins to communicate its valuable messages to us. In a calm and peaceful state, we access the channel for the higher information and start receiving important guidance. As the Subconscious understands us very well, it can show us exactly what is happening in the body and how we can transform it. This can become a very powerful healing practice.

In order to hear the messages from the body during meditation, we need to be quiet, calm and trusting. The best tip for this experience is to trust what comes first and listen to your intuition, which gives you images, feelings or inner knowing. Allow yourself time and don't doubt anything. Your trust will open the doors for more divine information to come.

This ability may come with time. In the beginning it may seem to you that you are making the messages up. Be patient. The more you do this work, the more you will learn to believe your inner guidance. Your own Subconscious will take care of you; you can trust it.

PRACTICE TIME
UNDERSTANDING THE MESSAGES OF THE BODY

◊ Find a quiet space where you feel peaceful and undisturbed. Take a comfortable position, close your eyes and relax.

◊ Start breathing deeply, imagining that your breath is travelling through all your body. Every part of your body is becoming relaxed and the breath is making you feel very calm. Take your time to connect and enjoy this peaceful state of being.

◊ Turn your attention inwards. Mentally scan the body and find the area that is calling your attention the most. Trust the first sensation that comes, allowing the body to naturally point you in the right direction.

◊ Breathe deeply and imagine that you are listening carefully to this part of your body. How is it feeling? What energy do you perceive from it? Try to connect to its inherent vibration, almost as though it is talking to you. What is happening there? Why is it happening? Ask these questions to your body and accept the first thing that you feel.

◊ Listen to the symptom and connect to the emotion behind it. What does this feeling remind you of? Is it sad? Is it nervous? Maybe it is lacking love? Ask the body to give you the right answer. Does this symptom remind you of anything that is happening in your life now? Believe the messages that you receive, even if they seem obvious or unbelievable. Trust your feeling.

◊ Listen to the symptom and ask it what you can do to make it feel better. Just feel the energy and sense how you could improve it. Let it guide you. Ask these questions: *What can I do for you? How can I help you?* Talk to it with a lot of love and care.

◊ Now act upon the messages that you receive, by using your own inner energy. For example, if the organ told you that you needed more relaxation, imagine that you are relaxing your body right now. If it said that you needed to breathe deeper, take several slow breaths and see how the energy of the organ responds to it. Perhaps your organ wants to cry the pain out and release the energy. Allow it to do so. Follow what feels right for you and spend some time changing the energy of the organ to make it feel better.

◊   At the end of your practice, breathe love into that part of your body. Express your care and support. Tell your body, "I love you. I am sorry." Imagine that you are caressing it as a child and making it feel very loved. Affirm to your body that you received the message and will act accordingly to the best of your abilities.

◊   Now breathe deeply again and start to wake your body up. Take your time to bring your awareness back to your physical self and to your space. Begin to slowly move your body, your feet, your hands, your head. When you are ready, open your eyes and come fully back.

WRITING DOWN THE MESSAGES OF THE BODY

Writing is another form of channeling the messages from the body. It opens a free flow of communication between you and your Subconscious and allows you to receive direct guidance for your healing journey.

Writing gives a great opportunity to talk to your body and let it express itself creatively. Your hands will connect to your heart and channel the right information from your inner self into the paper. It is almost like the energy of your body will be transmitted into the pen and will then take the shape of words and sentences that will explain exactly what you feel. It is a very powerful practice.

Writing doesn't have to take any specific form; it can be just a free flow of words. If you let your pen go in an intuitive way, it will allow your Subconscious to gradually take over and start writing for you. You will then see the patterns and connections that are present in your life now and will be able to get to the essence of the situation that you are trying to understand.

When you write intuitively, you are expressing the words of your own Subconscious.

Sometimes we may find it hard to admit certain things to ourselves. Maybe we have been holding a lot of pain and suffering inside of us, but we don't want to show it or talk about it with other people. Writing gives us a brilliant opportunity to express the deepest feelings that we keep inside, without being afraid of judgement from others. You may not even read again what you have written, but you will be able to express how you feel. Your body will be very grateful for this emotional release.

Writing can be used for healing purposes. In such cases, it is best to use a free-flowing form of writing, when you don't try to think and plan things, but just allow your pen to float and to write for you. Imagine that your hand has a consciousness of its own and wants to express itself in a unique way. Let it guide you.

You may wish to focus on a particular symptom or a part of your body that needs healing. You can write a letter coming from that part of yourself to you – for example, a letter from your eyes, explaining how they feel and what they have been through. Imagine that your body can talk and it wants to tell you a story. Begin with the way that you are feeling now and then allow your consciousness to open up and to start writing freely. You will notice that deeper information will surface soon.

Do not control. Do not plan. Just write.

Everything that you need to express will come out of you naturally in writing. Imagine that honest words and feelings are pouring out of you, like water from a deep well. The source of knowledge in you is abundant. Savour every moment of this sacred connection to yourself; it is a beautiful chance to hear your body speaking.

Write with love and writing will reveal your true self to you.

After you wrote a letter from your body, look at the paper and just connect to it. What is this energy telling you? What were you feeling while expressing it? What vibration is emanating from your writing? Look at it objectively and connect to the feeling that you receive from it. This is a part of your Higher Self talking through the writing.

DRAWING THE MESSAGES FROM THE BODY

Just like writing, drawing helps to express your inner self into the white canvas. It is a beautiful way of releasing emotions into the physical realm and getting to understand yourself better through intuitive colours and shapes. Drawing gives a wonderful opportunity to heal yourself because it allows you to connect to the energy of your creation like to your own mirror.

During the creative process, colourful pens are ready to help you in the best way. You only need to take them intuitively and start making your own work of art, based on the feelings and emotions that you have inside. The pen will begin to draw spontaneously and, as you let yourself go, the picture will appear exactly in a way that is needed to show you important messages about yourself.

You don't have to be a great artist in order to practise healing art. Even if it is the simplest drawing, it will still have a coded message in its energy, which will help you to answer your questions. You just need to connect to the feeling. *What do I feel from my drawing?* The pen will take care of the drawing and will reveal to you what you need to see at this moment. Trust the pen and let it take you on a journey, allowing it to move freely and spontaneously, without thinking too much.

Draw the first thing that comes to you and let the energy of the heart take over your pen.

You may wish to focus on a particular part of your life, for example, relationships, personal development or your goals, and then begin to draw using intuitive colours, shapes and textures. If you put the right intention in your heart, the energy will hear it and create a picture that will show you what is happening in that part of your life now. You can also just start drawing without any plan and let the energy take care of itself. This is my favourite way. I find that it then reveals exactly what you need to pay attention to at this time of your life.

You can explore a pain in your body through drawing. You can take a piece of paper, some colourful pens and sit for a moment connecting to the feeling in your body. Then take the first pen that is calling you and just start expressing your feelings on the paper. Imagine it is your body speaking through the drawing, making it flow. Draw what comes to you on the paper and spend as much time as you need depicting your feelings and letting them out of you. What comes first is always true. Trust it.

Let the pen guide you.

When you are finished, look at your drawing and feel it. What energy do you perceive from it? What is it expressing? How is your body reacting to it? Is there anything else that you would like to add to it? Connect to the energy and feel what colours and shapes you would like to add to the drawing to bring healing to your body. Imagine that you could transform your drawing with your hands. What would you do? Trust the healing process and move your hands in a healing way.

In the end, it is always best to just look at your drawing and connect to its energy. You can even touch it with your hands and imagine that you are sending a healing vibration to the drawing. At this moment a beautiful connection happens between you and your inner self. You are becoming one with your powerful energy and you are helping yourself to heal. Enjoy this magical moment!

Drawing is a wonderful way to communicate with ourselves and receive higher guidance. Many of these drawings will give you hints about how to heal yourself and what kind of energy to invite into your life now. Drawings are like little mirrors that will show you different aspects of yourself and point out where you need healing the most now. You can charge your drawing with your hands and benefit from your healing energy this way.

ACTING UPON YOUR INTUITION

Once the message has been received, the body invites us to act upon it and direct our energy towards fulfilling the task. It resembles a telephone call from a dear friend who is asking us for a favor. We listen to our friend and we want to help them by doing what they ask us to do.

Maybe you received a message that you need to relax and let go of stress. The body feels tense and tired. You can then ask yourself: "How can I help my body in this situation? What could relieve the tension?" Perhaps you need to rest for a considerable amount of time, without any distractions. Or maybe your body wants you to spend a day in the countryside, enjoying the natural surroundings. You can ask about it yourself.

We need to listen to the message and guidance that the body gives to us. Some healing may require us to change our habits.

If your body insists that some life situation is not good for you – maybe it is a harmful work environment or an exhausting habit – you need to look at ways to make it better for your body. Think and feel what you could do to improve your life, so you can be happier and more relaxed. Can you change your job setting? Is it possible to improve the conditions that you live in, maybe change the lights, bring more harmonic energy or add new colours? Are there any habits that are not serving you anymore, and you know about it?

Sometimes, on the contrary, the body may be prompting you to do something that you are not doing. For example, it may want you to follow your talents and express yourself more creatively. Maybe it wants you to sing, to dance or to draw; in other words, do an act of kindness for your spirit. The body is trying to connect you more to who you are, because this will make you happy and healthy.

Whatever the intuitive message is, it is our mission to listen to it and to help our body. Acting upon the message of the body is the sign of our love and appreciation to it. It is a small step that will count towards our general health and wellbeing in the long term.

Messages from the body are usually straightforward and they invite us to transform our life in a beneficial way. On a deeper level of our consciousness, we might already know these messages, but we need more awareness to start implementing them in real life.

Many times, we say: "I know I should be doing it." This phrase is the key. The word 'know' indicates that the voice of intuition is speaking to us. If we manage to act upon the intuitive messages immediately, it will bring us a lot of strength and power to make positive changes in our life. The more we listen to our intuition straight away, the easier it will be to stay in touch with our body on a regular basis.

These are some of the most common messages that the body gives to us on the healing journey.

THE BODY SAYS: "RELAX"

This is one of the most significant messages that the body gives to us. Relaxation is an important step for healing as it helps the energy in the body to flow. When we are relaxed, we naturally let go of stress and old stuck emotions. We give our body permission to be free and peaceful.

Relaxation feels good and promotes natural regeneration of the body. In the state of relaxation, the energy flows like a river, bringing nourishment to all the organs in the body.

Let's imagine for a moment that you can let go of all your worries and get completely relaxed. Imagine that there is no need to hold on to tension anymore and you can just release it and step into the dimension of relaxation. How would that feel?

You may notice how the energy immediately starts to move in the body. There comes a peaceful relaxing flow that reaches all the organs and supports them with life force energy. Wherever there was tension before, now it begins to dissipate and get released naturally. The whole body is changing just when we give it the command to relax. This is the beginning of the healing process.

The body needs to remember how to relax.

As we progress into relaxation, the body starts to remember its natural way of being. The organs come into alignment, the blood begins to circulate properly, the breath becomes free and full. We suddenly remember that we are supposed to always feel peaceful and relaxed. The body begins to naturally come back to its balance and restore the health.

How much can you relax now? Try the best that you can. Could you do it even more?

We begin to observe that relaxation comes from within. It is like a peaceful healing melody in our body that tells us that everything is going to be fine. If we listen to this melody, it will take us on a journey and begin to heal our body and soul.

Relaxation can be achieved by practising meditation, energy healing, breathing, massage and any other pleasant way of spending time with ourselves. The more we practise relaxation, the more our body will get used to this balanced and peaceful state. It is like tuning the guitar: we align the chords and create a wonderful song for ourselves.

Nature is a beautiful reminder of how to be relaxed. When we spend time with the trees and the water, we automatically tune in to the vibration of peace and release the stress from the body. The trees have the ability to take away our thoughts and remind us of how to be calm and present. This is the gift of our planet that we can use any time to naturally step into the healing mode.

Listen to nature – it will take you on a path of healing and relaxation.

In a state of relaxation, we connect more to ourselves and our inner core. We know exactly what we need to do and we trust the flow of life. The energy of worry or anxiety isn't harbored in us anymore as it doesn't survive in a state of relaxation. We are totally free.

We are rediscovering our true nature and coming back to who we really are. What does your body need and what makes it feel happy? What can you release from your life to make your body feel good? There are so many gifts that we can give to ourselves if we only listen.

PRACTICE TIME
RELAXING THE BODY

◊ Find a comfortable position in a place where you feel calm and peaceful. Close your eyes and relax.

◊ Take several deep breaths going through your whole body. Imagine that the breath is slowly beginning to release the tension and worries from the body. Enjoy the peaceful feeling for some time. Give yourself permission to just rest and breathe.

◊ Now we are going to relax your body. Focus on your head and imagine how it is getting more and more relaxed. Slowly begin to melt down all the thoughts and breathe out any tensions, relaxing the muscles in the head. Take your time. Imagine how the breath is cleansing the space in your head.

◊ Let us relax your face now and allow it to be soft and calm. Imagine how a beautiful relaxing energy is running through your skin and touching your forehead, your muscles, your cheeks and your jaw.

Let the eyes relax slowly, so they can release all the pressure and tension. Feel how the energy in your eyes is becoming replenished.

◊ Now let us move the relaxation down to your throat. Imagine how the muscles in your throat open up and the energy starts to flow freely. Release any old pain or fear from the throat, allowing it to be free. Imagine how, with every breath, you are returning the throat to its natural state of relaxation.

◊ The breath travels down to your lungs and your heart. Feel the relaxation in your chest as you allow yourself to breathe more freely and deeply. Imagine that any stress or tightness is leaving your body and you are creating more space for the energy to flow in the centre of your chest.

◊ The more you relax, the more flow appears in your body. You become more your natural self. Allow the energy of relaxation to spread from your shoulders down to your arms and your hands. Release any heavy weight that you may have been carrying in your life. Let it go. Say "Relax" to your whole upper body. Feel it happening.

◊ Now the relaxation is reaching your stomach and all of your digestive system. This is the space where we tend to hold tension and stress. Allow the energy to unfold in your digestive system and release it with your breath. Imagine that you are opening a window in your stomach and letting the stress float out through it. Let the peaceful breath untangle the energy in your body. Do it more, and more, and more. You might even start to hear the sound of your stomach – it is the sign of relaxation.

◊ Now let us take the relaxation all the way down the spine, like a free flow of spring water. Focus on your back and release the tension there as much as you can. Imagine that you are melting down the stress from the top to the bottom of the spine. Visualise it becoming free and happy. It is wonderful how much we can relax our body!

◊ The relaxation flows down to your reproductive system. It is ready to release all the tension there. Open the flow of your creative energy and feel it blossoming. Imagine that your reproductive system is completely calm and peaceful. Breathe out any old energy that may be there and allow your sacral chakra to relax completely.

◊ Now the relaxation goes down to your legs, through your thighs, your knees and your feet. Take the stress out of your system and imagine how it melts down through your legs. Release the pressure from your feet into the earth and leave it in the ground. Notice how you are feeling very light and free.

◊ Enjoy the pleasant feeling of relaxation in your whole body now. Stay in this state for some time and notice what it feels like to be completely at peace. Imagine that you are made of clear blue water that is free and flowing. Ask your body to remember this state of relaxation and keep it for as long as possible.

◊ When you are ready, slowly come fully back to the current moment and place. Take your time to return to your consciousness. You did a wonderful job!

THE BODY SAYS: "BREATHE"

Breath is a powerful healing ability of our body that we so often forget about.

The whole Universe is made from breath. All its beings are breathing with love, creating a beautiful movement of life: people, animals, trees, plants, even the air. If we listen carefully, we would hear that breath is the natural sound of the Universe. The planet is breathing, just like we do, every moment.

Breath is a natural rhythm of the planet.

This breath gives us a chance to realign ourselves with the vibration of the planet and recharge our powers naturally. As we breathe deeply, we reconnect to who we are and allow the breath to travel to the essence of our being, then we share it back with the Universe.

Breath unites us with everything that there is around us.

Breath gives us a chance to cleanse and renew ourselves every moment. It can calm down our energy and release our thoughts, spreading the feeling of harmony in our body. Breath is a wonderful tool that we all have since birth, and we can learn to use it to benefit ourselves physically and spiritually.

What is your own breath like? How do you breathe? Do you allow yourself to breathe fully and freely?

Breath is almost like a song that you are playing to yourself every other second. You can find magical mysteries and secrets of your being in your own breath. If you learn to listen to inner stillness that comes from the breath, it will teach you more about who you are. Your breath is unique and so are you.

Connect to the energy that you receive when you breathe. What does this energy feel like?

When you allow your breath to become deeper and fuller, you are inviting more energy and wealth into your life. You can then fully enjoy being part of the Universe and nourish yourself with this abundant energy. Breath is a gift to yourself, a magic wand that can lead you to so many revelations about life.

Breath is a shortcut to deeper experiences like self-awareness, meditation and visualisation. Breath allows us to go to a more profound state of being, beyond our mind and thoughts, and receive knowledge from our Higher Self. It is a doorway to higher dimensions and expanded spiritual awareness.

Allow yourself to breathe like a king or a queen. What breath do you really deserve in life?

Through the breath we connect, through the breath we release, through the breath we can see ourselves better. It is a mirror of who we are and how we interact with the outside world and with ourselves. Is our breath strong and powerful? Do we allow ourselves a full interaction with the world? By allowing yourself your own breath, you are establishing your presence in the Universe.

Breath offers so many possibilities to us every moment. We can learn to calm down our mind and bring ourselves to a state of inner peace and relaxation. Breath can be cleansing and releasing, if we direct it to a certain part of the body and help the energy there to move freely. Breath is like a fuel, a starter; it can make us feel strong and full of life.

Breath often reflects the way we feel about life. Sometimes we may experience shallow breath due to stress and worries. In the current times, many of us find it difficult to breathe fully. We align with the energy of the busy world outside and our breath can become superficial and shallow. We have to rediscover the power of the breath and return ourselves the ability to take in the energy of life in its fullness.

Many practices explore the power of breath and offer wonderful exercises to be in touch with this supreme power – for example, meditation, mindfulness, healing breath and others. There are a multitude of practices to choose from to your own liking.

Breathing is a direct way to get back to the flow and the heartbeat of the Universe, providing balance and relaxation to the body cells.

As with everything else, awareness and inner observation is the key for maintaining the deep breath throughout the body. Let us explore this exercise to find the unique vibration of your own breath.

PRACTICE TIME
YOUR OWN BREATHING

◊ Take a comfortable position in a quiet space. Relax your body completely and close your eyes. Observe your breathing and notice what it is like. Is it deep or shallow? Do you take long breaths or short? How does your breathing feel to you? Describe it to yourself.

◊ Listen to your own breath and begin to make it deeper and more relaxed. Focus on the energy of your breath and allow it to slow down. Observe how the body changes as you are starting to breathe deeper. Feel your mind getting relaxed and more peaceful.

◊ Ask your breath to show you what your natural breathing is like. What was it like when you came to this world? Align and tune in to your true breath, the breath of your soul. Let it come to you naturally, just by relaxing and trusting the inner flow. Who are you in your breath? What does it tell you about yourself? Just stay in your breath and listen.

◊ Notice how much more enriched you feel with every new breath in your body. Enjoy it and spread it all around your body. Give in completely to your natural healing breath. Become it.

◊ Practice this exercise for some time. After you finish, come back to your awareness and orientate yourself in the present moment. Observe the changes in your body. How do you feel? What is your inner energy like? Make an intention to remember your natural breath and carry it with you in life.

THE HEALING BREATH

Breathing brings natural healing energy into our body and helps us to achieve the balance in the organs. It is a simple way to make ourselves feel good and we can use it at any moment in our life.

When we were little babies, we used to breathe very deeply – it was our natural state. As we grew up, our breath became shallower and more stressed. At night, when we are sleeping, we go back to our natural state of being and switch to deep breathing. Bringing this ability to everyday life has incredible health benefits and can form an effective meditative practice.

Breathing deeply, we take in the full energy from the Universe, allowing it to flow freely through the body. As a result, all our cells become enriched by this breath and the stagnant energies can be removed from the body. When we direct the breath into the organ that is experiencing a lack of balance, we bring life force energy into this organ and purify it from within.

Breath cleanses the body and enriches it with healing energy.

Breathing helps to bring our awareness to the body. When we breathe fully, we become more present and connected with ourselves, feeling exactly which parts of the body are lacking energy and balance. This exercise will help you to direct the breath to the organs that need healing in your body.

PRACTICE TIME
THE HEALING BREATH
◊ Find a comfortable space, close your eyes and bring your awareness inwards. Take several deep breaths to completely relax your body and mind.
◊ Scan the body mentally and look for any tensions that you may be experiencing at this moment. Find a part of your body that is vibrating differently from the others – for example, it may feel denser or more stressed. Let this awareness come to you naturally; trust the first impression that you get.
◊ Bring your breath into this organ and direct the flow of energy into it. Focus on your breathing and imagine that you are dispersing and blowing away all the negative or stuck energies from this part of your body. Feel as though you are purifying

the organ with crystal-clear water and it is becoming renewed.

◊　Make this practice very slow and well-paced to allow every bit of energy to flow inside of the organ. While you are breathing, receive any intuitive messages that come to you about this part of your body. You may realise why it is feeling this way and what could be done to help it. Spend as much time as needed doing this practice, generously nourishing the organ with your breath.

◊　Feel if there are any other organs that need help in the body. Bring your breath there and do the same slow practice with these organs, keeping your awareness open for any intuitive messages. Enjoy every moment of healing your body with the breath.

◊　When you are finished, return to your normal breath and stay in the new replenished energy for several moments. Let it integrate back into the body completely and relax in the peaceful state of being. When you are ready, open your eyes and come back to your surroundings.

THE BODY SAYS: "LET GO"

Imagine that we are walking in the forest and we are looking at different plants. Some of the plants might serve us, so we pick them and put them in the basket. After a while the basket becomes full and we bring it home.

There we sort the plants out and decide which ones will stay with us and which ones have to go. There may be some plants that we have picked so long ago that they don't serve us anymore. But we don't want to throw them away as they feel important. In the same way, we hold on to some of our experiences in life as we get attached to them on our journey.

This basket is a combination of our life experiences and emotions that we have collected on our life path. Sometimes we carry this basket so full that we forget that it is time to let go of some of its ingredients.

Do we need everything that we carry with us every day? Is there anything that we can release and leave behind?

Letting go is an ability to free ourselves from the past and release the unnecessary emotions from our body.

Perhaps some of the feelings and memories that you carry do not align with you anymore. Maybe these experiences served you at a certain time in your life, but now it is time for them to go and set you free. What would happen if you let them go? How would you feel?

Ask yourself what truly belongs to you and what you can release now.

If you decide that there is a feeling or an experience that you would like to release, imagine placing it in a beautiful bubble of light and letting it go up into the sky. Feel it leaving your body as you are blowing the old feeling into the bubble and safely removing this energy from yourself. You will find an instant relief in your heart when you set your old emotions free.

Life is about change and a constant flow. We are always moving from one place to another, both physically and spiritually, like shifting between dimensions. Travel is an integral part of our life experience and, in order to move safely to a next step, we need to let go of some of our past experiences. We can't carry everything with us.

Letting go is a natural ability that helps us to stay balanced and be ready to step into a new stage of our life. It is like playing a ball game; once we catch the ball, we send it back very quickly. We don't hold on to the ball in a game. This is exactly what letting go is about. It is like a breath – we breathe in and then we breathe out. We can't keep the breath inside of us.

Sometimes we are afraid to let go as we think that we will lose something when we do it. Maybe we are holding on to a certain feeling that we experienced a long time ago, for example, a feeling of hurt as a child, when we were upset by our parents and couldn't express ourselves. We may not want to let it go as it has become part of our habit and personality. We get used to a feeling and each time we get a similar experience, we automatically hold on to it again. If we were to remove the layers of these feelings, underneath them we would find a very pure and light being that doesn't need to hurt itself anymore.

We just need to honestly ask ourselves: *Does this feeling really belong to me? Does it make me who I am? Am I happy with this feeling?* And then make a decision whether to keep it inside or not. Once we decide to let the feeling go, the energy will instantly begin to give us the power and ability to do so. The Universe is very wise and supportive. It will find a way to help us release what we need to.

The body wants to let go. It doesn't want to hold on to old feelings. We make this choice.

Letting go is an art of being free in ourselves. It is a reward that we give to ourselves, a sign of recognition of who we really are. We express love to our true self when we remove what doesn't belong to us. We also open the doorways to bringing the energy of freedom into our life.

How do we learn to let go? Awareness and relaxation are the clues to mastering this sacred ability. When we are present in the moment, we can easily notice the things that do not serve us in the best way. For example, we can catch the moment when we are just about to get a negative reaction and we can choose to let it go at this time. Observing the feeling can help us to release it back to where it came from, like the ball in a game.

Maybe I don't need to get upset this time?

After some daily practice, we will begin to build more awareness of what serves us and what doesn't. We will be able to define the energies that come into our life and decide whether we want to keep them or not. Small steps of practice will help us to shift larger layers of complex feelings that may have been there for a long time.

There are many ways to work with letting go, including meditation, hypnotherapy, energy healing and breathing exercises. All of these techniques offer an excellent opportunity for inner growth and bringing the balance into the body. This is a powerful visualisation exercise that will help you let go of the energy that doesn't serve you anymore in your life.

PRACTICE TIME
LEARNING TO LET GO

◊   Find a comfortable space where you feel peaceful and quiet. Close your eyes and relax. Take several long deep breaths and allow the relaxation to flow through your body.

◊   Turn your awareness inwards and focus on your inner self. What is happening in your body now? How do you feel? Just become aware of it, as an observer, and connect deeply to your breath.

◊   Now, in your inner world, imagine that you are walking in a beautiful forest. There are trees and plants everywhere around you, and you are taking a path forward. This is your journey of life. It shows all the experiences that you have had and all that you have been through. Observe what your forest looks like. What can you see around you?

◊   Now look at yourself and notice what you are wearing as you are walking in the forest. What does your clothing look like? Are you carrying anything with you? Observe every detail and connect to the emotions that your clothes give to you. Do they feel light or heavy? Are they comfortable? Notice how they feel.

◊   The path is taking you to an open clearing in the forest. It is a beautiful sunny place where you can have a little rest. Walk into the clearing and find a place to sit down and relax. Notice how light and pleasant it feels there.

◊   Now focus on what you are wearing and feel if there is any clothing that you would like to change or let go of. Even if it is just a feeling, listen to it and trust your impressions. Is there anything that needs to go? Is there any old clothing that doesn't serve you anymore? Now imagine yourself taking off the clothes that feel heavy, uneasy or giving you unpleasant sensations. Take them off slowly, feeling every motion of release in your body. You can say: "I now release with joy and love everything that doesn't belong to me." Repeat it as many times as you like.

◊   Notice how your body feels as you are removing the old clothing. Does it feel lighter and freer? Just observe and connect. Affirm to yourself that you are safe and protected without this clothing. Notice the positive change in yourself. What do you look like when you have removed the old energy? How does it feel? Maybe you can even transform the old clothes into new ones. What kind of garments would you like to wear to feel good about yourself? You can imagine yourself wearing light sparkly clothes that uplift your energy. Choose magical clothes that match your new vibration.

◊   Enjoy your new being. See how shiny and beautiful you are. Connect to the feeling of being rejuvenated and full of light. See what you would like to do now in the forest to have a good time. Imagine being very free and open, allowing your new self to have fun. Maybe you would like to dance, maybe you feel like running and jumping; do whatever comes to you now. Spend as long as you need enjoying your beautiful new energy.

◊   When you are finished, just relax in the sunny clearing and begin to prepare for the journey back. Start taking deep breaths and orientate yourself back in the current time and space. Feel your physical body waking up, move your hands, your head and your feet. Return to your full awareness here and now. Congratulations! Your energy feels wonderful!

This is a transformative exercise that will help you to shake off the weight of your past experiences and reconnect back to who you are. You can repeat this exercise from time to time, and it will assist you to create a positive habit of letting go and being free in your spirit. If you want to, you can ask a friend to read this meditation for you, so you can completely relax in the process and follow the instructions slowly.

THE BODY SAYS: "REST"

Rest is a beautiful opportunity for the body to relax and let go. It is a natural state of replenishment that is so needed by our physical body, mind and soul.

Rest is available to us at any time and it allows us a deep nourishment of energy. Rest can be seen as a conscious gift to ourselves rather than a sign of weakness and procrastination.

With the help of proper rest, we can learn how to heal ourselves naturally and ask the body to reprogram itself by using our own healing buttons. When we rest, we create a healing sanctuary for our body and give it an opportunity to restore the balance in its own way.

Rest is a natural state of being where our organs recharge and heal of their own accord.

A true rest is a time spent on our own in peaceful and calm surroundings. It is not just a break when we turn to outside distractions, like phones or television; this takes our energy away and muddles our thoughts. A true rest is a sacred time for ourselves when we consciously create a relaxing environment and disconnect from any distractions.

65

Turn everything off, even your thoughts and your responsibilities, and allow yourself a space of complete emptiness for some time.

A proper rest can be short, but if it is done in the right way, with respect to ourselves and our body, it will replenish us much more than a long rest with a distracting environment. You can create a sacred portal for yourself, which you enter every day for a short period of time, to have your special rest with your attention completely devoted to yourself.

When we allow ourselves to rest, we enter a divine state of nourishment for our soul from above. At this moment the healing powers of the Universe come to help us in the best way. We give higher powers an opportunity to reach out to us and work on our bodies to bring the balance. When we free our mind and turn off our busy activity, the systems in the body can come back to agreement, helping each other to realign and grow in strength.

Rest is not a weakness but a necessity. The body knows exactly how much rest it needs to renew and function well.

Rest is absolutely needed by everybody in current times. There is so much emphasis put on a busy lifestyle nowadays, that we often sacrifice our bodies to the illusion of constant race in this world. Stress can be damaging for health as the natural state of the body is supposed to be peace and relaxation. Once we agree that rest is a beautiful, rewarding and actually a more productive way of being, we can create a healing environment for ourselves.

You only need to find several opportunities per day to allow yourself to switch off. It is the intention and the repetition of the resting process that works so well. The body will be grateful to you and will reward you with new ideas and a stronger power.

It is OKAY to rest.

The body carries its own wisdom and its own buttons that we need to press in order to turn the healing process on. Some of them are very natural and easy to do; we just need to provide the time and opportunity for the body to heal. If your body says: "Take a rest", please listen to it – it really needs your attention at this moment.

THE BODY SAYS: "MOVE"

Our life is a journey of movement: we are born, we grow, we go through experiences and move to different stages in life. In order to transit from one experience to another, we have to move, physically and metaphorically. Life is about constant change and flow.

In the same way, our bodies are made to move and keep the motion in order to progress on our journey. Only when we move do we discover new things and attract new experiences in our lives. The body knows about the importance of the constant flow and it enjoys when it is given a chance to move.

The body needs to move in order to make the energy flow freely and experience changes.

Everything in the Universe likes to move: the clouds, the Earth, the birds, the animals, even the flowers and the plants. Life is about movement and change and there is wisdom in every single motion.

Our bodies are equipped with the gift to move; they can synchronise with our inner rhythm and the outside world. When we move our body, we give it a chance to speak and open itself up. This is how the body can express itself: it shows its emotions and feelings through motions.

Movement allows our inner self to come out and express itself fully.

When we move, the energy flows in the body and reaches the parts that need to be nourished. It is almost like feeding the body with the breath of the Universe. Movement helps to release the stagnant energy and open the centres in the body.

Movement is not just about improving the body physically. It is an opportunity to clear the mind and balance the emotions. We can understand ourselves better when we move. It becomes a precious opportunity for our soul to express itself.

Spiritually, movement of the body represents our movement in life. When we feel stuck and we don't want to move forward on our path, the body may start experiencing pain and stiffness. It wants to remind us about the essence of the constant flow of life. Movement means opening up to new experiences, meeting new people, allowing ourselves to go to new places and exploring life. Letting go of fear and just going with the flow can increase the healing power of movement in our life.

Allow yourself to move in life by following your intuition.

One of the most beautiful forms of physical movement is dance. Dance is a magical process that gives us a chance to express ourselves freely. When we dance, we forget about our mind and let our spirit show itself. Dance helps us connect to our inner freedom and creativity.

Everybody can dance if they listen to their own body and their inner calling. The body already knows how it wants to move; it just needs an opportunity to demonstrate its talents. We can let go of the restrictions when we dance if we completely trust the expression of our spirit. We just follow it.

Through dance we receive the energy from the higher powers. They connect to us in this precious moment and help us to release any blockages and stagnant energy. We become our own healers when we dance freely from the heart.

Intuitive dance releases the emotions and connects you to your Higher Self.

Yoga is another beautiful gift that we can give to our body. Nowadays yoga has become very popular as it truly helps people to realign and become more balanced physically and emotionally. Yoga is a great way to cleanse the old energy, rejuvenate all the body and make a clearer contact with our inner selves. Yoga is incredibly healing: it balances the organs and directs the flow of energy into the body.

Every time we practise yoga, we feel calmer, more centred and aligned with our life path.

You can practise your own intuitive body movement at home as a part of your healing ritual. When you listen to your body and follow your inner rhythm without thinking, you can reach a state of deep relaxation. Just listen to the body and ask it how it would like to move now. Your intuition is your teacher.

PRACTICE TIME
INTUITIVE MOVEMENT

◊ Find a comfortable place where you can practise free movement without feeling restricted. Begin by closing your eyes and tuning into your body. The breath will connect you to your inner self and allow you to receive guidance from within.

◊ Start moving your body gently as if you are following your own breath and inner rhythm. You may choose to sway your hands in slow beautiful motions or turn your body softly from side to side. Let the intuitive feeling come to you as you start moving the body naturally.

◊ Continue to move and feel what your body needs the most at this moment. Is it a stretch? Is it a turn? Maybe your body would like to balance itself by repeating circular motions with your arms. Do not have any doubts at this point and feel how your inner self is taking over completely. Dance with your energy!

◊ During every move, become aware of what you feel in the body. How is this move helping you at this moment? Is it releasing the old energy? Is it replenishing your body? Is it helping you to balance your system? The body will tell you. Let your inner self remember what it feels like to be free. Feel the transformation and the joy in your body as you explore the natural ways of healing.

◊ Note that gentle circular movements are very good for balancing the body and aligning the left and the right sides. You can make slow circular movements with your hands, your upper body, your lower body or your head. It is a beautiful meditative way to connect to yourself as you are moving. You are creating a portal of energy that feeds you with nourishment and stamina.

◊ Explore any type of intuitive motion that comes to you naturally. Spend as much time as you like in each position and feed yourself with expressive energy. Your body really deserves it. You can finish your practice sitting cross-legged with your eyes closed or lying down. Feel the gratitude to yourself and your body for doing this exercise and make it a regular practice, if you wish.

INNER ANCHOR

Every ship sailing in the sea needs an anchor to keep it steady and grounded at times. In the same way, we, as physical beings, need an Inner Anchor to stay connected to our true inner state.

Inner Anchor is a metaphor that can help us stay focused and calm no matter what circumstances we find ourselves in. It is a state of being when we feel peace and connection to our true self. Inner Anchor is a reference point that we remember and can go back to if we drift away and experience a lack of emotional balance.

Everybody has an Inner Anchor inside as we all have the ability to find inner peace. The key is to locate the Inner Anchor within us and remember what it feels like, so we can bring it back when it is needed.

What is it like when you feel harmony inside? When are you at your best? What circumstances provide you with a feeling of peace, tranquility and inner knowing?

If you imagine the scales, where the movement of the left and the right sides can represent feeling too emotional and swayed by the circumstances of life, the Inner Anchor would be the place right in the middle. It is a neutral state that helps you to stay focused, calm and present.

Inner Anchor is a tool that you can master in order to help you deal with life situations. We are very used to having reactions when different events happen in our life, especially if they are sudden or traumatic. In these times, it can be difficult to remember the peaceful state inside, as we get distracted by strong feelings. If we learn to maintain the Inner Anchor in everyday simple situations, it will be easier to come back to it in more complex scenarios that may appear on our path.

Knowing your Inner Anchor will help you to move through the waves of life without being swayed or depleted energetically. It is a natural state of inner rest and stillness.

In order to find your Inner Anchor, you need to ask your body when it feels the best and experiment with it until you achieve the state that feels naturally peaceful.

PRACTICE TIME
FINDING YOUR INNER ANCHOR

◊ Find a comfortable position, close your eyes and relax. Start breathing deeply, allowing your body to release all its tensions and stress. Begin connecting to your inner self.

◊ Spend some time bringing the inner peace and relaxation into you. Imagine that everything inside of you is calming down, like waves in the ocean turning to complete stillness. Look within and ask your body to show you your Inner Anchor. Let it come as a feeling. What is your Inner Anchor like? Become aware of it and allow it to come to you intuitively.

◊ Expand that feeling in your body. Imagine that your whole being starts to emanate peace and inner knowing. You are becoming your Inner Anchor. Observe this state; enjoy every moment of it. Spend some timing being in it. Try and remember this feeling, so you can come back to it any moment that you like.

◊ As you come out of the meditation, imagine that you are taking your Inner Anchor with you. Set the intention to maintain this peaceful feeling for a longer period of time. Make an inner note that this is your anchor and that you can go back to it whenever you want. The more you focus on this feeling, the easier it will be for you to recreate it.

◊ As a subsequent practice, observe yourself daily and notice how your inner state changes throughout your life experiences. Which experiences make you lose your balance? When do you feel peaceful? Stay present and listen to your body and observe how you feel in every moment. The state of inner observation is the key for learning about yourself.

◊ Remember your Inner Anchor and have it as your remedy when you need calmness and serenity. Practise going back to it when you experience a strong emotion or a lack of balance inside. Imagine that it is a metaphorical road that you are taking within you so you can come back to your true home.

◊ You may even make a drawing of your Inner Anchor – a symbol that you can keep in a visible place that will remind you of your natural peaceful state. Let your Inner Anchor help you whenever you need it.

THE DIARY FOR THE BODY

Connect to your body in meditation and write down the answers to the following questions. Keep updating this material regularly as you evolve on your healing journey.

Questions for the body in general:
– How are you feeling today?
– What emotions are you experiencing?
– What energy do you feel in your body?
– Is there anything that is bothering you? What kind of a feeling is it?
– Are there any parts of your body that feel weaker or in need of help?
– What would you like to bring into your life the most now?

Questions for a particular organ in the body:
– How are you feeling?
– What are you trying to tell me?
– Which area of my life are you connected to?
– Which emotions do you represent?
– How long have you been feeling like this?
– What can I do to help you feel better?
– What shall I do more or less of?
– Do you have any dietary or lifestyle advice?
– What can I change in my life to heal you? Please guide me.

INTUITIVE GUIDANCE FOR DIFFERENT PARTS OF THE BODY

Each organ performs a certain physical function that has a corresponding spiritual meaning. The physical aspect of ourselves is a mirror of the energies that we are experiencing in our life.

In order to understand a deeper message that lies behind a certain symptom, we need to look into what that organ actually represents on a metaphysical level. It becomes clear when we ask ourselves how this organ helps us to function in life. This is general guidance that will help you to connect to some of the spiritual meanings of different parts of our body.

THE HEAD

The head is the dome of the body. It represents our mental activity and the process of creating thoughts. The head is responsible for how we function in the world; it helps us to reason, make decisions, perceive the world and communicate with other people.

The head is like a sacred temple that holds the wisdom and guidance for our life. We communicate with it to receive ideas and inspiration. Sometimes we put a lot of responsibility on our head, when we burden it with our thoughts, plans and decisions. The head can get overwhelmed and tired from too much pressure.

The wellbeing of our head is related to what is going on inside of us on the mental level – that is, what we think about, how we think, and how our thoughts make us feel. An overthinking head can create an energetic imbalance in this area and lead to discomfort and tension.

One of the common ailments related to the head is migraine. In metaphysical terms migraine can be explained as the accumulation of dense thoughts, often of a negative nature, which creates an energetic cloud in the head and manifests itself as a physical sensation. Stress and pressure can also contribute to the discomfort in the head.

If you are experiencing problems with the head, it is important to look at the way you think and process thoughts. How pleasant are your thoughts? How light are they? Do you carry any heavy thoughts in your head? Can you substitute these thoughts with happier ones?

A clear mind and relaxation are very important for the health of the head. The head functions best when it is in a peaceful environment and it is given love and appreciation. When we balance our thoughts in the head, we can receive higher messages of wisdom and connect to our inspiration.

Meditation is a wonderful way of becoming friends with the head. With practice, we can gradually develop the ability to maintain a clear and focused mind. In the beginning, it may seem that there are too many thoughts in the way; however, with time, this exercise will become easier and easier. Meditation will help to rebalance the energy in our head and make us feel calm.

In the same way, tranquil activities are very important remedies for the head – for example, a walk in the park, a relaxing massage, gardening or doing something creative. These soothing activities will release the pressure from the head and help to focus the energy in a balanced way.

You can also visualise the space in your head as a house where every room is beautiful and in a perfect order. Imagine how you would decorate your ideal house, what energies and objects you would like to bring there to make it comfortable and pleasant. If you feel that there is anything in your house that you don't need anymore, simply breathe it out and let it go. You head will really appreciate it.

In order to find your own preferred balancing remedy, you just need to ask your head at times when it feels the calmest and most peaceful. When you meditate, connect to your head and listen to its messages – it will give you the clues as to how to relieve the pressure and be happier. It already knows it.

My dear head, what would you like me to know now? How do you feel? What are you experiencing? I would like to know more about you...

Questions to ask yourself:
– How does your head feel most of the time? Is it light, neutral or heavy?

– If you ever experience discomfort in the head, how would you describe it?

– What does this feeling remind you of in your life? Are there times when you feel it more?

– When are the moments when you feel calmer in your head? What helps you to feel clearer?

– What are the majority of your thoughts like? What kind of energy do you feel from them? (For example, pleasant/tiring, peaceful/anxious, inspiring/depleting, light/dark, fast/slow/well-paced.)

– Can you single out the thoughts that make you feel good and include them more in your daily life?

– What can help you to create a better relaxing environment for yourself?

THE EYES

My beautiful eyes, what do you see? What would you like to see now? How can I assist you in the best way? I love you very much.

Eyes are the organs of vision that are responsible for both physical and psychic seeing. Through our eyes we perceive the world, interact with other people, differentiate colours and shapes in our reality. Eyes can also help us to connect to our intuition and see beyond the physical world when we tap into our psychic abilities and perceive auras, energies and vibrations around us.

Every time we are looking at something, the vibration of our eyes is connecting to the vibration of that object, and they interact on an energetic level. The vibration of the object literally travels to the frequency of the eyes and has an effect on them. This is why it is important to observe how various objects make us feel. The energy of the image can affect our eyes in different ways.

Let's say that we are looking at something pleasant, like a beautiful flower or our favourite animal. Our eyes are becoming happy and are smiling to themselves when they see something positive. They are receiving a high frequency from that image, and this has a good effect on the cells of the eyes.

If we are looking at something sad and upsetting, our eyes also react on an energetic level. They can pick up the low frequencies and get sad too. The eyes can even become ill if they see a lot of something they don't want to see. They are conscious beings that can react to what is going on around us, just as we do.

Our eyes can accumulate feelings from the experiences that we go through.

When we are reluctant to look at a certain aspect of our life, we may choose on a subconscious level to limit our ability to see things. This is when our eyes can create problems with the vision. Maybe we are afraid to see the future or we don't want to look at our special gifts and talents? Perhaps we hold on to the hurt from the past? The eyes carry valuable messages for us and we can talk to them in order to understand what we need to heal in our life.

Sometimes we can get used to having a weaker vision and wear glasses to help us to see clearly. However, is it really true that our eyes need to continue carrying the weight of the past or the fear of the future? Perhaps we can just allow our eyes to start seeing again and clear the pain that they have been storing. Our eyes certainly deserve to see all the beauty of the world.

It is important to pay attention to how we treat our eyes in everyday life. What pictures and scenes do we show them? Do we nourish them well by sharing happy moments and beautiful images? Do we give them enough rest daily? All these gifts are valuable for the health of our eyes.

Nowadays the rise of technology has entered our lives. A lot of our daily activities are connected to the internet and we often find ourselves glued to a screen. The truth is, technology emanates a lower frequency that can affect our eyes on an energetic level. It can make our eyes tired and less focused. We need to be careful with the amount of time that we spend with technology. When using a screen, always remember to ask your eyes how they feel and, if they are tired, give them a little rest. It is important to take balance into consideration.

After you have had contact with technology, especially for a long time, you can wash your eyes and hands with clear water. Just imagine that you are releasing the residue energy from the screen and replenishing your skin and eyes with water. You can also wash your energy in your imagination, just by passing the white light through your eyes. Feel how the light is cleansing every cell of your eyes and allowing them to rest. Then you can look at something beautiful in your reality, for example, a plant or a tree. This will clear the dense energy of technology.

The eyes can be strengthened in a meditation: just imagine the white light bathing them.

In order to be healthy, the eyes need to be rested and filled with positive emotions. It is a good idea to give your eyes some rest every day and to hold your hands over them so they can receive some of your soothing energy. This will cleanse your eyes and fill them with more power to heal. The eyes really need our support and encouragement, as they do so much for us every day.

Give your eyes some rest today.

Damaged eyes want to remember what it is like to see again. They want to learn to perceive the world in its fullness. You can practise imagining what it is like to have a perfect vision and establish this feeling back in the eyes. For example, in a meditation you can ask your eyes to show you what it is like to see perfectly. Try and connect to the time when you could see clearly and ask the cells to retrieve these memories and rejuvenate again. In other words, tune your eyes into the frequency of seeing.

Exercises and meditation for clearing the eyes with energy will significantly improve the process of healing. You can imagine bathing your eyes in the white light and helping them to release accumulated energy and tension. This practice will release the pressure from the eyes and contribute to the healing process.

Questions to ask yourself:

– How are my eyes feeling today? What kind of energy do I perceive in them?

– Do I enjoy seeing what I see every day? How does it make me feel?

– Are there any negative emotions stored in my eyes? (For example, fear, tension, tiredness, sadness.) If so, where do they come from?

– Can I release the emotions from the past? Have I seen anything that upset me in life? How can I let it go in the best way?

– Do I see my present and my future with openness? Do I like looking at all the aspects of my life?

– How do I treat my eyes? What do I do to make them happy? Do my eyes get enough love and rest?

– How can I help my eyes in the best way?

THE THROAT

My dear throat, what would you like to sing? What words of love would you like to say? Is there anything that you would like to express now?

The throat is a beautiful part of our body that was given to us so we can express ourselves through words and sounds. Our throat is like a tunnel of light where our ideas get formed into sounds and then are shared with other people.

The energy of expression travels through the throat and determines how well we communicate our feelings to the world. When the energy of what we want to say is not freely expressed, it can manifest as an unpleasant feeling in the throat. Energies like fear, doubt, lack of belief and unexpressed truth can accumulate in the throat and potentially lead to blockages in this area.

The wellbeing of the throat is related to how comfortable we are with expressing ourselves.

Self-expression with a healing intention can create a beautiful energy in the throat, which will awaken the stagnant energies and allow them to move out of the body. We can use uplifting and loving sounds to help our throat reach the balance and be free emotionally again. Saying words of love and truth to yourself will raise the vibration of the throat and transform its energy in a positive way.

A very effective visualisation for the throat is imagining a tunnel of light that is dissolving all the blockages there. You can imagine any colour that you like – blue, purple, green or white – and spread it everywhere in your throat. This will cleanse and renew the cells, helping your energy to express itself beautifully.

Deep breathing through the mouth helps to alleviate the tensions in this area, especially when you are breathing consciously with the intention of healing. You can visualise the light cleansing your throat while you are taking deep slow breaths; this will strengthen the effect of the meditation even more.

Speaking your truth to other people or even to yourself will also help to release the stuck energy from the throat. If you find it difficult to express your feelings openly to others, you can just practice closing your eyes and saying what you feel to yourself when you are on your own. After a little while, the words will start flowing and it will get easier for you to express your deepest feelings. We are giving the body a chance to release its emotions.

Just open your mouth and begin to express how you feel. Let the words, sounds and emotions flow.

And, of course, singing is a wonderful way to balance our throat chakra. You can create gentle loving sounds that make you feel good or hum some of your favourite songs. Our throats love to sing! Think of all the animals and birds that constantly make sounds and express themselves – they naturally feel that it is the right thing to do. Singing is healing.

Questions to ask yourself:

– Am I expressing myself fully in life? Do I allow myself to say what I really think?

– Is my creativity expressed well? Are there any projects or ideas that I want to create but I am holding back?

– Are there any lower emotions related to my throat and self-expression, like fear, doubt, worry or pain? How could I express them better? Ask the throat to guide you.

– Is there anything stuck from the past that I couldn't express at the time? Was I not able to say something that I felt? Can I say it now?

– If I was completely free, how would I express myself now? Would I sing, play or write?

THE LUNGS

Thank you, dear lungs, for helping me to breathe! I can experience life fully this way. Is there anything that I can do for you to heal? What would make you feel better?

The lungs are the trees of life that were given to our bodies to help us breathe. With the lungs we connect to the world and breathe the air into our body. The lungs are intrinsically connected to the heart and the blood and help to spread the oxygen in our system.

Spiritually, the lungs represent the freedom of the breath and the ability to enjoy life without limitations or restrictions. If we can breathe fully, we can establish our presence the way that we like in this life. If we restrict ourselves, we are putting a limitation on our experiences and thus our breath can become shallower too.

Breathing also represents our connection to the current life situation; the air that we breathe is a symbolic metaphor of the circumstances that surround us. If we find ourselves in a situation that is emotionally suffocating us, this may be reflected in a way that we breathe.

The lungs represent the ability to breathe fully in life, both physically and emotionally.

When the circumstances in our life become stuffy and restricted, this may affect our lungs on an energy level. For example, a certain situation may not give us enough space, like limiting circumstances at work, problems at home and in relationships, or perhaps even our own restricted view on life. These feelings of suffocation can spiritually affect our ability to breathe and make us feel enclosed.

The lungs need plenty of air and space to breathe. The more they can embrace the fullness of life, the happier they will become.

Freedom and opportunities to breathe without fear will help to bring the balance to our respiratory system.

Working on freedom and self-expression can be a positive step to balance the energy in the lungs. It may be worth looking at the current life situation and finding if there is anything that may be preventing us from enjoying our life fully. Perhaps a change is needed or more space can be created in order to allow us to breathe in a comfortable way.

Sometimes the external situation can't be changed immediately, so instead we can focus on developing a feeling of inner freedom. While practising deep breath, you can affirm to yourself: "I can", "I am free", "I allow myself full life", "I can make my own decisions" and see how the energy of these words is helping your body. Imagine that you are free and you can do anything that you like, despite the circumstances that you are in. You will feel a sense of inner joy at this moment and the energy of freedom will have a positive effect on your lungs.

Natural healers, like trees, plants and the earth, are very good remedies for the lungs. The purpose of nature is to bring us fresh air and cleanse our body from within. Walking in nature and breathing deeply, while observing the green colour of the trees, will help us to purify the lungs and synchronise with the healing power of nature.

Cleanse your lungs with breath and the energy of nature.

Breathing exercises are wonderful for healing our respiratory system as they help to release the stuck energies from the body. You may visualise that you are breathing the air full of bright light into your lungs, helping them to cleanse internally. Imagine the white light in every cell of your lungs and visualise them getting balanced, both physically and emotionally.

You can also think of the situation in your life that makes you feel stuck and suffocated. Imagine that you are directing a breath of pure light to this situation, dissolving the difficulties and letting go of the stuck energy. This will bring you more freedom and will help the situation to move forward.

Questions to ask yourself:
– Am I breathing fully in life? Do I feel free in every situation?
– Are the circumstances in my life giving me enough freedom? Is there anything that may be restricting me and preventing me from full breath?
– Are there any thoughts or beliefs that give me a feeling that I am restricted? How can I change them?
– Is the physical environment around me healthy and natural? Do I get enough fresh air and connection with nature?
– Are there any past traumas related to emotional stifling and feeling claustrophobic? How can I release them?
– How can I make my lungs happy?

THE HEART

I can hear you pumping in my chest… You are so beautiful! Thank you for being here for me and for helping me to love and be loved. Is there anything that I can do for you to make you happy? Tell me!

The heart is the most beautiful and loving organ given to us by the Universe. It has the purpose of creating love and sharing it with the world around us.

The heart is our centre; it gives birth to wonderful ideas and brings us the joy of loving. When we listen to our heart, we feel happy and elevated from within. The heart whispers to us messages of truth and inner knowing all the time. It helps to guide us in the right direction as it contains an eternal source of loving energy. We can share this energy abundantly with the world.

The heart is always right.

When we are centred in our heart, our decisions and thoughts become love-based and reflect true compassion for the world and for ourselves. Living from the heart allows us to be intuitive, because this way we can hear the voice of our soul without the boundaries of the thinking mind.

Listen to the heart to hear the messages from your soul.

Our heart is very powerful. We can direct the healing energy from the heart and help ourselves and other people to feel better. The heart can release the pain, melt down lower feelings and clear stuck energy. We can use the heart to shine light on our path and manifest the wishes of our soul.

The heart is a natural healer.

Ailments arising in the heart are connected with feelings of love and appreciation of ourselves and other people. It is related to our ability to live freely and limitlessly, receiving and giving our feelings to the world. The heart reflects how much we trust ourselves, other people and life in general, and how much we open the gateways of our soul to the world.

Tension in the area of the heart can be related to stored emotions of hurt and being closed off from the experiences in life. Sometimes we go through a difficult relationship and the pain stays in our heart, not allowing it to open again to the beauty of life. Fear of getting hurt can also cause an imbalance in the heart. We need to bring these energies to the light and heal them with love.

Love and trust are the most wonderful medicine when it comes to healing the heart.

The heart loves to be open and trusting. It jumps at the idea of doing the things that you love doing and communicating with the world on the level of compassion and kindness. The heart loves the energy of forgiveness; it wants us to release the old emotions of pain and hurt and be open to trust again.

"Please, let go of your pain and let me love again," asks the heart.

You can support your heart by breathing love and trust into it. Every time you focus on your heart, it becomes stronger and vibrates with your true soul energy. You can visualise your heart having wings and flying freely, allowing you to create a loving relationship with yourself and the world. Imagine the beautiful birds of paradise flying out of your heart and reaching all the places in the Universe, spreading your love everywhere.

Sending love energy to the heart will automatically release the fear and pain from past experiences. Allow the light to shine brightly in your heart and envelop it in a sparkling ball of loving energy. Carry it with your every moment of your life and let the heart guide you on your path.

Questions to ask yourself:

– What do I feel in my heart now? Is my heart open? Are there any restrictions there?

– How can I make my heart be more open and trusting now? Ask the heart to guide you in this healing process.

– Am I listening to my heart? What is my heart telling me?

– How do I interact with the world around me? Am I open to life experiences and other people?

– Is love flowing freely in my life? Am I loving to myself?

– Is there anything that I need to let go from the past? Can I fully embrace my expansive self?

THE BACK

My dear back, I really appreciate and love you! What would make you feel stronger and more balanced? Is there anything that I can do in life to support you more? I would love to help you!

The back represents the pillar of our body and helps to maintain other important organs in balance, playing a major role in our general wellbeing. When the back is healthy, the whole body feels strong and energised.

Our back is carrying powerful energy for our body, like the trunk of a tree or the stem of a flower. Through our legs and feet, it draws the energy in from the earth and then spreads it to all the other organs, feeding them with natural power. This helps us to feel grounded and safe in life.

On a metaphysical level, the problems with the back can represent the weight that we carry and accumulate in our life. Just like we put heavy bags and rucksacks on our shoulders, we put the invisible energy of responsibilities and duties on our backs. If we want to heal our back, we need to release the weight that we have put on ourselves in life.

Set your back free by releasing the feeling of burden inside of you.

The back is communicating with all our body at once and lets us know if something goes wrong or loses balance. It shows us when the energy doesn't flow freely in the body or if there are blockages and constraints. For example, if the body is experiencing too much stress, the spine may give us a message in the form of pain or tension. It prompts us to look at our life and understand if there is anything that we need to change or release.

Sometimes the spine may indicate that we need more movement in our life, for example, if we spend too much time sitting down in one position. The spine may give us a signal that our spirit wants to come out and dance and be free. In this case, we can listen to the language of our spine and move our body in a way that it wants. Our inner spirit will guide us to release the tension from our back.

If we are experiencing problems with the spine, we need to see how much love and support we give to ourselves.

The spine loves freedom and lightness. It wants to release any extra weight that it carries in life, be it heavy responsibilities, obligations or worries. The spine likes open movement and self-expression, just like everybody else does.

On our healing path, it is important to recognise the beautiful support that our back gives to us and express our gratitude to this organ for holding all our body together. We can show our love to the back by giving it rest, some exercise and care. This will help our spine to feel appreciated and loved, and it will respond back with the same positive energy.

You can imagine that you are releasing the weight from the back by removing any invisible chains or shackles that may have been attached to it. This will help you to let go of any energies that don't belong to you anymore and set yourself free. You can also visualise that the heaviness and weight is melting down through your spine into the earth, leaving your back in its perfect, pure and light state. Our imagination with a healing intention is a very powerful tool.

Visualising white light in your back will help you to release the tension and bring back the balance to the body.

You may also wish to imagine a pair of beautiful wings that appear on your back. They can take any shape and colour that you like.

Enjoy having magical wings of freedom and let them move in a playful and liberating way. Imagine that you are flying and that you are free to do whatever you like. This visualisation will help to heal your back and bring the feelings of freedom and happiness into your life.

Questions to ask yourself:
– Is my back fully appreciated and nurtured in life? Do I respect and love my back?

– What energy am I holding in my back? Are there any tensions or worries that reside there? What is my back telling me?

– Do I carry any extra weight on my back? Do I hold responsibilities that belong to other people? Where are they located? How can I release them?

– Am I feeling supported in life? How can I show support to myself?

– Are there any heavy burdens from the past in my back? How can I release them?

– What would make my back feel better? Do I get enough rest and relaxation in life?

– Would my back like more physical activity? What kind of movement would it like to have?

THE STOMACH AND THE DIGESTIVE SYSTEM

My dear stomach, you are so wonderful! You help me to digest my food and my emotions in life. I am so grateful for your beautiful work. Tell me, what can I do to make you happy? Can you guide me? What food would you really like and what is not for you? What emotions would you like to have? Please tell me; I would love to be your friend.

Our stomach is a precious part of the body that is responsible for the vital process of digesting what we eat. It breaks down the food and helps to move it through the body. On a metaphysical level, the function of our stomach is similar: it digests the experiences and situations that we go through in life. When strong emotions and stress come into our life, the stomach takes the responsibility to digest it, just like it processes the food that we eat.

If the stomach is being exposed to low energies – for example, difficult life situations, negative emotions and unhappy food – it may feel a lack of power and show the need for a proper nourishment. We may experience heaviness, discomfort or blockages in the digestive area. The energies in the stomach affect the whole body as this is where we receive our nutrition from. It is like the sun spreading its rays all around the planet – the brighter it shines, the happier the people on the planet are. When our stomach is being fed with high, uplifting energies – for example, positive emotions, organic food and a relaxing environment – it starts to heal from within.

Our stomach needs love and relaxation; it has so much stress to deal with.

As the stomach is responsible for digestion, it is important to nourish it with the right energies. Everything that we take in as food becomes a part of us vibrationally. This can have an effect on our physical body and emotions. Hence, it is helpful to observe what vibrations we introduce into our body daily. What is our diet like? How does the food that we eat make us feel? You can even make a list of the products that make you feel uplifted, for example, fruit and vegetables that you like. Also make a note of the products that bring your energy down and don't feel right for you, for example, too many sweet things or processed food. You can listen to the intuitive feeling of 'yes' or 'no' when you are taking the food into your hand and beginning to eat it. This will confirm the right choice for you.

Interact with your stomach and let it guide you on your path of nutrition.

At the same time, our stomach is digesting everything that we go through in life: our life situations, our relationships, our jobs and our environment. When working on healing our digestive system, we need to see if our life situations are balanced. Is there anything in your life that is giving you pressure? Can you change it in any way? We can always ask our body for guidance during a meditation and listen to what can be done to improve our lifestyle.

The body already has a perfect plan for your wellbeing. You just need to listen to it.

We can make it easier for our stomach if we learn to regularly relax and let the tension out. You can practise deep breathing and relaxing the stomach as much as possible. Every time you are breathing out, imagine that you are allowing more and more relaxation to come to your digestive system. You will be surprised by how much tension can be released in this simple way.

Just like any other part of our body, our stomach loves feeling appreciated and cared for. The energy of gratitude helps to release the stress from the stomach and bring a healthy flow of energy into our digestive system. You can even place your hand on the stomach and ask it with all your heart: "My dear friend, what would make you feel happier?"

You can also imagine cleansing the stomach with a beautiful white light that is spreading through the whole digestive system. Visualise all the toxins leaving the body safely and allow only the high energies in your system. Imagine that you are filling every organ with pure white light and it is bringing the balance and power back to you. While doing this work, you can ask your stomach what type of nutrition would be the best for it.

Another version of this exercise is to imagine a bright golden yellow light inside of the stomach. This is a powerful healing colour for the solar plexus chakra, as it connects you to the energy of the sun. Visualise the sun in your stomach and imagine that it is spreading multiple shiny rays all around your digestive system, touching your organs with the healing light. The energy of the sun is very pure and empowering; it will help to disperse any negative energies from your solar plexus.

Questions to ask yourself:

– Are there any situations in my life that my stomach finds hard to digest? What can I do about them?

– Is there any tension or stress in my life? How can I release it?

– How do I take care of my digestive system in the best way? What can make it happy?

– Am I spending enough time to relax my stomach? How can I better relax myself?

– If I listened to my stomach, what would it tell me? What kind of a diet is good for me?

– How can I nourish my stomach better? What energies are good for it?

– Do I breathe deeply enough? Can I direct my breath to the stomach to release the tensions?

THE REPRODUCTIVE SYSTEM

My flower of joy, how are you feeling today? Am I giving you enough love and care? What would you like to create in my life? What are you giving birth to? You have all my love and support for your special creations. You are beautiful!

Our reproductive organs are a wonderful gift from the Universe. They help us to connect to the person we love and to start a new life. When we experience bliss, our sacral organs can be the direct channel for our higher spiritual connection. What can be more miraculous that that?

Nevertheless, a great deal of lower emotions can often be attributed to these organs, such as shame, pain, worry, lack of self-love. We are often brought up with a feeling of guilt and shame about our physical body and we don't tend to talk much about our reproductive organs. It is considered a secret subject, something that is not right to discuss openly and share. This creates a lot of hidden emotional energy in the sacral chakra, also contributed by the effect of mass media and low-vibrational words. The physical connection between two people is rarely portrayed from a spiritual perspective, which, in fact, when approached with love and gentleness, can be a powerful healing experience.

Our reproductive organs are so beautiful and so important for our happiness. They are the epitome of our expression of masculinity and femininity, like a wonderful flower that we carry with us all the time. This flower is capable of expressing love, creating new projects and bringing spiritual experiences. If only we could give support to our love organs by nourishing them, accepting them, bathing them in our appreciation and kindness, while doing the same for the person who we love, this would transform our lives and society.

At the moment, it feels like the whole energy of physical unity has gone far from its essence, tarnished by fear and the imbalance of power. People have forgotten how to see gods and goddesses in each other. They have forgotten that they can heal with the power of love and use the gentle touch that radiates pure kindness and affection. When we have an intention to heal and uplift during the physical connection, we can create a magical experience for each other. And it is not only about the body; it is also about channeling the right energy and connecting on the level of the heart and the spirit. We get a beautiful chance to see the divine power in ourselves and each other when we connect this way.

Miracles can happen when the physical connection is nourished with high healing energies. When the partners show each other love, respect and appreciation by sharing healing energy, kind words and a gentle touch, the spirit of both elevates and expands. Then the creative power of the two comes together and it is ready to produce something beautiful into this world, be it a new creation, a flow of inspiration or just loving energy.

Reproductive organs are portals for love and spiritual growth. They need to be treated with respect and appreciation.

A lot of problems with sacral organs can be connected to confusing emotions, such as guilt, shame and fear, and to one's masculine and feminine expression. Sometimes we don't want to accept who we are and we feel blocked in our sacred expression. We can carry hurt and shame from past experiences in our life. Letting go of lower feelings and accepting our divine expression in this lifetime can help to create a beautiful space for our sacral organs to blossom.

You can connect to your reproductive organs by talking to them, feeling them and saying wonderful things to them. If you show them love through the kindness and gentleness of your energy, while having high-frequency thoughts, it will begin a healing process. Imagine that your reproductive organs are like a flower and they are blossoming inside of you with the most beautiful iridescent colours. Connect to every petal of the flower and give it love and appreciation. Your energy of kindness will heal your sacral organs.

Try and say to them: "You are beautiful. I love you so much. You make me feel happy. You create beautiful things. I trust you. I like you. I believe in you. I am so happy that you are with me." And then see how the energy in the sacral centre changes and transforms. You will soon feel a pleasant energy of love coming to you and dissolving all the negative frequencies. You can also ask your reproductive organs how you can help them and what makes them happy. Then just listen. The answer will come as a feeling.

Another side of the health of the reproductive organs is connected to our relationships with other people, especially our love relationships. If something is not working well or is out of balance in our love life, if there is tension or irritation there, it may manifest as an imbalance in our reproductive organs as a reminder that something is not right for us. It is a good idea to listen to your sacral organs and their response to a particular person in your life, as this is a true guide to how your energy feels about this connection.

On the whole, a loving and caring approach is what our reproductive organs really need. You can express it by allowing them to speak in a meditation or in writing. Let them express their feelings and release all the energy that has been accumulated there for years, starting with the emotions coming from your childhood and continuing to adult life. We tend to store feelings in our sacral chakra. Ask your reproductive organs to release any old pain and sorrow that may have been there and let them speak the truth of who they really are.

Then you can send all the love that you can imagine to your reproductive organs. Nourish them with love, tell them beautiful words, give them all the precious energy that they deserve. Imagine that the highest energy of love is flowing through your body and enriching your sacral organs. You can tell them that everything is going to be alright and that they are safe and looked after by you. Focus on the flower energy there and imagine it opening up, blossoming and radiating pure love and happiness. You can create miracles for your own body!

Self-acceptance, love and care are the healing energies for the reproductive organs.

Questions to ask yourself:

– How do I feel about my reproductive organs? What emotions are stored in them?

– Do I express my femininity or masculinity well? Do I feel comfortable in my own body?

– Have I experienced any trauma, lack of appreciation or oppression as a child? Where is it stored in my body? Can I release it now through self-love?

– What are my relationships like? How do I feel about them?

– What could make me happy in a love relationship? What does my heart say?

– How can I help my sacral organs to be happier? What makes them feel uplifted?

– If I could imagine that I was a flower, what kind of a flower would I be? What would I look like? What scent would I emanate? What colours would I have?

– What projects am I currently working on in life? How is my creative expression flowing?

– Do I love and accept myself as I am? How can I show it to myself now?

THE LEGS AND THE FEET

Where are you carrying me, my beautiful legs? Where is my path going? Do I feel supported and encouraged on my journey? Do I enjoy exploring new places? Show me where my true path is.

The legs and the feet represent moving forward in life. They carry us to our destination, help us to cross the roads and choose different pathways, depending on where we want to go.

Metaphorically, our legs mean a change in our life, something new that we are moving forward to. In order to shift from one place to another, be it in a physical dimension or on a spiritual journey, we need to make a move and go somewhere.

What happens if somebody feels reluctant to move? Or if somebody doesn't want a change in their lives?

Then our joints can become stiff because the energy is not encouraged to move. Our hips, our knees and feet may develop a discomfort – only to remind us that our spirit wants to grow and move on. Many people refuse a change in their life and stick to the old ways because they are afraid to take the next step. The legs are there to remind us that we have to be brave and go where the feeling is taking us.

Move forward. Make a change. Follow your heart and its calling.

The change doesn't always have to be significant, sometimes it can be just a small transformation that will help to shift the energy – perhaps a new hobby or activity. Maybe all your life you have wanted to do something but you never thought it was the right time. Or perhaps you felt that you were not good enough to pursue a certain career or path. If you know deep inside of you that you really want to do something, then go for it. Any time is good for it and it is never too late. The energy of the Universe will adjust to your decision and help you.

Ask your legs how they feel and where they would like to go. You can explore guided meditations, where you connect to your life purpose and receive messages for your path. Meditate more and take the advice from your intuition and your body. Your legs will be very grateful and will gladly take you to your new horizons.

You can visualise your feet becoming very light and having wings attached to them. Imagine that they are taking you anywhere you like and that you are floating effortlessly to any destination. See yourself exploring different paths that open new possibilities for you. Enjoy this feeling of lightness and welcome the energy of change into your body. The legs will listen to this visualisation and begin to feel better.

Take good care of your legs and nourish them with love as you walk. It is important to give a lot of appreciation and gratitude to the legs for carrying us to our preferred destinations. You can help your legs by taking them to the places that they really enjoy, maybe a park or a forest. These intuitive ideas will come from your body.

Questions to ask yourself:

– How do I feel about a change in my life?

– Where would I like to move on my journey? Which destinations are calling me?

– Am I resisting any changes? Why am I feeling this way?

– Where do my legs take me quickest? Where do they go slower? Observe them.

– What do my legs really enjoy? Is there any type of activity that makes them feel light and happy?

– Am I connecting enough to earth? Do I spend enough time in nature breathing the energy from the ground?

THREE

THE 2ND WONDER OF THE SELF: WE CAN SEE

The Creator has gifted us with the most beautiful organs that help us to perceive the world in its colourful diversity – our eyes.

The eyes are the mirrors of our spirit and our inner energy. They contain information about who we are on a soul level and what experiences we have had on our journey. Through the eyes, we can express ourselves and understand others telepathically.

The eyes are incredible organs that help us to function in the world and to decode the reality that is happening around us. Our eyes can choose how they want to perceive the world, depending on the way they look at it. They take in different energies from the outside reality and form them into pictures, which are then deciphered in our mind into names and concepts.

Our eyes are also a conduit of energy. Every time we look at somebody or something, we share our energy with them. The more loving our look is, the better the receiver will feel. It works the other way round too. The eyes receive the energy from the people and things that we are looking at. It is a constant exchange of energy.

We communicate energetically with people and objects that we are looking at.

Our eyes are the purest form of expression, which is beyond words and thoughts. They are quick to show what is really happening within us and can reveal our genuine feelings and intentions. It is really through the eyes where the most truthful communication between people takes place.

When we are open to the intuitive realm, we can learn to see the non-physical world with our eyes: the energy of people, plants, animals, stones, crystals and more. Our eyes have the power to go beyond the visible realm and tune into the subtle energy frequencies. This ability can be used for healing and balancing our life and body. We can understand what energy emanates from the objects surrounding us and then choose the appropriate energies for ourselves. We can also play with the energy inside and outside of our body to create beautiful energy fields that will protect and heal us.

When we start perceiving the world on the level of energy, it turns out to be a magical place where every object emanates a frequency and talks to us in an intuitive way.

A wonderful gift of our eyes is the ability to visualise images, creating them in the non-physical space and bringing them to life through our intention. With the help of our eyes, we can imagine our body being healthy, we can travel to the places that we dream about, and we can achieve things that we really want. Anything that we would like to manifest in our life, our eyes can create it.

If we direct enough energy and intention into our creation, it will take a physical form and manifest in our life.

The eyes are a blessing, both on the level of vision and on the level of intuition. They allow us to be nurtured by the beauty of the world: vibrant colours, harmonic shapes and magnificent nature. At the same time, the eyes can help us to change the way we see things and transform our reality into a magical place.

EVERYTHING SHINES WITH ENERGY

If we were to defocus our eyes and tune into the world on an energy level, we would see that everything around us is vibrating at a certain frequency. People, animals, objects, sounds and even thoughts – they all have energy, which is moving and communicating with us all the time.

We would be surprised to see that there is an energy field surrounding everything that we come across in life, such as the food, the water, the trees, the birds, even the objects that appear to be inanimate. They also have energy. If we practise looking at them long enough, we would begin to differentiate between various types of frequencies – for example, uplifting and happy ones or the ones carrying a more dense and unbalanced vibration. We would understand what energies are good for us and which ones are not in harmony with us.

One of the things we would see is that our body is also made of energy. All our inner organs have energy and the body itself is surrounded by a vibrational field called an aura. This is a sphere of light protecting our body that helps us to communicate with other energies around. Through our aura we interact with other people and exchange our energy with the outside world.

In this energy world, where everything affects everything on a vibrational level, our eyes have a very important role. They can transform things as we look at them. With the help of our eyes, we can send light and positive emotions to an object, and this will bring a healing effect to it. When we look at somebody with a loving intention, it changes their energy in an uplifting way. A person can start feeling better and a flower can blossom beautifully, just because it is nourished with a good vibration from our eyes. This is pure magic that is happening on an everyday level; we just don't always realise the power of our energy.

In the same way, positive visualisation works for our own body. We can direct our loving eyes and kind imagination inwards and benefit from our own healing energy. Imagining a healthy body and looking at it with love will help to bring it power and balance. You will find some techniques of how to visualise a healthy body in this chapter.

SEEING WITH YOUR INNER EYE

Our eyes have an ability to see the spiritual realm as well as to perceive our everyday reality. When we look at something, we are capable of tuning into the energetic field of this object and picking up its particular vibration.

This way, clairvoyants can see the auras of people and objects: they tap into a different dimension where everything exists as energy. This dimension is very close to us, we just don't always look beyond the physical realm. If we decide to look into the energy world, we would be able to see the energetic structure of every object and perceive messages from the subtle world.

Everybody can train themselves to see energy through their feeling and intuitive perception. It takes some energy awareness to develop the ability to tune into the vibration of objects; the more we observe the energy, the more it begins to speak to us. This can be a very helpful tool in the healing process, as energy awareness will let us intuitively understand how our body functions.

In order to practise seeing with your inner eye, you can experiment with looking at objects without focus and concentrating on the energy that is emanating from them. Imagine that an object has a certain vibration, which appears like a gentle glow around it. Focus on that glow and listen to the feeling that it gives to you.

Visualise the aura of that object, trusting the images that come from your intuition. Your first sensations will help you to connect to the energy of that object.

For example, you can use a candle to practise this technique. Look at the candle very softly, just perceiving its energy and colour. Allow your eyes to defocus and be very receptive. Try not to think at this moment, just feel and sense. Communicate with the candle through energy. What kind of vibration is emanating from it now? How would you imagine its aura? How does the candle make you feel?

In the same way, this technique works when we look at ourselves and other people. With our eyes we can perceive the energy field of another person, including their vibrations, their body, their emotions and their mental state. After some practice, it will be possible to tell precisely where the body may contain an imbalance and what can be done to heal it.

The power to see intuitively develops with practice.

In this practice we learn to really trust ourselves and our inner guidance. It is always good to start with ourselves and practise on our own body first, so we can get accustomed to this technique and learn how to trust our intuitive seeing. You will always know that you are on the right path, if the message that you receive resonates on a vibrational level with you.

Our body is a beautiful learning field with so many secrets, mysteries and revelations. We can explore so many healing practices just by looking at ourselves and listening to our inner guidance. It is simply great that we have a chance to practise our skills on ourselves and receive healing this way.

When we work with energy in all its various aspects, we need to remember to be very gentle and loving. Use the heart as our guide and be very kind to ourselves and other people. If you are talking to somebody else and trying to help them, imagine that you are talking to yourself. What would be the best way to say what you want to say? How would you treat yourself in this situation? It is always nice to be gentle. A loving word reaches the heart and is the most healing form of communication.

A wonderful way to practise inner seeing is to look at your own reflection in the mirror. Find some time to practise this exercise and let your intuition be your guide. Your clairvoyant abilities will benefit from this exercise and you will get a deeper understanding of the energy inside of your body.

PRACTICE TIME
TRAINING YOUR INNER EYE

◊ Stand in front of a mirror. Let's begin by looking at yourself in the eyes and connecting to yourself. Take your time. There is so much that you can learn from your own eyes! Imagine that there is a current of energy running between your eyes and their reflection in the mirror. It is made of a beautiful light. Tune into that channel. Feel what your eyes are telling you. Let your inner self shine through your eyes. Be with it for some time.

◊ Now let's start to visually scan your body. Imagine that your eyes can see beyond the physical realm and perceive the subtle energies in your body. Focus on the top of your head and feel it. What energy is emanating from it? What do you feel? Is it harmonious or does it feel like it needs more balance? Perhaps you could perceive some colours or vibrations there. Scan the top of your head with your eyes and trust your feeling.

◊ Now let's move to your forehead and your eyes. Go beyond the physical reflection that you see in the mirror. Perceive the energy of your body. It will speak to you through your feeling. What energy do you feel in your eyes? Do they look happy or tired? Is the energy in your forehead flowing well? Connect to the frequency in your eyes and feel its vibration.

◊ If you feel that an organ needs balancing, for example, the energy may feel low, stuck, cluttered or heavy, you can ask this organ telepathically for the best way to clear it. Trust the first answer and then use the message that comes to you to help heal this organ energetically. You may wish to imagine bathing it in a colourful light, or perhaps release some extra energies from it by moving your hands in a cleansing way. Trust what feels right and visualise it happening simultaneously in the mirror.

◊ Be very free in this exercise and really believe your own sensations. You will get more confident with practice. How does it feel when you are doing it? Is the body experiencing a relief? Does it feel good? Then continue. Listen to your body as your guide; it will tell you everything that you need to know. You are your own healer.

◊ Repeat the same process with the whole body, scanning and balancing all the organs (the throat, the lungs, the heart, the stomach, the reproductive system and others). Pay special attention to the organs that often feel unbalanced and need help. Be creative and follow the first intuitive sensations that come to you.

◊ In the end, place a beautiful shiny aura around your body and see it glowing like a sphere of light around you. Believe that this energy will stay there and protect you with its luminous light. Say thank you to yourself in the mirror for this lovely work! You did so well! Your body will be very grateful to you.

VISUALISING IS CREATING

Our eyes do not just receive the information from the outside world but they also have the capacity to create our experiences. Every time we direct the energy from our eyes to our reality, we create energy. The quality of this energy depends on the frequency and the intention that we focus on. For example, if we look at something with love, it can become more beautiful in our reality. If we judge something with our eyes, we can make it look dimmer and lose its light.

Our talented eyes can also create a dream inside of us. It is a vision that we would like to come true in our life – a perfect scenario, a happy outcome, a successful event that we want to happen in the future. Our mind can fill this vision with colours, shapes, motions, scents, sounds and feelings. This is part of the constant creation process that helps to form our reality.

We create our reality all the time with the help of our imagination and feelings.

Daily we visualise a lot of things: future events, memories from the past, being in different places and meeting other people. Many times, we don't even realise how much we imagine every moment of our life. It is a constant process. When we begin to observe what kind of scenes we visualise every day, we start to realise how these images may be affecting our reality. What kind of scenes are our eyes creating? How does it feel when we imagine them?

If we direct our natural process of visualisation towards our desired goals, we can reach our dream destination quicker. The truth is that energy is alive and, as soon as we create something in our mind, it begins to vibrate on an energy level and has the potential to become real. After doing it repeatedly for some time, especially with a strong belief and action, we can bring this energy physically into our life. This is a gift that our eyes have. They start the creation process. So why not use our natural ability to create a positive reality for ourselves?

The practice of visualisation can accelerate our healing journey if we send positive images to our body. Just like we manifest our life goals, we can create a healthy body by using our imagination. This is a gift that was given to us from birth and that is not used to its full potential. Nobody taught us as children that we can improve our health with our own vision.

Spend some time imagining how your body is getting healthier and more balanced. It wants to see this image so it can adjust to the new version of you.

Visualisation is best when it is coupled with positive feelings and a strong belief. Think of a team of helpers who can assist you on the journey of creation: vision, intention, feeling, belief, action. Each one of them will help you to accelerate your creation process.

QUANTUM REALITY

We live in a quantum reality where everything is interconnected and interchangeable. The way we perceive the world can change how we experience it. Our eyes affect our own reality.

You can try to look at something with a lot of love and see how the energy of this object begins to change. You may notice how it warms up and opens just in front of you. When you look at something with kindness and appreciation, a part of this energy goes to this object and enriches it with these qualities. We are transforming the object with our eyes and giving it more brilliance. Imagine how uplifted everybody would feel if we were to do this consciously for each other.

Every time you are looking at somebody or something with love, you are helping them.

On the contrary, if we are looking at something with disapproval, this feeling can travel to this object and shift its energy in our reality. It may not appear as wonderful as it could have been for us. It is almost as though we have special filters in our eyes that help us to perceive the Universe. We ourselves choose the filters that we want to see the world through: a filter of love, a filter of joy, a filter of magic, or perhaps a filter of sadness and dislike.

Because everything appears to be solid only on the illusionary surface level, the reality around us has the power to change with the help of our intention. We can literally look at the same object with two different filters and it will transform accordingly. Nobody knows ultimately what the reality is; maybe it is all a product of our eyes and imagination? If that's the truth, we have a lot of power over what we are projecting into our reality.

Imagine that you have an invisible energy of love coming through your eyes. Direct it to what you are looking at now and notice how it changes.

For example, if we bring the energy of joy and happiness to our eyes, the reality will reflect back in the same way and will show us the signs that our life is wonderful. It is as though we put miraculous sparkles into our glasses and everything starts to look colourful and uplifting. People will seem friendly, nature will begin to appear alive and full of light, there will be a feeling of magic in the air. All because of our energy.

In a similar way, if we wear sad glasses and choose to perceive the world through darkness and negative impressions, it will likely reveal such qualities to us. The reality will find ways to challenge us and, by the law of attraction, we may begin to see the negative energies that we focus on. People who wear unhappy glasses will get more confirmations that the world is a sad place; they will have more reasons to complain, feel down and encounter difficult situations.

Life is ultimately a dream where everything manifests with a speed of light, but it can take time for us to realise it and see the results. We can create miracles when we put the right filters in our eyes, such as love, appreciation and kindness, and help the Universe to bring us uplifting experiences.

VISUALISING A HEALTHY BODY

We already know that we live in a quantum reality and that everything that we see and feel affects the reality around us. Now we can use this awareness to benefit our being. For example, we can use the eyes to transform our body and improve our health.

Our body has both a physical and an energy form. On the surface, it appears that the body is solid and is made of bones, muscles, blood and skin. This is true for the physical reality that we currently focus on. However, if we were to look deeper with our inner eye, beyond the physical side, we would notice that our body is also made of energy.

We have a subtle energy body that projects itself into our physical body.

It is this subtle energy form that is ultimately so important for keeping the balance in our body. It is like the mould where everything gets shaped: our feelings, our experiences, our thoughts, our soul memories and our visions. All these ingredients produce the end result known as our physical body with all its systems and the way that they function.

First comes the energy form, then appears the physical form.

When something goes wrong in our life on an energy level – for example, we experience lower emotions or stress – it first starts to show itself in the subtle body. This is why psychic people can perceive a possible illness long before it manifests itself on the physical level. They see that the energy vibrates in a different way in that part of the body and seems out of balance. Thus, clairvoyants can indicate correctly where the body may have a problem and suggest possible ways for healing.

It can take a while for the energy to shape into the physical form.

If the change in the subtle energy is noticed on time, it will be easier for the person to shift that imbalance by releasing it from the body and moving on to a higher vibration. This way they can clear the lower energy and prevent a physical result in the body. The body always intends to cleanse and heal itself naturally when it sees a problem, so it will cooperate with our positive intention and action.

If the energy has not been cleared and it continues to persist in the subtle body, it has more chance to manifest into a physical symptom. It may not necessarily happen; sometimes the energy may stay in the body for many years and just exist on the subtle level. But if the energy gets accumulated too much and doesn't have a chance to leave or balance itself out, it can create an ailment with a visible discomfort. We may experience pain, heaviness, changes in the body, fatigue, weakness and other symptoms. Then more work is needed to release the initial cause of the disruption and balance the energy in the physical body.

So, this brings us back to the main point – healing starts with energy. If we want to change the way our body is on the physical level, we have to address those issues on the energy level first and bring them back to balance.

Think of making a snowman in winter. We take the snow from the ground and begin to create the shape of a snowman. Depending on what kind of snow we pick up, its texture and amount, the snowman will turn out differently. We can shape him big or small, rounded or elongated. We can add different objects to it, like a carrot or sticks of wood. Metaphorically, the snow represents our emotions, feelings and experiences that we carry every day. The snowman is the physical result. Thus, it is important to see what energies we pick and how we distribute them in our body. Are we balanced inside? Do we carry the energies that serve our highest good?

We can use healing visualisation to bring the balance back into our body and transform our organs on the level of frequency. By doing that, we create a new energy form for our organ and start projecting it inside of our body so it can become real on a physical level. When it is done with consistency and a strong belief, the body begins to listen and respond positively to our visualisation. It starts to change its vibration to match the image that we are showing to it.

Visualisation is the projection of the energy form of our consciousness into the physical reality.

Let us imagine that a person is experiencing discomfort in the digestive system. One of the techniques that they could use is to visualise their organs being healthy and functioning well. They can imagine that the stomach is filled with beautiful healing light and that all the cells are happy and in full balance. This can take the form of a meditation, which includes visualising a perfectly shaped and perfectly functioning organ that brings delight to the rest of the body.

Focusing on the harmonious function of your organs helps to bring more health into your system. It is like setting an example to your body of what you would like it to be.

The more we visualise a healthy organ, the more of this energy we bring into the body. We are working on the subtle energy level and transforming the frequencies with our inner vision. It is almost like our eyes are sending a special energy to the body that helps it to form a new, healthy and balanced organ in the physical reality.

You can prepare for this practice in advance by looking at pictures of healthy organs in their perfect state. Once you have connected with the balanced energy of a healthy organ, you can start projecting these healing visuals into your body. We need to convince the body that it is going back to its original balanced form and that it is time for it to function perfectly well now. The body will follow the vibration that we are projecting to it and will start remembering again what it is like to be healthy.

By visualising a healthy organ, we are creating a happy future for it.

If you are open to energy, you may start feeling the positive changes in your body very quickly and this feeling alone can help you to build confidence and belief in your healing work. This type of practice likes repetition, because it will take some time for you to get used to a new perception of your body. It may also take some time for your body to adjust to the new energy that you are creating for it. So, persistence, patience and love coming from you will work wonders.

It is also important to add the ingredient of a positive feeling while you are doing the visualisation. This will help to bring even stronger energy to your creation. Dreams, which are accompanied by a feeling, are much more powerful and can manifest quicker. You can visualise the newly transformed organ with feelings of joy, love and confidence. These energies will speed up the process of healing and help you to enjoy the meditation even more.

You can ask yourself: "What would it be like to have a healthy organ now? How would it feel?"

PRACTICE TIME
VISUALISING A HEALTHY ORGAN

◊ Take a comfortable position, close your eyes and relax. Take several deep breaths to release the thoughts and breathe the tensions out of your body. Decide which part of your body you would like to work on today.

◊ Take some time to connect with the subtle energy of that organ. How is it feeling now? What do you pick up from it energetically? Just feel it, get to know it with your intuition. Become aware of what energies are vibrating there right now.

◊   Now imagine a completely healthy version of this organ in your mind. See it in full detail. What would a perfectly balanced organ look like? Create a 3D version of it and make it very clear in your imagination. See it functioning perfectly and emanating healthy energy. Imagine placing this image into your body where it is supposed to be. What does it feel like to have it there?

◊   Spend some time visualising the healthy organ in your body. Bring back the power to this organ. Imagine that it is very happy and balanced. It is almost like you are placing a perfect drawing into your body, and it replaces any old energy that doesn't serve you anymore.

◊   Bring a feeling of confidence and belief that healing is happening right now. Imagine that this organ is very pleased to be in your body. It is so wonderful to be healthy! If you have difficulty visualising, focus on the feeling and transmit the energy of a healthy organ into the body. Feeling is as important as visualisation.

◊   Repeat the same with all the other organs that you would like to focus on. Keep the new energy in your body and feel how the positive change is taking place. Spend a moment to enjoy the perfect balance and harmony inside of you. When you are ready, slowly begin to orientate yourself back to the current place and time. Bring full awareness to yourself. You did a wonderful job.

VISUALISING A HEALTHY ENERGY FIELD

If we had special glasses to see the world from an energy perspective, we would notice that every person has an energy field around them. This energy can be perceived as a sphere of light that is emanating from the body of every person, animal, bird, tree and stone.

The energy field is also known as the aura, a colourful projection of our energy that is present around us all the time. The pattern of the aura can change depending on what mood we are in, on our past and present experiences, our thoughts, our emotions, our relationships with other people and our interaction with the world. It is like a bright mirror of ourselves that is alive and constantly moving.

Our energy field helps us to protect our body when we interact with the outside world. The stronger our energy field is, the more shielded we are from the unnecessary energies that sometimes come our way. It is like the invisible immune system of the body, which, when it is bright and powerful, can be less affected by lower energies, such as fear, stress or judgement.

Building a strong energy field improves our health.

Our energy fields help us to communicate with other people. As we interact with each other, we form invisible energy links between our auras. Through these channels we can send the energy to each other and communicate telepathically. This interaction happens all the time, whether we are aware of it or not. We constantly exchange energy with the outside world and the people that we meet, sending powerful telepathic messages to each other.

The energy field helps us to communicate with other people.

The beautiful quality of our energy field is that it helps us to recharge our own energy through the universal source of power. We constantly receive the energy from the cosmos, which nourishes our body from the top of our head to the feet, cleansing us and filling us with strength. We also receive the energy from the ground, from the earth, and this magnetic power enriches us with support and love from the planet.

When the energy around our body is clean and moving smoothly, it positively influences our health and maintains a natural balance in our body. The aura is like our little house that we carry around us all the time. We create the atmosphere in our house by adding beautiful objects, colourful paintings and pleasant energies.

In the same way, if our aura is clean and balanced, it creates an uplifting space for our body.

A clean, balanced energy field promotes healing in the body.

Our energy field can become influenced by the world around us. Every day we go through a lot of different experiences: we meet various people, exchange energies and feel emotions. Some of these energies can stay in our energy field and, if they have a lower frequency, they can have an effect on our body and bring us down. We may experience sudden tiredness and lack of energy, or may feel sad or upset for no apparent reason.

The same negative effect can be produced by our own thoughts and emotions. If we tend to have a lot of low vibrational thoughts – for example, angry thoughts, stressed thoughts, annoyed thoughts – and experience lower emotions like frustration, pain or sadness, we create a cloud of this energy around us, which can affect our aura. Other people would be able to read our thoughts and feelings by just connecting to our energy field, as it is written there vibrationally.

If there is an illness in the body, it can also show in the energy field. The vibration of that organ will stand out in the aura – for example, it may have a different frequency or a darker colour. Sometimes psychic people perceive holes or dents in the aura; these are the places with weakened energy that may contain an energy imbalance. In these cases, the aura also needs healing because if it is damaged it can deplete the energy in the body. The body and the aura are interrelated and can affect each other, both positively and negatively. Healing the aura can actually improve our health as it will provide more energy nourishment for our body.

Our energy field needs looking after as it gives support to the body.

What is important to know is that we can change, transform and heal our energy field. With the power of our vision and imagination, we can cleanse our aura and release the lower energies that may be found there. We can then add the colours, lights and positive emotions to our energy field to make it luminous and powerful. Expanding our aura will make it stronger and will help to protect our body. All these abilities are within us – we just need some practice and dedication to master them.

Visualisation is one of the most powerful ways to strengthen our energy field. We can imagine that the energy around us is pure, sparkly and uplifted. We can fill it with colours like pink, orange, purple, green and yellow, depending on what comes to us at the moment. We can even play beautiful music in our aura and grow divine flowers of majestic shapes there. The energy field will listen to our visions and respond by changing its vibration. The miracle of energy is that as soon as we give it a positive image, it starts adjusting to it. It will become what we imagine. We can even program our energy field to heal us during a certain time – for example, at night – and it will do so accordingly.

When we hold a higher vibration in our energy field, it starts to heal us on the physical level.

It is recommended to clean the energy field every day to help process the energies that we encounter in the outside world. Looking after our aura is an act of love towards ourselves. We care about our bodies, our relatives, our houses, our pets. In the same way, we can enrich our aura with positive vibrations and allow it to strengthen our immunity.

PRACTICE TIME
VISUALISING A HEALTHY ENERGY FIELD
◊ Take a comfortable position, close your eyes and relax your body. Begin to breathe deeply, releasing your thoughts and

worries. Feel how they are leaving your body. Keep breathing slowly until you reach a pleasant meditative state.

◊ Now imagine that you have an aura around your body. You may perceive it as a sphere of light, a warm glow or just an energy field. Tune into your energy. Observe what it is like. How does it feel? How far does it stretch? What energies are present there? Slowly scan the front of your aura, then the left and the right sides, the back, above your head and below your feet. What areas are calling your attention? Are they evenly strong or do some of them feel weaker? Are you holding any important life experiences in your aura? Focus on the energy field around you and let it tell you a story.

◊ Let's begin to breathe the light into your energy field and imagine that it is blossoming like a flower. Feel that your aura is getting lighter and stronger as you are breathing in this beautiful energy. Imagine that you are mending your energy field from all sides, making it balanced and protected. If any of your life experiences – for example, a relationship or a sad feeling – is located in your aura, you can choose to release it. Just cleanse that part thoroughly with the light until it becomes pure and sparkling. Feel the increase of energy and light around you. It is healing and safe to be in this high energy.

◊ Now that you have created a beautiful energy field, enjoy being in it for some time. Appreciate this moment. Imagine that you are being lovingly embraced by your own energy. Feel how your body flourishes with the majestic, divine light around you.

◊ Breathe in your newly created aura. If you like to, allow the energy of the body to open up and take in some of that light. Imagine that the high vibration of your energy field is healing your body. Rejoice in this delightful feeling.

◊ When you are finished, ask your aura to remember this feeling and to keep nourishing you. Know that any time you remember about your light, it is going to be there for you. Slowly come out of the meditation and orientate yourself fully in the physical time and space. Enjoy wearing your wonderful aura!

CREATING THE FUTURE WITH YOUR EYES

We can direct visualisation towards creating a positive future for ourselves. Our minds are so powerful that when we constantly imagine the perfect version of our future, we create this energy in our life and it begins to manifest in our physical reality.

Daydreaming is a very useful technique that helps us to align with our goals and project our positive vision into the world. It can take the shape of a meditation or just imagining the scenes from our future life when we have a free moment. Precise visualisation – which includes imagining all the details of our dream, like feelings, colours, sounds and scents – will help the Universe to connect to the vibration of our vision and present it to us in the best possible way.

Our eyes have an incredible ability to tap into our future, as they can connect to several variants of our future development. When we meditate on creating our future life, we just select a particular pathway that we would like to take on now. Think of it as already written somewhere; by changing your vibration, you are moving closer to that scenario of your life that already exists in another dimension.

We can use the power of our eyes to visualise a perfect future for ourselves.

There is one important ingredient in the visualisation process – the energy of belief. Belief is like a fuel that powers our imagination and our goals in life. Without belief, our dreams feel weaker and may need a longer time to manifest. Imagine that your dream is like a car and in order to make it move, you need to add fuel to it, which is essentially the energy of belief. Accept that what you want to create is entirely possible and it is absolutely natural for you to have it.

It is recommended to practice a short ten-minute creative visualisation every day to connect to the energy of your dreams and manifest them in your reality. This meditation will also help to develop your psychic powers and understand what you really need in your life on a soul level.

PRACTICE TIME
CREATING THE FUTURE WITH YOUR EYES

◊ Take a comfortable position, close your eyes and relax your body. Begin to breathe deeply and slowly to connect to your inner self, delving fully into the world of your dreams.

◊ Imagine that you can see your perfect future. Tune into this vibration and feel it in your heart. What kind of a vision comes first to you? How do you see your positive future? Connect to the first feeling that comes and let your intuition show you what you need to see.

◊ Now let us go deeper and develop this vision even more. What details do you see in your perfect future? Imagine yourself being happy and content. Where are you? What are you wearing? How are you feeling? See yourself doing what you would love to do the most in your life. Just allow this vision to come and submerge yourself completely in it.

◊ Focus on the dream that you would like to create in your future. Perhaps it is a successful project, a new relationship or just a happy moment. Feel the dream in your heart and allow this energy to be projected into your vision. What does it feel like? How do you imagine it? Accept that it is completely possible now and recreate this vision in your imagination. Feel your whole body buzzing with the energy of your dream.

◊ Visualise your dream as though it is happening right now. See yourself in your happy life, healthy, joyful and abundant.

Imagine what you would like to be doing and who you would like to see around you. You can add sounds, scents and movement to your vision. Imagine that you are living it at this very moment. What would it be like to experience it now?

◊ Breathe this energy into your aura and imagine having this vibration in your body. Align with the vibration of your dream and invite it into your body and spirit. Imagine that it is already here and now. You are your dream. Say thank you to the Universe for making it come true for you.

◊ Take long calm breaths to slowly bring yourself to full awareness. Begin to feel your physical body and orientate yourself in your space. Bring yourself back to the current moment and open your eyes, when you are ready. What did you see?

VISUALISING FOR OTHERS

Visualising positive energies can be done not only for ourselves but for other people too. We have the ability to change the frequency of the world around us with the help of our positive intention and vision.

Let's imagine that we are walking in the street and we are seeing a lot of people passing by. Perhaps some of them are happy and smiling, others may feel sad or stressed. We may intuitively feel that some people need support and encouragement. If you feel that you can do something good for another person and your intuition says 'yes', then you can help them through visualisation and directed positive energy.

You can imagine that you are sending beautiful white light to this person, for example, in the shape of an energy ball. You can project this light with your eyes and see it appearing as a sphere around this person. If you add a positive feeling to the image, like love or happiness, it will intensify and strengthen the healing effect. You may also wish to say a silent prayer and ask the higher powers to help them. Every kind intention counts.

Imagine, if we were all to help each other with positive energy, even just on the level of visualisation, the world would become a much more peaceful and loving place. Truly, the energy travels in the realm of time and space, so every drop of this positive essence accelerates the healing process for everybody.

If you want to help somebody instantly, visualise a beautiful light around them.

In a similar way, you can help a relative or a friend who needs healing if you visualise them getting better. This sometimes may be a little challenging to begin with as your mind might be preoccupied with worry about that person. But as soon as you start the visualisation, you will begin to feel the healing effect and you will know that you are doing the right thing. Imagine that this person is full of white light that is travelling through their body and helping them. Feel how the light is bringing them health and balance, both physically and emotionally. Energy travels through time and space and your light will reach the person in need instantly.

You can also imagine this person being happy and having a good time in a wonderful place, like a garden or a flowery field. Imagine them without any worries, already healed, in a safe space full of light and happiness. The person will receive your loving energy and it will have a positive effect on them. Also, you will feel more at peace yourself after doing this helpful visualisation.

You can support the healing process of others by visualising them happy and healthy.

SENDING LOVE WITH YOUR EYES

Our eyes are the channels of energy that can exchange frequencies as we look at each other. When we look at somebody or something with a certain feeling, this energy travels from our eyes and delivers our intentions to the receiver. This is why, when somebody is looking at us intently, we can feel their presence instantly and we turn our head to see who it is. The energy of the look interacts with the energy of the receiver.

The energy of the look can knock us off our feet when it is very strong or it can make us feel warm and pleasant when somebody is sending us good vibes. Every energy is different and the effect depends on the intention of the giver.

There is a great healing potential in our eyes and the way we look at each other.

From our eyes we can direct loving energy to the other person and make them feel comfortable, nourished and protected. Just by looking at somebody with appreciation and encouragement, we can transform the way that person is feeling at this moment. It is like an invisible blessing that we are sending with our look.

You can develop this ability if you practise looking at people with love and directing your healing light to them. This is a beautiful exercise that will increase the power of your intuition and also give healing to your own eyes. Imagine that you are bathing people in love and sending them kindness from your heart. You will notice how the energy changes in the air, and the place gets lighter and happier.

You can experiment with different positive frequencies when you send the energy with your eyes, for example, you can use the vibration of joy, peace, encouragement, acceptance, admiration, kindness and so on. Each one will add a special healing flavour to the person's aura and will help them in a unique way. As always, just follow your intuitive choice. If you like, you can just shine pure light from your eyes and spread it to nature, people, streets and houses. The eyes can heal everything.

Sharing light with our eyes is a powerful healing practice to raise the frequency in the world around us.

You can also practise this beautiful technique with the people who you love. While sitting down together, you can silently direct the love to each other's eyes and express your feelings this way. Focus on your positive intentions and shine your most delightful feelings to another person, imagining them in their highest state of being. You can visualise the person being happy, doing the things that they love doing and fulfilling their life purpose. It is a wonderful practice that will help you to uplift each other and bring healing energy into your relationship.

Of course, we shouldn't forget about ourselves when it comes to loving with our eyes. Every time we look in the mirror, we have a beautiful chance to express kindness to ourselves. Instead of judging the way that we look, we can direct the most loving energy from our eyes to our reflection. The waves of positive energy will give us healing and will help us to connect to our inner self.

FOUR

THE 3RD WONDER OF THE SELF: WE CAN TALK

The Universe has presented us with a magical gift of making sounds and sharing them with the world. Almost everything that we do is accompanied by a sound and it can make us all feel differently, depending on the frequency of the sound. Some sounds make us feel happy and peaceful, while others may not be in vibrational alignment with us.

As the creators of our life, we are constantly producing ideas, thoughts and projects in our mind. Some of these creations are manifested into a sound so the world can hear about them. Words help us to express our opinion and have meaningful conversations with each other.

Every sound that we produce becomes a part of the Universe and affects all that there is around us, including ourselves. Making a sound is like weaving a special pattern into the fabric of our reality. Depending on the quality of the sound, a certain colour and shape is added to the tapestry of the world that we live in. Sounds carry frequencies and can transform our reality.

Many of the sounds that we make are produced unconsciously as we don't always realise what kind of music we are playing to the

Universe. However, everything that we say, whisper, sing or mutter becomes a part of the world and starts to live a life of its own. This is why it is important to notice what sounds we are giving birth to every moment of our life.

Like everything, the sound is a vibration and can have different qualities, depending on the energy that we put into it. The sound can be uplifting and happy, warm and kind, soulful and loving. The sound can also be sad and lonely, angry and frustrated, heavy and distorted. Even our thoughts, which have not yet manifested into the voice, can still carry a strong energy and have an invisible sound in them. This energy can have an effect on the way that we feel and on the people around us.

We are the directors of the sound orchestra in our life. We can sing a harmonic song to the Universe and uplift the energy in our space.

Words can also carry different meanings and have different energies attributed to them. When high-vibrational words are said with love and a positive intention, they can change the molecular structure of the cells in our body and make them harmonious and healthy. Lower-vibrational words, said with the intention of hurt, can affect our energy, lower our stamina and have an upsetting effect on our aura.

When we make a sound, we change the molecular structure of the world around us on the level of energy.

We can make a big change in the world around us if we choose to share an uplifting melody with the Universe. This can include saying good things to other people and to ourselves. It also includes producing any sounds of positive nature, like playing music, singing, praying and laughing. Happy sounds are wonderful tools that can heal the energy around us.

Being in a state of awareness allows us to observe our speech and create the sounds that we want to be a part of our reality. We can begin to notice which sounds we are surrounding ourselves with daily and what energy would be beneficial for the world. Then we can consciously make a beautiful and healing song to the Universe.

AS WE SPEAK, WE CREATE

The sound is the start of the creation. When we make a sound, we bring a new energy to life. The effect that we produce when we speak is much stronger than we ever realise. The vibration of the sound reaches the Universe and affects the energy structure of the things around us.

There have been experiments showing that higher-vibrational sounds, such as the words of love, appraisal and appreciation, bring harmony and beauty to the water; while the words of a lower vibration, like hatred, irritation and unloving energy, destroy the natural frequency of the water and make it distorted. The same effect happens not just with the water, but with everything else around us, because energy is the essence of all. Like water, every living being is influenced by the newly created energy of the sound.

When the sound is accompanied by a strong emotion, the effect of the sound is significantly intensified. It works like magic – a positive intention added to the sound can bring cure, while a bad intention can curse the sound and lower its vibration.

We are responsible for the sounds that we give to the Universe and to each other.

All the beings in the world, including inanimate beings, have invisible ears. They can all hear what we say even when they are far from us. The energy travels through time and space and reaches our consciousness telepathically. The same works for our own body, our physical spaces, even the air and the water.

For example, if we have a plant at home and we keep saying good words to this plant, it will feel our love and become happier. The energy of the plant will get nourished by our good intentions and it will help its growth and wellbeing. Who doesn't like to hear the words of love? Who doesn't feel good when they are appreciated? We can even sing to the plant and play it some lovely music; it will definitely feel our kindness.

The energy of good words will reach the ears of the people in your life, whether they are close or far from you. We can elevate each other's energy by sending a good thought or a happy word to each other. This is especially healing when we are sharing the same living space, as the positive energy of the sound permeates the air and spreads to everybody who lives there.

The same concerns inanimate objects in our life: our food, our clothes, our furniture, our documents, our photographs. They all have invisible ears and take on the energy that we produce with the sound. We can make our house a magical place if we speak beautiful words to our objects.

Observe the sounds that you create, as they become your neighbours.

AS WE THINK, WE CREATE

Our thoughts, although seemingly not alive and pronounced, have a strong inner vibration, too. As soon as we have a thought, especially if it is charged with an emotion, we create a new life. Some thoughts can have a good influence on us – this happens when they are positive and contain high-vibrational energy. Other thoughts may be unbalancing and disturbing and they can energetically affect our body, like a whirlwind.

The majority of our thoughts pass through our mind unnoticed, as we are often so used to having a constant chat in our head. We don't always realise the number of thoughts that we think during the day and their quality. The so-called repetitive thoughts that we harbour in our head for a long time, sometimes for years, are especially powerful. These thoughts literally create the space for us to live in as they can linger in our energy and affect our existence. Then our actions can become governed by these thoughts, even though, perhaps, they may not have been true from the beginning.

Thoughts produce a strong energetic effect in our head. When we create a thought, it starts to vibrate in the aura of our head and can bring a similar energetic resonance into our body. If it is repeated and intensified, it can affect the whole body and its organs on an energy level.

Thoughts are real; they have energy and can be transmitted to your body and the minds of other people.

Imagine that a thought of a low-vibrational character has been present in a person's mind for many years. For example, a thought with the energy of 'My life isn't fair'. This thought can acquire a strong power through constant repetition and occupy the body of the person, bringing their energy down. It can also affect their life as, by the law of attraction, this thought can magnetise a similar frequency in their experiences. In order to find proof for that thought, the mind will look for more confirmations in the outside world and will, most probably, find them. This can bring even more upsetting feelings to this person.

Now imagine if a person has a happy repeating thought, for example: "I am a wonderful being." This thought is cleansing, uplifting, inspiring. The energy of this thought is healing in its own nature and it will bring a positive effect to the person's emotional state. It will also help them to see their life in a positive light and will naturally attract better energies on their path.

It is a good idea to look within ourselves and see what thoughts we are creating on a daily basis in order to understand what power they have over us.

Make a list of the thoughts that you tend to think the most during the day. This will show you what kind of energy you give to yourself on a daily basis.

Becoming aware of the thoughts that you create is a first step towards changing them. The light of awareness dissolves the negative aspect of the thoughts, because you step above them and consciously make a choice of producing happier and more balanced thoughts. We can master our mind and direct the thoughts for our healing and wellbeing.

BECOMING FRIENDS WITH YOUR THOUGHTS

Mastering the energy of our thoughts can be compared to physical training – it can take some time and diligence to achieve a good result. The conscious mind tends be stubborn. In the beginning, it may try to control the situation and distract us in every way possible. However, patience and regular practice can bring good results and shift the long-term patterns in our mind.

The first step towards working with our thoughts is observation. We need to understand what is going on in our head and what kind of thoughts occupy most time of our day. When we observe our thoughts as detached from us, we free ourselves from their control and can see what is happening in our mind objectively. This gives us a good perspective of what energies we create in our mind in our daily life.

We need to connect to the energy of our thoughts in order to understand what effect they have on us.

Through careful listening to our thoughts, we may notice that each thought carries a certain energy. It can have a different effect on how we feel, for example, some thoughts elevate our being and make us feel excited, while others can drain us and bring our confidence down. We can also observe that one thought often attracts another one of a similar kind, and then it can become a chain of thoughts, sometimes repeated over and over again.

Every thought has an energy and a life of its own. It is like a seed that can grow into a plant or a tree and create many more other life forms from it. The thought has a possibility to turn into a sound and then it will create even a stronger vibration, which will permeate our space.

When we observe our thoughts, we notice that perhaps some of them are not serving our highest potential. Maybe they are there just because we are used to them, but on an energy level they deplete us and don't allow us to move forward. If we catch ourselves having unloving thoughts, we can direct the energy of kindness to our head and dissolve our thoughts with love. The power of our heart will heal the insecurities of our conscious mind.

We need to look at our thoughts without judgement and bathe them in the love of our awareness.

Thoughts can be powerful beings and may not want to leave immediately, especially if we have been giving them permission to be there for a long time. It may sometimes be wiser not to fight a particular thought, but direct our love and awareness to heal it naturally.

Thoughts are like little children; they need our love as they are feeling unsafe.

When we work with the energy of our thoughts, it is useful to separate ourselves from our mind and look at the processes in our head as an observer. We can then write down the thoughts that come to us during the day – and sometimes during the night – and understand what kind of energy they are bringing to us.

This exercise will help you to understand what thoughts are going through your head daily and explain how you can connect to their vibration. You will gain more control over your thoughts and learn how to manage them with love and awareness.

PRACTICE TIME
HEALING THE ENERGY OF YOUR THOUGHTS

◊ Find some free time to work with the energy of your thoughts. Preferably dedicate a whole day to do this practice; this will give you a good overview of how your thoughts change during the day.

◊ Spend the day in a state of awareness, observing yourself and your thoughts. Imagine that you step out of your head and pay attention to what thoughts come to you every moment. Try to maintain a position of a third-person observer, as though you are doing a research. If you forget and get carried away in thinking, simply go one step back in your practice.

◊ Notice what thoughts come into your head. What are they like? What energy do they have? How do they make you feel? Do you like your thoughts? If you were to choose your thoughts, which ones would you rather have?

◊ Write your thoughts down. Focus especially on the repetitive thoughts that visit you a lot. What are they about? What are you saying to yourself? Make the list of the most common thoughts that come to you during the day. Feel the energy of your thoughts. What are you trying to achieve with them? What is the intention behind your thoughts?

◊ Look at the list of your thoughts and mark them according to the type of energy that they represent – for example, happy, sad, uplifting, demanding, questioning, encouraging, disturbing, frustrating, exciting. Make them go through your mind again but now in a state of awareness and watch how your body reacts to each one of them. Notice the tiniest sensations that you get as you are connecting to these thoughts. See which thoughts make you feel good and which ones give you stress.

◊   Look at the paper with the written thoughts and send your love to them. Imagine that you are not judging or assessing them, but just bathing them in your love and acceptance. If you like to, you can open the palms of your hands and direct your healing energy to the thoughts. Embrace them with the love of your heart. Imagine how your thoughts become softer and kinder and the negative ones become smaller and disappear.

◊   Repeat this exercise from time to time to maintain the awareness of your thinking process. Every time that you practise it, do it with love and kindness, and your thoughts will respond with the same energy.

CHOOSING THE RIGHT THOUGHTS

Thoughts are food for our mind, as they provide the energy nourishment for our body. Choosing happy and uplifting thoughts will help us to feel balanced and empowered. Now that we have figured out which thoughts visit us during the day, we can look at them and decide which ones are good for us and which ones we need to release.

> *The next step for healing your thoughts is choosing the right ones and welcoming them into your life.*

Let us look at these examples of happy and sad thoughts. Read them slowly and carefully, with a feeling, and notice what effect they have on your body and mind.

Happy Thoughts	Sad Thoughts
Today is a wonderful day.	Nothing is working out for me today.
I am successful in everything that I do.	I am not good enough.
My body functions perfectly.	I am not happy with my body.
I love myself and accept myself just the way that I am.	I am not worthy. I don't like myself.
I believe that everything will work out perfectly.	It's never going to work.
I am surrounded by wonderful loving people.	People don't like me. I can't trust anybody.
I take very good care of myself and give myself love.	I have too many things to do. I don't have time for myself.

What do you feel from each one of these thoughts? How does your body respond to them? Feel the ones that resonate with your energy. Can you sense what effect they have on you vibrationally? You can repeat the same exercise with your own list of thoughts.

As you can probably feel, the energy of happy thoughts is very uplifting and makes you feel good, even just by reading it. Imagine if these thoughts could be in your energy field every day and every hour – they would do an incredible healing job!

On the contrary, sad thoughts can be really destructive for our mind and body. They are like strings that pull us down to the ground and don't allow the good energy to flow inside. These thoughts can create a blockage that doesn't always let us see the goodness in our life.

Every thought has a direct link to our body. If we change the thoughts that we have every day, our body will change the way that it feels. Like the chords in a guitar, our thoughts will play a different song for our body.

Happy thoughts are a gift from the Universe and a powerful remedy for healing the body.

We can form a habit of thinking happy thoughts if we repeat them regularly in our mind. This way we will slowly substitute the negative beliefs that we have developed in this lifetime. It is like removing the layers that were acquired by old experiences and coming back to the purity of our soul. Going through life, we inevitably tend to take on the opinions of other people, the words said by our parents, teachers, friends and even ourselves. This can be transformed with the power of our own mind.

If we replace every negative thought with a positive one and keep repeating it, in the end our minds will get used to thinking a happy thought and will get rewired. We learn a lot by repetition and sometimes we need to be very patient with ourselves in order to change the habit for the better.

When you make your list of thoughts and then grade them by the type of energy, select the ones that make you feel happy. You can also transform the negative ones into positives by reversing them completely (for example, "I am not good at it" to "I trust that I can do it"). Then read this new happy list to yourself and make a conscious decision to include more of these thoughts into your daily routine.

Practise bathing yourself in happy thoughts, imagining that they are going through your body like a shower. Take your time and enjoy the energy of every positive thought healing your mind. Even if some of these thoughts are not a part of your belief system yet, they will nourish you with good energy and, with repetition, will become an important aspect of you.

THE ENERGY OF WORDS

Every spoken word that we use carries energy as well. It is a unique combination of letters that were brought together to create a special meaning. Throughout the centuries this word has been used by billions of people and it has acquired a particular energy that we spread out when we say it. A word is really an incantation – we create magic when we pronounce the word and we can turn it in any direction – a positive or a negative one – depending on how we say it.

We have to be careful with the words that we choose to say to the Universe.

Some words are high-vibrational because they carry a pure uplifting energy. These words are made for expressing love and admiration, for depicting beauty, for connecting to our positive qualities and bringing them out into the world. Other words are low-vibrational, as they are used to connect with our negative emotions; some are used to represent the darkness or even to hurt other people.

Every time we say a word, it begins to live in our space and interact with us energetically.

While all the words have their own place and are needed for different reasons, we have to be aware which ones we are using in our own space and in the space of other people. Try not to say something if you feel that it will hurt someone unnecessarily and you will regret using this word and emotion later. Take a deep breath and connect to your intuition, asking your heart to give you the right words to express your situation with kindness. You can understand the vibration of the word by listening to it energetically and feeling how your body responds to it.

Use your heart as a measurer for the selection of the words that you choose. If it feels right, say it. If it doesn't feel right, leave it out.

We can accelerate the power of the word with the help of the energy that we attribute to our speech. This way a simple phrase can sound differently, depending on the emotion that we put into it. We can say a word lovingly and it will reach the heart of another person and make them feel kind and appreciated. We can say something in a cold manner, and this person will feel this intention behind our words. It is all about the energy of how we speak.

The more we direct the energy of our heart to our speech, the more loving our words will become.

It is an interesting practice to feel the energy of different words and compare the way they make you feel. Let us look at these various words and connect to their energy.

love	fear
happiness	destruction
delight	disgust
sunshine	clutter
wonderful	rubbish
glorious	anger
harmony	menace
singing	frustration
soul	hate
angels	revenge
freedom	worry
flying	upset
breathing	greed
magical	anxiety

Try reading these words out slowly, one by one, feeling the energy of each word. Imagine that you forget what the meaning of the word is and just focus on the energy emanating from it. What does this energy feel like? Imagine that the vibration of this word is going through your body and your space. Focus on the smallest sensations. How does this sound affect your body and energy?

You can continue your own list if you have more favourite words to add to the first column or if you want to explore some other low-vibrational words in the second column. We learn when we compare different energies, so it is helpful to experiment with various types of words. This exercise will bring an awareness of the power of our speech and show how quickly words can affect the space around us.

Every time that you speak, imagine that you are singing a beautiful song to the world. Then the right words will come.

Our intuition is the main guide in discerning what needs to be said when we speak. Sometimes excessive talking is not necessary. We can express the precious energy of our soul in just a few words. It is how we say things that changes the energy in the room. At other times, we might want to expand on what we are saying and allow the flow of our speech to become free. It is important to feel the moment and sense what words need to come out right now.

Try and focus today on the words that come from your heart. What would you really like to say to yourself and to the world?

TALKING TO YOUR BODY

Let us imagine that our body is a temple and we are the Masters of our Temple. Day and night, work goes on in the Temple to keep it balanced and well-functioning. As we are the Masters of our Temple, everything that we think or say gets echoed in the walls and all the inhabitants can hear it.

Whatever we think or say our cells accept as the truth.

The body is constantly listening to us. It is a natural process, as our voice is a part of our system and it acts like the main commanding force for our cells. Saying things to our body is like giving it an order; the body listens and believes everything that we say, whether it is good or bad.

Our body is like a sponge: it takes in everything that we give to it, energetically and physically.

We have an incredible power to change the way our body feels by using special healing words. It is almost like planting seeds into the ground and then watching them grow into beautiful flowers. In fact, we are doing this all the time. Sometimes we praise the body and let it know how much we love it, when we say things like "I have a beautiful body", "I love my body very much", "Thank you for doing a great job". At other times, mostly unknowingly, we can plant negative suggestions to our body – for example, "You are not doing very well", "It's getting worse", "How tired I am of feeling like this!".

Every word that we say to ourselves is received by the body and is energetically absorbed by the cells. So, if we believe that our body is healthy and well-functioning, it will respond to our words and will give us more confirmation of our good health. If we are constantly not happy with the body, the cells may get upset and struggle to keep the balance. After all, this is just an order from the Master.

Observe how you speak to your body and what energy you give to it.

The body needs emotional food just like it needs physical nourishment. Words of love, kindness and support are the best remedies that we can give to our dear body. Like any other being in the Universe, our body wants to be loved and taken care of. And we are the ones who can give this love in the most beautiful way.

Sing the song of love to your body.

Positive conversations with the body have a strong healing power as we can literally convince the body that healing is happening now. The cells are very responsive and they will happily receive the information that the body is getting better. For them it is like listening to good news! Even if you are not feeling a hundred percent at the moment, you can begin by using the healing words, and your body will start adjusting to this vibration. It is almost like tuning into a radio station where the energy of your body has a perfect frequency already.

When you are talking to your body, imagine that you are talking to the person whom you love. How would you talk to them? What would you say to somebody you love? Treat your body as a precious treasure given to you by the Universe; it deserves words of appraisal and kindness from you.

It is also important to observe what messages we receive from other people and the world around us daily. What do you hear from others about yourself every day? Is it uplifting you or bringing you down? Are the people in your surroundings giving you emotional nourishment and love? Do you receive information from television, internet, radio, books? What kind of suggestions do they put in your mind? Does your body like what it is hearing from the world around? These are the questions that you can ask yourself in order to understand what energy goes into your body on a daily basis.

We have the power to change what energy we receive into our body in the form of words and suggestions.

So, let's say that a television program upsets your energy and makes you feel sad or angry. Maybe it is just distracting you in the background and not letting you truly connect to yourself. In this case, perhaps you could switch to another channel that has a happier message, or change the activity to something of a more positive vibration, like writing, dancing or drawing.

The same holds true for your social surroundings. Do your friends make you feel uplifted and inspired? How do you feel when you are in the company of the people whom you meet often? Maybe you could invite more people into your life who will help you to step on a healing path and grow spiritually.

Surround yourself with high energy in all possible forms.

Nowadays the healing power of words is used in many different therapies, for example, hypnotherapy, when positive suggestions are given to the mind of the person. With the help of a specially worded script and guided imagery, the therapist relaxes the conscious mind of the client and then gives them the positive suggestions that go straight to the subconscious mind and create a beneficial effect for the body. In the state of relaxation, it is easier to receive healing directions, and with repetition, they can become ingrained in our system, so the body accepts the positive change. This is a very powerful way of transforming the old patterns and beliefs that don't serve us anymore.

In my experience of working with QHHT, I witnessed many times how the Subconscious works with the positive power of words. The Higher Self often purposefully repeats the positive healing suggestions in a very stern and confident way, until the person begins to accept them. This helps the conscious mind to believe that change is happening, and the person to trust in their own healing power. They can feel how the energy begins to literally shift in the body and bring the balance back.

On one occasion, I was asked by the Subconscious to repeat these words myself to the client and affirm that the cells in their body were healing and transforming. They said: "Please, say it strongly several times, she needs to hear it from you." I kept repeating powerful suggestions for some time, until the new healing energy was incorporated in the body. This experience gave me a good overview of how to use positive affirmations in my guided meditations and hypnotherapy.

Say positive affirmations to the body with a lot of belief and power; this will help the conscious mind to trust that healing is taking place.

LOVE AND APPRECIATION ARE THE MOST HEALING WORDS

There are many different healing vibrations that we can share with our body. We can uplift it with joy, bathe it in happiness, nurture it with peace and care. Among all the possible energies, love and appreciation is what our body enjoys the most. It reminds the body of the moment it was created – through love and kindness.

The most powerful healing energy for our body is love and gratitude.

When the body feels love, it begins to open up, release the stress from the past and collaborate with us in the best possible way. Just imagine how our body is faithfully performing its functions every moment of our life to give us different experiences. How do we express our gratitude for this incredible amount of work?

In many cases, we take the functions of the body for granted, because we are just so used to them. We are used to the fact that our body can walk, can digest food, can speak, can help us to touch objects and see reality. It happens so naturally that we forget what a brilliant team of diligent workers is behind it. There are millions of cells that are responsible for these beautiful processes and they are alive and listening to us right now.

This is what sometimes our body is missing the most: the

appreciation of its goodness. Like a flower, it needs attention and looking after. You can nourish your body with the words of love and gratitude. The body would love to hear how much you appreciate it; these words will change the energy in the body and start the healing process.

The body needs to know how much you love it.

You can repeat the loving words to the body throughout the day, affirming that you appreciate it and feel grateful for what it is doing. You can also say some loving words before going to bed – this will target your Subconscious and will help these words to stay in your mind for a longer time. We enter a special state just before going to bed, a zone between sleep and awakening, where our visions and intuitive perception are activated. This is a perfect time to place healing suggestions into your mind. You may also get a clear idea of what you need to do to help yourself in this meditative state.

Sometimes, if you wake up at night, you can also remember to nourish yourself with loving words. This will help you to still your mind and fall asleep with ease, receiving powerful messages in your dreams. Magic can happen when we enter the state between sleep and awakening and consciously work with our Higher Self at this moment. This is the time when we receive the most healing from the higher powers.

This exercise will help you to express love to your body and benefit from this beautiful healing energy.

PRACTICE TIME
TALKING TO YOUR BODY

◊ Find a comfortable position, close your eyes and relax. Take several deep breaths, going through your whole body, and allow yourself to breathe out all your thoughts and worries.

◊ Turn your attention inside of your body and focus on its energy. How is your body feeling now? Spend some moments connecting to it energetically.

◊ Find the feeling of love in your heart and begin to spread this beautiful energy through your body. How does it feel? Imagine that love is travelling to every part of your body and sending appreciation for everything that your body is doing for you.

◊ Now bring together all your positive intentions and start saying beautiful words to your body. You can repeat several times: "I love you", "You are wonderful", "I appreciate you so much", "I am very grateful to you", "Thank you for helping me in my life", "Thank you for being with me", "You are a such a great body", "I care about you." Say it slowly, lovingly, meaning every word that you say. Pronounce the words with a lot of feeling, let the body really receive your good intentions and your love. Enjoy every word that you say and feel how the energy in your body is transforming.

◊ Notice how you feel when you say these beautiful words to your body. How does the body respond? Try saying different magical words and find the ones that make you feel the most wonderful. Say a word and then feel the immediate response of the body. You will know what works best for you.

◊ If there are more things that you want to say to your body, you can do it. You can go through your whole body and express gratitude to each organ if you like. Make a note of which words make you feel really happy. Try to repeat them regularly in your daily life; let them be your own mantra.

POSITIVE AFFIRMATIONS FOR THE BODY

Affirmations are the words and sentences that we say repeatedly in order to tune into a healthy way of being. They can include positive words that are related to our general health and different organs in particular. Affirmations are great tools that can bring the energy of our positive wishes together and manifest healing in the physical body. By repeating the affirmations, we state to the Universe how we want our health to be and provide a framework for our wellbeing. Then, together with other healing techniques, it helps to adjust our body back to balance.

Affirmations are powerful instruments to boost our health and wellbeing.

Positive affirmations work really well for several reasons. First of all, they are creating a positive energy in the body that helps us to attune to the frequency of health. Secondly, we are reprogramming our mind with a new belief about our body, which, with repetition, becomes a part of our system. Also, saying an affirmation makes us feel really good about ourselves; as soon as we say the healing words, we are stepping into a different dimension, feeling strong and open to a positive change.

Working with affirmations can take some time as we need to convince the body and mind that change is happening. Patience, persistence and belief are very helpful factors in our work with positive affirmations.

When we say an affirmation, we give a formula to the Universe and it responds with a corresponding result in our reality.

Creating an affirmation is really easy; you just need to feel what you would like to change in your body to make it feel better. Think of the situation that you have now and then think how it could be positively resolved. Connect to your intuition to find the words to express the desired feeling in the most uplifting way. It is recommended to use the words that make you feel really good, as they will carry the necessary high energy to your body and mind. This is your personal creation, so use your imagination the way that you like.

Here is a list of sample affirmations that you are very welcome to use for yourself in your healing practice. I recommend choosing the ones that feel right and that bring a change in your body when you say them.

The Head	◊ My mind is calm and relaxed. ◊ I choose to think happy, positive thoughts. ◊ I allow only beautiful energy in my head.
The Eyes	◊ I have a perfect vision. ◊ My eyes are rejuvenating all the time. ◊ I choose to see light and love around me.
The Throat	◊ I express myself freely. ◊ My throat is cleansing and healing right now. ◊ It is easy for me to speak the truth.
The Teeth	◊ My teeth are strong and beautiful. ◊ My teeth have the power to regenerate themselves with ease. ◊ I have the ability to repair my teeth naturally.
The Lungs	◊ I allow myself to breathe freely and deeply. ◊ My lungs are being cleansed with every breath. ◊ I am completely free to do whatever I like. ◊ I enjoy my life fully.
The Heart	◊ My heart is strong and safe at all times. ◊ My heart functions perfectly. ◊ My heart is open and loving to the world. ◊ I trust my heart completely.

The Stomach	◊ My stomach is relaxed and feeling wonderful all the time. ◊ I easily digest everything in my life. ◊ I completely release all the stress from my stomach now.
The Digestive System	◊ I release all the old energies from my body. ◊ I easily let go of everything that I don't need anymore. ◊ I welcome new wonderful energy into my life.
The Sacral	◊ My sacral area is blossoming with love and joy. ◊ I am open to creating new things in my life. ◊ I love and accept myself the way that I am. ◊ I trust my intuition and my own sacred energy.
The Blood	◊ My blood is pure and healthy. ◊ The blood flows freely through my body, supplying all my organs perfectly. ◊ The cells in my blood are renewing and healing constantly.
The Bones	◊ My bones are strong and healthy in my whole body. ◊ My bones receive wonderful nutrients and keep strong for all my life. ◊ I feel balanced and supported in life.

The Back	◊ My back is straight and strong; it holds my body perfectly.
	◊ Each vertebra in my back is fully balanced and aligned.
	◊ The healing energy runs freely through my spine and supports my whole body.
	◊ I release any extra weight from my back right now.
General Wellbeing	◊ I am happy and healthy at all times.
	◊ I communicate regularly with my body and understand its messages.
	◊ I speak lovingly to my body and express my appreciation to it.
	◊ I am full of energy and power; my body feels great.
	◊ My immunity is superb and functioning well.
	◊ My cells are renewing and rejuvenating right now.
	◊ My body heals itself immediately.
	◊ I am in divine connection with my body; we understand each other perfectly.
	◊ I love my body so much! It is wonderful!
	◊ I am very happy with my body.
	◊ I take care of my body and my cells; I give them plenty of love and attention.
	◊ I support my body with happy, positive thoughts.
	◊ I am best friends with my body!

These affirmations can be read aloud three times each to increase the effect of the healing energy. Make sure that you include the feeling when you say these words – for example, delight or happiness – and repeat them slowly with joy. Every time you read an affirmation like this, your body will receive a positive suggestion. You will naturally attune yourself to the healing mode and will start to feel, think and act in the way that your affirmation says. Have you noticed that just reading these sentences makes the body feel uplifted?

It is a good idea to read the affirmations when you are in a peaceful mood, for example, early in the morning, when you don't have to rush and can do this practice with full awareness. You can start by reading them out slowly, in a very uplifting voice, absorbing every word that you are saying. You can imagine that you are playing beautiful music to your body and that it is changing at this very moment. As you pronounce the healing words with love and care, it becomes a special meditation for you.

After each affirmation give your body a little time to fully integrate the energy of the words. Do not rush. Feel the energy of each sentence and let it bathe the body and mind in its healing power.

Give your body a chance to listen to you; sing a beautiful song to yourself.

TELLING THE TRUTH TO YOURSELF

Sometimes the energy of truth is hiding inside of us and we don't have enough courage to express it to ourselves and other people. Perhaps the truth is too powerful and we don't want to face it, so we put it deep inside of our body, trying to mask it under other feelings. This can create an energy imbalance.

The energy of truth can get trapped in our body when we don't acknowledge our true feelings. Sometimes for the sake of another person or for our own peace of mind, we swallow the truth and keep quiet. Perhaps we don't want to hurt somebody or it is a delicate subject that we don't feel like sharing with other people. But the truthful energy inside of us still wants to come out and is looking for a way to be expressed. It doesn't understand why we can't be honest with ourselves.

We can help to release the stagnant energy from the body by speaking our truth. It doesn't necessarily have to be shared with another person; it can just be expressed to ourselves in a private way. This will release the pressure inside of us and help the energy of truth to flow better in the body. It will also help us to connect to the true voice of our soul.

The truth doesn't always have to be something bad or embarrassing; sometimes it is just expressing a natural need that we haven't been allowing ourselves to speak about. Maybe we are spending too much time with other people, but in reality we need more relaxing time for ourselves. Or perhaps we are afraid to say 'no' to somebody so as not to upset them, but this is exactly what our energy is telling us to do. In this case, telling the truth becomes a gift to ourselves as we are responding to our inner need and taking care of ourselves. It is an act of self-kindness, which is healing in its own nature.

There is a beautiful exercise that can help you to connect to your truth and understand how you really feel about a certain situation. You don't have to confide your secrets to anybody here, you can just do it for yourself. During this practice, your Higher Self will be activated and it will help you to find the right words to express your feelings. You will experience a wonderful sense of relief when you speak about something that you have been holding inside for a long time.

You can start by lying down comfortably and closing your eyes. As soon as you close your eyes, you will enter a deep state of relaxation and begin to connect to your inner essence. This process will help you to express your true feelings. Find the subject that you want to speak about and focus on your feelings. Then just open your mouth and start talking about it. Say whatever comes first, without thinking or controlling yourself in any way. Speak truthfully from the heart and let all the emotions and feelings come out the way that they are. This is ultimately your truth.

Just keep saying whatever comes to you for some time and you will notice that, at some point, your inner self will start to take over and speak. It will happen naturally; just trust it. There is a higher power within us that is knowledgeable and wise. It will wake up during this practice and guide you to express your feelings.

This exercise is very healing. You will connect to your true self directly. You may find yourself crying or expressing different emotions during this meditation. This is perfectly fine. Just be free and allow yourself to say anything that comes. Spend as much time as needed to do this practice; you will feel a lot of lightness in your body afterwards. Great job!

PROGRAMMING THE SUBCONSCIOUS

Our Subconscious is the guardian of all information about our body; it knows exactly how our organs function and why they are experiencing certain symptoms. The Subconscious also holds all the memories, feelings and beliefs that we have acquired in our life.

We can ask the Subconscious to explain the reason for a certain ailment in our body and it will look for the underlying cause for it in this life or past incarnations. The Subconscious has the capacity to heal our body naturally as it has a direct access to all the systems of our body.

When we access our Subconscious, we can connect to our divine wisdom and receive messages about our body.

We can communicate with the Subconscious on a daily level and plant the healing suggestions to reprogram the way our body feels. The words that are received by the Subconscious will be taken inside and will help our body to heal. It is particularly effective to repeat the words with a lot of confidence and power; this way we can help our mind to change its beliefs and assist the healing process.

The best way to talk to the Subconscious is during a meditation when you are in a deep, relaxed state. When the conscious mind is quiet, the Subconscious has a chance to come forward and activate the healing suggestions in a powerful way.

It is recommended to do this work when you are completely on your own and you have some time to devote to self-healing. As you can go quite deep during this meditation, it is best if you don't have any distractions and allow plenty of time for the healing process. You may find it more comfortable to lie down during this practice for complete relaxation. Make sure you that follow all the steps in the meditation, including the last one to orientate yourself back.

PRACTICE TIME
COMMUNICATING WITH YOUR SUBCONSCIOUS

◊ Lie down in a comfortable position, close your eyes and begin to take deep breaths. Allow the breath to release all the thoughts and worries from your body. Spend several minutes just breathing calmly until you reach a state of deep relaxation.

◊ Start counting slowly from one to ten and notice how you go deeper with each count. You can say to yourself: "1, 2 – I am going deeper and deeper; 3, 4 – my body is getting more and more relaxed; 5, 6 – I am feeling comfortable and at peace; 7, 8 – going deeper and deeper; 9, 10 – fully relaxed." Know that by the time you reach ten you will access your Subconscious.

If it helps, you can visualise the numbers as you are counting them.

◊ When you reach ten, ask your Subconscious to come forward and speak through you. Release any expectations and just imagine that your deeper, wiser self is coming forth, taking you over like a wave of powerful energy. This is your Subconscious. Notice what sensations you receive in your body at this moment. Trust your feelings.

◊ Ask your Subconscious if there are any messages for your body. Listen to any sensations or images that come first – they contain the most important messages. Connect to your inner knowing and feel how much love and support your Subconscious has for you. Just feel it.

◊ Now ask if there is any information about how to heal a particular organ. Let the Subconscious show you an image or give you a sensation about how to help your organ in the best way. Receive the information in any way that it comes to you: a visual image, an inner knowing, the first feelings or intuitive words. You may already begin to feel that your body is being healed at this moment. Spend some time bathing in this powerful energy.

◊ Now it's time to give some positive suggestions to your Subconscious. Choose the words and phrases that you would like to give to your inner self to make you feel better. For example, you can use the following affirmations: "I am in perfect health", "I am in perfect harmony", "My body functions very well", "I am healing right now", "My body is healing naturally", "My cells are rejuvenating and renewing", "I am starting the healing process now", "Healing is happening now", "Healing now".

◊ Say these words aloud with a lot of conviction and belief, almost like you are giving your body an order. Do it lovingly and fully believe in what you are saying. Feel that the healing process is

152

already happening in your body. You may experience positive changes in your energy as soon as you start saying these words.

◊ After saying each phrase, stay there for some time and enjoy the healing effect in your body. Imagine that you are pressing the healing buttons inside of you with every word and observe how your body is changing in response. When you are finished, just bathe in the beautiful energy that you have created. Enjoy the healing effect of the positive suggestions and let your body keep the memory of this change.

◊ Now let's thank the Subconscious for all its help and reaffirm that you will stay connected with it. Express your gratitude for this powerful collaboration and feel that you are working together with your Subconscious for your highest good.

◊ Now ask the Subconscious to return to where it belongs. You can slowly count back from ten to one, affirming that you are coming back to your physical body. You can say: "1, 2 – I am becoming more and more present; 3, 4 – I am returning my awareness back into the body; 5, 6 – my body is fully waking up; 7, 8 – I am completely present here and now; 9, 10 – I am fully awake, back in this time and place." When you finish counting, take a couple of deep breaths and slowly open your eyes. Always spend enough time to bring your awareness fully back into your body.

Working with the Subconscious is a beautiful gift that can bring positive changes to the body. With regular practice, this exercise can become your tradition and will strengthen your connection with the Subconscious. You will be able to get clearer messages about yourself and your path and receive natural healing from within. The Subconscious is a very kind, loving and cooperative power and it always works in your best interest.

Here is a list of healing words that you can use for working with your Subconscious and creating positive affirmations:

Healing Words			
Nouns	**Adjectives**	**Verbs**	**Phrases**
rejuvenation	uplifting	cleanse	perfect health
light	healing	renew	radiating light
health	sparkling	heal	healing energy
abundance	joyful	purify	pure energy
balance	powerful	rebalance	divine energy
love	beautiful	transform	free flow
harmony	brilliant	release	white light
joy	wonderful	let go	instant healing
regeneration	cleansing	align	natural healing
alignment	magnificent	connect	full harmony
connection	bright	empower	higher power
peace	delightful	encourage	complete healing
magic	miraculous	shift	magical energy

You can use any combination of these words and add more healing words that naturally come to you during this process.

SINGING TO YOUR BODY

Another way of giving positive messages to the body is singing. Singing is a wonderful form of healing that helps us to express ourselves freely and attune our body to high vibrations. It is a light but very powerful means of communicating with our energy that can be done in a playful and jolly way.

When we sing, our heart opens and we let go of the conscious mind, entering a special place where we can release the old energies and create a new frequency in the body. It is like all the cells of the body are listening to the song and singing with us, responding to the very powerful healing effect of the words.

Singing to our body is good for inner alignment and balance as it helps us to connect to the voice of our soul. It is also a beautiful way to express love and nourishment to our body. Because of its free nature, singing can help to release old emotions that we have kept inside for a long time, in a light and easy way. Repetition in the song helps to program our Subconscious for a positive change.

You can use any happy song for this exercise, providing that it has an uplifting vibration and contains the words that make you feel good. You can also create your own healing song, including specifically the words that will target your situation. For example, if you feel the need to reconnect with your body, you can write a song about how beautiful and special your body is. Or, if you need to heal a particular part of you, you can include the healing sentences referring to that aspect of you in an uplifting and balancing way.

The song that you create doesn't have to be perfect or rhyme; it can be written in any way that you personally like. It is the energy of your chosen words that will do the magic for you. This is an example of a small verse to show you how simple it is to create a self-healing song:

I wake up in the morning and I am feeling great,
I heal my precious body, I reach a balanced state,
My body is so special, it brings me love and joy.
My beautiful creation, there is so much to enjoy!

You can sing the verse to yourself several times per day and this will help you to attune your energy to the chosen healing words. The words in your song will become a magical incantation that will have a powerful effect on your body and mind. You can make the song fun and easy so you can enjoy singing it to yourself every day.

SAYING HEALING WORDS TO OTHER PEOPLE

Healing words work wonderfully for people around us too. Every time we are talking to another person, we have a chance to bring something good into their life. What we put into our words reaches the mind and the heart of another person, and we can choose to give a message that will make the other person feel happy.

We are all sensitive people and we take in the words that we hear, knowingly or unknowingly. When somebody says something to us, we receive the message on many levels: in our mind, in our body and in our soul. Our cells are also listening to these words. This way we can receive beautiful energy from another person, such as love, kindness, gratitude and appreciation, or we can hear lower energy – for example, anger, judgement, blame, hurt and so on.

We have the power to change how we speak to other people and what kind of energy we bring to them.

Whereas we can't always control what other people say to us, we have the power to choose what words we say to them. This power is available to us every moment and everywhere we go: at home, in the street, on public transport, in a shop. We can change what we say and how we say it. We can choose to say uplifting words that will strengthen the person's self-belief and remind them of their gifts. We can give hope to a person and let them know that they have the power to change their life if they want to. Healing words are like mirrors that will reflect the right aspect of that person – their strength, courage, beauty – and will allow them to shine even more. We can also add special energy of love and kindness to our words that will touch the person's heart.

Look for the good in the people around you and remind them of their power with your kind words.

Everything is connected to everything. We are like stones that are thrown in the water of life, creating ripples and bringing resonance to all that there is around them. Every seed that we plant goes to the soil of the person's heart, so why not choose to plant a positive one?

If this resonates with you, you can start to choose healing and uplifting words to say to other people. Imagine that you talk from your heart and allow the energy of your speech to flow gently and lovingly to the heart of another person. As you are looking at another person and perceiving their energy, let your intuition tell you what would be really good for them to hear right now. Be kind and generous, from the heart.

This practice can help to improve the relationships within the family and focus on the positive sides of each other. You can sit down with somebody close to you and exchange the words of love with each other. For example, you can do it in turns and talk about the beautiful qualities of the other person, say what you love about them and what their talents are. Focus only on the positive and you will notice how the energy rises and becomes very loving between you. You can practise this game of kindness in a circle of friends and see how wonderfully it uplifts the energy in the group.

We bring a magical transformation to each other just with the words of love and appreciation.

FIVE

THE 4ᵀᴴ WONDER OF THE SELF: WE CAN FEEL

Everybody is born with a beautiful gift of feeling in their heart. This talent helps us to understand ourselves and the world around us. Throughout our life we experience different feelings that serve us as inner navigation. They are a signal of how our heart responds to various people, places, situations and a kaleidoscope of life events that we come across.

Feeling is the first impression that we receive about a new situation. It is like a sense of knowing that helps us to discern our experiences and make the right choices for ourselves in life.

Feelings can have many different colours and hues: love, happiness, joy, excitement, peace, sadness, pain, regret, disappointment. Some of these feelings, such as the feelings of love, excitement and joy, are the signals on our navigation board that let us know that we are on the right path. Listening to these markers can help us to find our way in life intuitively, because when we feel a positive resonance, it means that we are moving in the right direction.

For example, if you feel drawn to nature and experience a peaceful feeling when you are surrounded by trees, it could be an invitation from the natural world to spend more time with it. Similarly, if you feel magnetised to a particular book, perhaps a book about spirituality or healing, it is likely that this book has something special for you and is calling for your attention. This is how our feeling is guiding us.

Listening to the feeling is very important as it provides the direct guidance from our intuition.

It is interesting that in QHHT sessions, the Subconscious always repeats the same message about the feeling: "You have to listen to your feeling. This is how we speak to you. Trust yourself and connect to your feelings." This message is given to the majority of people who come to a session and it shows how important it is to listen to our inner navigation.

While the mind thinks and analyses, the feeling gives us a sense of knowing.

When we remember to listen to our feelings, we open a path of connection to our inner self. This way we learn more about our body, our soul, our true mission and the vibrations that we encounter on our journey.

In this chapter we will look at the ways we can understand different feelings inside us and learn to work with them to improve our wellbeing.

FEELING IS OUR BEST GUIDE

Feeling is a powerful gift that reflects to us what is happening in our lives. In every situation we receive a feeling that acts as an immediate vibrational response to the outward circumstances. This makes feeling a very precious ability that can truly show what a particular situation means for us.

For example, when we are walking in the street and passing by different people, buildings and trees, we receive feelings about every one of them. It is a natural reaction that we get inside of us, however we don't often pay attention to it. We can get so busy in our minds that we don't notice the energy of the world around us. But it is there, all the time, waiting to be heard. When we begin to listen to our intuition, we can pick up plenty of vibrations around us and understand the true cause of our feelings.

The ability to sense energy can be developed if we begin to pay attention to how we feel every moment of our life. It takes some observation and presence in the current moment, as well as curiosity to learn about the world of energy. The more our awareness grows, the more we can sense the vibrations around us and understand how they connect to our own energy.

We all have built-in antennae that help us to read the reality on an energy level.

Every time we meet a new person, we open an interesting book. We begin to receive information about their energy, thoughts, emotions, experiences, sometimes even their health. It all happens intuitively and comes as a feeling or a 'knowing'. This is because, on an energy level, we have already picked up these signals and they have now reached our minds as conscious awareness. We are very telepathic beings by nature and we communicate with each other energetically all the time. It is useful to practise these abilities and develop an intuitive feeling so we can help each other with guidance.

When we receive an offer or a suggestion to do something, we also get a feeling about it. We may get a pulling sensation of a 'yes' that magnetises us to the experience, or we may feel that it is not for us. Listening to the feeling in the moment of making a decision is important because it shows if it is a beneficial experience for us. Usually, a positive experience would be accompanied by a feeling of love and excitement, and one that is not for us may feel more like a closed door.

The signals can vary in different situations, but this simple practice of listening to your feeling will improve your intuition and connection to yourself. The vibration of truth speaks in our body as a wave of energy. When we direct our attention to this energy, we automatically release the attention from the mind and open to our inner knowing.

HOW DO WE FEEL ENERGY?

We can sense the energy in our aura when we come across a certain vibration. Every time our energy field touches another type of energy, we receive a reaction. It can be particularly strong when we are in the presence of a new or a very prominent energy, for example, a powerful person or an old building with an intense history. Usually, this feeling comes as a 'knowing' or as a sensation on our skin.

Some people are particularly good with an intuitive feeling; they get an immediate sense of a person or a situation. Other people are stronger visually and they can see clear images in their mind when they connect to energy. There are also some people who receive sounds or voices as a way of communicating with the invisible realm. Every way of receiving information is equal and valid. The most important thing is to trust the very first sensation that comes to you. This way, you will discover your own technique of feeling the energy around you.

If you were to imagine that an invisible energy is touching you at this moment, what would this energy be like? How would you perceive it? What feeling does it bring to you? You can connect to this invisible energy with your heart and listen to what comes to you intuitively.

The more you listen to the feeling, the more information about the energy will come to you.

Let us say that you are walking in the presence of beautiful trees in a park. If you focus on the sensations in your body, you may sense that this energy is relaxing, calming and allowing you to breathe deeper. It may feel like the trees are helping you to release your worries and uplift your mood. Following this feeling, you can learn more about the energy of the trees and receive healing from nature, bathing in its peaceful energy.

You can also practise feeling energy in different social situations. Imagine that you enter a room full of people who are involved in a conversation. As you enter this space, before you speak to anybody, feel what the energy in the room is like. How does it resonate with you? What are your first sensations? This simple practice can increase your ability to feel the energy of people and places.

Open to the energy with trust and the energy will open to you.

One of the most powerful ways to read the energy is with the help of our hands. This is what I teach in my Energy Creation courses. Our hands have an incredible ability to feel the energy every time we come into contact with something. This way we can scan our own body, understand other people's vibrations, read the objects that we touch, and connect to nature around us. Every time our hand touches something, there appears an invisible bridge between the hand and the object, and we begin to receive telepathic information about it. At this moment we are connecting to a very truthful and unique vibration of the object, which tells us exactly what qualities it has.

Our hands are like sensors that receive energy from everything we touch.

Opening to the energy dimension is a fascinating journey, as it leads us to profound discoveries of ourselves and the world around. We can learn to understand our body with the palms of our hands and communicate with other people in a more sincere and powerful way.

FEELING THE BODY

One of the main benefits of feeling the energy comes when we apply it to our own body. Trusting the feeling from our body is a very important part of the self-healing journey. The body has already prepared an important message for us and it tries to communicate it through our own sensations.

Feel your body and what it wants to tell you.

Feeling the body is a completely intuitive process. When we interact with it, we don't think but we feel; we connect to the energy and the vibration within each organ. This helps us to build a bridge between our mind and our body, and allows us to understand ourselves in a better way.

We can perform a mental scan of our body every day to make sure the energy is balanced in each organ. It is a very simple exercise that will help you stay in touch with your body and respond to every little signal that the body gives to you if the energy is going out of balance.

In the same way, we can work with some of our symptoms. If you get a message from your body, you can meditate on it and feel the symptom. You can ask the body how it is feeling and why it is showing you this symptom. You can then talk to the symptom itself and ask it for a message. A lot of interesting and revealing information can come this way if you trust what you are feeling at this moment.

Let us practise this exercise together now.

PRACTICE TIME
FEELING YOUR BODY

◊ Find a comfortable position, close your eyes and relax. Take several nice deep breaths to allow your body to release all the tensions. Bring your awareness inwards and connect to the feeling in your body.

◊ Let us start with the area of your head. As you are breathing, sense the energy of your head. How does it feel? Is it relaxed or tense? Does it feel light or heavy? Listen to it. You can ask your head how it is feeling right now. Receive any words or messages that come to you first (for example: "I need a rest", "Breathe deeper" or "There are too many thoughts"). Connect to your sensations. Ask your head what you can do to make it feel better, and move the energy in an intuitive way to heal it.

◊ Now let's focus on your eyes. Feel your eyes, connect to the energy in them and around them. What does this energy feel like? What does it remind you of? Does this energy feel healthy and relaxed? Or is there any stress in it? Just feel it. If you were to help your eyes, what would you do? Maybe you could give them a rest or perhaps you could imagine cleansing your eyes with the light and dissolving the old energy. Work on your eyes in the way that your feeling tells you to.

◊ Now let's move to your throat. Feel the energy of your throat. How is your throat feeling today? What do you sense in this area? Feel every part of it: the lower, the middle, the top. If you feel that there is some tension in the throat, breathe it out. Relax your throat and connect to any messages that come to you. What can you do to make your throat feel better? You can even open your mouth slightly and imagine that you are letting out all the old energy that has been kept there.

◊ Now feel the energy of your heart. What does your heart feel like? Is it calm? Is it open? Does it feel at peace or is anything bothering it? Listen closely to the energy of your heart. Ask yourself what would help it the most now. Then follow the guidance that the heart gives to you.

◊ We are now moving to your digestive system. Sense this area as a whole. How is it feeling now? Does it feel balanced? Or do you feel any tensions or worries in this area? Connect to your digestive system through your feeling. If you wish, you can place your hand on the stomach to help this communication. Ask your stomach what it really needs right now and listen to the messages carefully. You may have pictures or words appearing in your mind. Trust them. This way you can scan every organ in the digestive system (the liver, the colon, the gall bladder, etc.).

◊ Now we are going to your reproductive area. Feel the energy in this area. Does it feel calm or are there any tensions? Sense if there are any feelings in your sacral chakra (for example, happiness, joy, peace, sadness, stress); you can scan it with your intuition. Ask these organs if you could help them in any way. Talk to the energy for a moment. Then spread the healing vibration into the sacral chakra as directed by your feeling.

◊ Repeat the same procedure with any other organs that you would like to feel in your body. This exercise may or may not include the whole body; you can just work on the organs that you feel drawn to at the moment. Notice that every time that you do this practice, you will get better and better at receiving the messages from your body. You have to really trust what you hear inside of you – this is your bridge to healing.

◊ After the practice is finished, say thank you to your body for doing such a wonderful job. Now you know how to connect to your body and shift the energy inside. Take several deep breaths to start bringing the awareness back into the body and take your time to return to the physical world. Slowly start to move your arms and legs and, when you are ready, open your eyes.

THE FEELINGS INSIDE

During the day we go through different feelings and emotions, which create a certain frequency inside of our body. Some of them may be uplifting and balancing, others may be distressing and low. Emotions interact with us on an energy level and have an effect on our physical self.

> *Emotions have a direct effect on the body; they create a pool of energy inside our organs.*

For example, a feeling of joy and peace is good for the body. The cells positively respond to the energy of these uplifting feelings and balance themselves naturally. Peaceful energy has a healing effect on our body, releasing the tension and bringing harmony inside. It creates a balanced living environment for our cells, as they take this energy in like a sponge. Everything that we feel is registered in the body and is passed on to our cells.

> *We create the positive environment for our cells by choosing the emotions that are good for us.*

A lower-energy emotion, like anger or frustration, can negatively affect the body and bring its energy down. The frequency in the body becomes distorted and loses its balance, almost as though the protective energy is becoming weaker. This unbalanced energy can lead to problems on the physical level. There is always a link between the affected organ and an emotion that caused its disturbance – for example, anger and irritation can cause discomfort and inflammation in the body.

Some feelings can be trapped in the body for a long time. This is especially true for strong feelings of a dramatic nature that couldn't be dealt with at the time when it happened. For example, a child who experienced deep hurt and couldn't cope with it on their own may have kept the painful feelings inside. Perhaps at the time there was no chance to express how they felt and there was no emotional support available from adults. So, as they grow older, this lower energy can still continue to have an effect on their life.

Depending on where this emotion has been hidden, it may affect the part of the body that is linked with the emotion. For example, if a person is used to taking a lot of stress in their stomach, the emotion will go to this organ first, trying to digest the situation. If a person takes a lot of pressure from other people, the emotion may lie in their shoulders or back as this is where we tend to accumulate the weight from life. Every signal has a reason and is very symbolic.

Understanding the emotions and talking about them can assist us on the path of discovering who we are. Every emotion has a certain energy and, if we connect to this frequency and ask it for a message, we can understand the deeper causes for this feeling. We can also learn how to transform this feeling into a lighter one. This is why such techniques as communicating with the body and emotional release are important for healing.

Don't judge yourself for feeling a certain emotion; rather, explore and understand it.

Some feelings, like sadness or pain, can come to us like teachers and help us to learn more about life. As challenging as they can be, these feelings can sometimes help us to navigate through physical life and broaden our senses and perspective. We can learn to empathise through these feelings and become more compassionate to other people. We can also learn to move to the lighter vibrations and go beyond the illusion of fear to the vibration of peace and love.

Lower-frequency feelings help us to learn more about ourselves and understand the range of emotions on the Earth plane.

Sometimes it is important to sit with the feeling and embrace it when it comes along. When we accept a certain feeling, it becomes easier to listen to its message. After the feeling has been acknowledged, we can choose what we want to do with it – explore it, let it go or shift to a higher frequency.

Awareness can help us on the journey of working with our emotions. In the light of awareness, we can cure old feelings that have been with us for a long time. Once we step above the tormenting feelings and watch them as an observer, we can begin to understand what they are teaching us and how we can release them. The more we practice meditation and spiritual techniques, the more aware we become of energy, and the better tools we acquire to achieve inner balance.

PRACTICE TIME
UNDERSTANDING YOUR EMOTIONS

◊ Find a comfortable position, close your eyes and relax. Take several deep breaths to allow your body to release all the tensions. Bring your awareness inwards and connect to the feeling in your body.

◊ Think of a situation in your life, either in the present or in the past, that you would like to work on and heal. Imagine this situation and recreate it inside of you. What feelings come to you first? Pay attention to what happens in your body as you connect to this energy. Allow your feelings to come out to the surface.

◊ Describe to yourself what you feel. Try and name your emotions – for example, frustration, sadness, pity, loss. Ask yourself: "How does it make me feel?" Relax completely and allow yourself to say whatever comes to you at this moment; imagine that you are connecting to the deepest part of you. Be free in your expression.

◊ Ask the feeling how you can work with it. Can anything be

changed in this situation? What can you do to make it feel better? For example, you could imagine the bright light surrounding this feeling and dissolving any negative effects. Or perhaps you could breathe it out of your body and let it go? Let the feeling guide you. Connect to the part of the body where this feeling is located and cleanse it with your energy.

◊ Make a mental note of what you need to do in life in order to work with this feeling. Maybe you could change your focus or do something in a different way. Let your inner wisdom guide you.

◊ After you have finished the practice, take several deep breaths and allow the awareness to come back to the body. Take your time to slowly come out of meditation and bring all your consciousness to the current time and place. If you would like to, write down what you experienced on paper so you can remember it later. In some cases, you may need to work with a particular feeling more than one time.

POSITIVE FEELINGS

Positive feelings are gifts that come into our life to uplift and encourage us. They are almost like good friends who point us in the right direction and make us feel better inside. Positive feelings allow us to know ourselves better. When we have a positive feeling about something, it is an indicator that this situation is good for us.

Positive feelings represent the true nature of our soul. Deep inside we want to feel love, joy, peace and unity. Positive feelings are a calling from our soul asking us to look within and pay attention to what makes us feel happy.

When we have a positive feeling, we are being ourselves.

We can connect to a positive feeling and invite it into our life. When we spend more time with a positive feeling, it begins to grow and transform our everyday experiences. We start to see life in a happier way and appreciate all the good things that come to us. Positive feelings bring a beautiful colour into our life and can make our experiences much lighter and easier.

Positive feelings have a healing frequency as they belong to a very high vibration. When they enter the body, they cleanse it naturally and rejuvenate the cells, bringing us inner balance. We can bathe in positive feelings, like in the river of light, and allow them to heal our body. Just spending time with love, laughter and joy can help to raise our vibration and make us feel much better.

The more we allow positive feelings into our energy field, the more we cleanse and heal.

Positive feeling is a sign that we are moving in the right direction. Let us say that you are thinking of going to a meditation class and this idea gives you a feeling of joy. This inner feeling is a sign that you are doing the right thing. The more you listen to the feeling, the more obvious it is going to become, and it will bring you other experiences of a similar high vibration.

Positive feelings can be induced by doing something that you really enjoy doing. You can find hobbies and activities that allow your energy to flow and make your soul happy – for example, drawing, singing, walking in nature, meeting beautiful friends. Everything that your heart responds to is the right step on your path.

What makes you feel uplifted and happy? What is your favourite positive feeling? When do you feel it?

We can learn about positive feelings from the world around us. The trees and nature remind us of the feelings of peace, joy and freedom. We can observe the animals and receive the positive feelings of love and sweetness from them. Animals are naturally attuned to their instincts and emanate strong spiritual energy. We can connect to the wisdom of animals through their eyes and learn more about the positive feelings that they share with us.

In the same way, spending time around water, air, earth, fire, crystals and other elements helps us to reconnect to the natural positive energy within us. The elements already know how to reach harmony and peace and they naturally transmit this frequency to us when we are in their presence. There is a lot that we can learn from the world of energy around us.

In this chapter we are going to explore several types of positive feelings and discover what kind of energy they give to us.

HAPPINESS

Happiness is an uplifting feeling that brings high-frequency energy into the body. We feel happy when our soul knows that it is doing the right thing and we feel elevated from within.

Happiness is a beautiful energy that has a positive effect on everything that we do. When we are happy, creativity flows better and everyday simple activities, such as walking, singing, dancing and taking care of ourselves, bring us joy.

Happiness is a sign that we are doing something that we are supposed to do. Our soul responds to the fact that we are on the right path and prompts us to smile to express our happiness. There appears a natural vibration of joy in the body and the light starts to shine inside of us.

When we are happy, we project our own positive feelings onto other people and on the situations that we find ourselves in. This makes even darker moments appear lighter and easier to go through. Happiness is a true healer and can help others to feel better too.

The world around us can also remind us of our own happiness. We can see, hear, touch, perceive things in the outside reality that make us feel uplifted. For example, when we hear the laughter of a child, see a funny dog, smell a beautiful rose, we encounter doorways to our own feeling of happiness. These open-hearted moments sparkle the energy of truth inside of us and help us to remember how to be happy.

A simple remedy to promote the feeling of happiness in your life is to include more things that you enjoy doing. This can be, for example, doing creative arts, looking after your body, meeting cheerful friends, drawing, dancing, performing. Allowing yourself to do something that makes your heart sing. Sometimes it is the small things in our life that bring the big energy wave of happiness.

It is worth asking yourself a simple question. What makes you feel happy? How often do you feel happy? If you could invite more happiness into your life, what would you do?

LOVE

Love is a beautiful feeling which reminds us of a state of bliss. When we feel love, we become our natural selves and we activate our heart to transmit high-frequency energy to each other.

The energy of love changes things instantly – it creates a special vibration that makes the world appear kinder, more familiar and comfortable. With love we become more accepting and we open our heart to other people and situations in our life. Love really helps us to see the magic in the world around and expect miracles to happen.

Love creates the light inside of us and paints the world in the brightest colours.

The source of love is our heart. This is where we generate this high-frequency energy that we then direct to ourselves and other people. Love helps our energy to flow and become free. As we open our heart to love, we begin to embrace ourselves and our special gifts. This helps our projects and creations to flourish, like a special fuel that brings energy to everything that we do.

The energy of love is so strong and high-vibrational that it can bring healing to our body. Like beautiful sacred water, love disperses negative feelings of anger, hatred and sadness and brings the balance back into our system. In many healing practices, including meditation and Energy Creation, love is used to heal the energy in the body and recreate harmony on a physical, emotional and mental level. Love helps us to release the energy of the past, forgive ourselves and other people, and in this way become free.

Love is the most powerful healing energy.

When we fall in love, we connect to a beautiful part of ourselves that wants to be kind and giving. We begin to feel joy, excitement and a willingness to express ourselves in a loving way. Love shows us the truth about ourselves – how kind-hearted and sweet we really are from within. In a way, when the world invites us to fall in love, it gives us a chance to connect to the feeling of love that we already carry deep within us.

Love is the driving force of our life, almost like invisible clay that puts everything together. It connects the people, the animals, the nature, all parts of the creation together in one big majestic ball of light. When we feel love, we begin to recognise that we are all similar, irrespective of the shape that we chose for our incarnation. Love unites everyone.

We are always safe and protected when we feel love.

When we feel fear, we temporarily forget that we are made of love. We get into the illusion of darkness and the unfairness of the world. While this can be true on one level, staying in this vibration can take us away from the feeling of love that is our true essence. We need to remember that there is always a doorway of love just next to us and we can open it to enter this dimension and experience the magic of transformation.

Love is a magical switch that can completely change our experience of living on Earth.

Love is always there and it is waiting to connect to us. There is a lot of healing energy in love and it is not only about loving another person. It is about completely accepting ourselves in all that we do, loving the world around us, holding the higher frequency for each other and surrounding everything that we touch with the energy of love. Love is in every moment and every millimeter of our reality.

Since the olden times, fairy tales have taught us that the power of love changes evil into goodness. How many times have we read about a hero with a kind heart who made the wicked witch disappear? This is the story of our life in general. The energy of love and kindness can melt down the illusion of fear and malice.

When we are in the vibration of love, we can perform miracles for each other. We can generate and share brilliant ideas that come from the heart and manifest our dreams. The beings who look after us always support our dreams that are based on love. They say that if our wish is empowered by love, it will always come true. There is no greater gift that you can give to yourself than the energy of love.

What makes you feel love? When do you feel love the most? How can you express love to yourself and the world in the best way?

GRATITUDE

Gratitude is a way of positive communication with the Universe. It is a state of appreciating what we have in our life and saying 'thank you' to the world for giving us our experiences.

Gratitude brings us inner content. It helps us to see the good in everything around us and notice the small positive things that come our way. When we feel gratitude, the Universe recognises that we appreciate our life and sends us more of the same positive vibration.

Send gratitude every day and you will receive presents from the Universe.

Gratitude is very fulfilling – it opens a flow of kindness and warmth in our hearts. When we appreciate our life, our energy changes and begins to sparkle with light. Like magic, gratitude can instantly elevate our mood, improve our relationships and bring beautiful experiences into our life. It rewires our existence from the state of need to abundance.

When we feel gratitude, we are encouraging the Universal flow to give us more of the same kind. We uplift our own energy and become even more confident that we are on the right path.

"Thank you, the Universe, for making me happy today!"

Expressing gratitude can be difficult when we focus on something that we don't have or something unpleasant that happened to us. This way we can temporarily forget about gratitude and move away from the loving heart to the thinking mind. When we shift the focus back to gratitude, it helps us to flow with ease in life and find the positive sides in all our experiences.

Practising gratitude can take the simple form of saying 'thank you' to the Universe every moment of our life. It is about finding small things that you feel grateful for and acknowledging this feeling. When you say 'thank you', the doors of positive energy open and more abundance flows your way.

You can experiment by listing the good things that happened to you during the day or the week. For example, maybe you received a beautiful gift from a friend, or perhaps you met a nice person who made you feel good. These positive happenings will help you to focus more on the happy vibration and invite it into your future.

What are you grateful for in your life? Did you experience any positive changes in the last several years? How does gratitude make you feel?

JOY

Start feeling joy… Where is it coming from? How does it feel? Sense its presence in your space now.

You will probably notice that joy feels like a wave of pleasant energy in your body, bringing a message that something good is happening now. It is a feeling that makes your energy elevate and your spirit uplift. Joy is always a welcome guest in our life and it helps us to enjoy the current moment.

When we feel joy, we experience a pure sensation of happiness that appears naturally within us and spreads through the whole body. It is such a wonderful emotion that it creates a positive healing effect on the body, making our organs smile and feel good.

Joy brings the energy of elevation and alignment into the body.

We first experience joy as children as we are discovering this world and finding the simple ways to be happy. In the beginning of our life, we feel joy just by seeing something exciting around us. Now, as adults, we can connect with the energy of joy in our daily experiences. We can find it in the smiles of other people, in the rustling of the leaves on a tree, in the sunshine on our path, in the achievements that we have.

Joy is a universal feeling that is available to everybody. It doesn't matter whether it is big or small, joy is always a pleasure and a great healer. We can spend time with our family, admire the beautiful colours of nature, bathe in the sea and enjoy the current moment. Joy is everywhere.

There are many reasons to be joyful, we just need to find them.

It is wonderful how easily joy can travel from one person to another. When we see somebody happy or smiling, we naturally start to feel better ourselves, receiving this jolly energy in our heart. In the same way, we give some of our special sparkle to other people when we feel joyful. It is good to remember that we can be the beacons of joy and have a positive effect on the world around us.

Like happiness, joy is also an indicator that we are on the right path. When we feel joy, our spirit naturally uplifts and we feel more in tune with ourselves. Joy is a simple ticket to feeling more confident and courageous, as in this moment we just follow our inner excitement.

Joy brings us in alignment with our soul.

The good thing is that joy can be invited into our life. Just like a friend who comes for a cup of tea, we can sit down with joy and have a little interaction. We don't always have to wait for a moment when something good happens, we can purposefully channel this positive energy into our day. Just ask for joy to come. One or two happy ingredients per day will make us feel much better.

Remember the moments when you feel joy. What are they like? When was the last time that you felt joy?

PEACE

Peace is a serene and tranquil state of being. When we are feeling peace, our energy is in harmony and is not affected by the events in the outside world. Peace is like a beautiful surface of a lake, always calm and glistening.

When we are at peace, we focus on our inner world and allow tranquility to be our guide. We take things as they are, without letting the stormy waves of life affect our inner harmony. The energy of peace is good for the body and prevents us from getting nervous and worried. It has a healing effect on us because it calms down any distorted or inflamed energy in the body.

Peace is a natural healer.

The most perfect example of peaceful energy is nature, because it already emanates a serene frequency. The trees, the sun, the flowers – they all know how to be peaceful and they teach us this way of being just by their presence. When we are in the company of nature, we automatically attune to the energy of peace and remember what it is like to be still and calm.

Nature is a wise teacher of the energy of peace.

Breathing is a beautiful way to achieve inner peace as it connects us to the natural rhythm inside of us. When we breathe deeply and listen to our inner selves, we get in touch with the expansive source of knowledge within. This wise energy is always calm. Deep inside we know that in the bigger picture everything is alright; we just need to connect to this feeling to remember it.

As you invite peace inside of you, the outside world starts to calm down too.

Inner peace is a form of art that sometimes takes time to achieve. In the constant buzz of the modern world, we can lose touch with our serenity and begin to depend energetically on what we see around us. However, when we turn to peace inside of us, we naturally attune to our knowing self and our perspective starts to shift. We begin to see the world as a happier place and find acceptance in different situations in life.

What makes you feel peaceful? Can you recreate the feeling of peace inside? How does peace make your body feel?

TRUST

You know it's true, you know it's right… You have *a feeling* about it. What does this feeling tell you?

Trust is a feeling that lets us know that we are on the right path. It shows an alignment with our inner self and helps us to embrace our intuition. Trust represents our own support of our beliefs and actions and is an incredibly powerful force for positive creation in life.

Trust is like a staircase that takes us to new heights and achievements. In order to go up that staircase, we need to believe that it is there and that it can hold us safely. Sometimes the staircase may not be that visible and obvious, but as soon as we begin to walk up, the new steps appear and help us to go higher.

Embrace trust and let it take you to the next step on your journey.

Trust helps us to fulfil our dreams in life. Sometimes what we want to achieve may seem daunting and implausible in our head, but the energy of trust has a special quality of making it happen. When we let go of worries and believe in the process, the waves of life take us lovingly into their hands and bring us to the desired future.

There are many ways to practise the energy of trust in our life. We can learn to trust ourselves and our gifts, we can open ourselves to trust other people, we can embrace the flow of life and surrender to it. Everybody has a magical quality – an inner sense of direction that is guiding us at all times. And it can be heard with trust.

It is easier to live with trust.

Trust is the absence of worry and a belief in the natural flow of things. When we are in a trusting state, we let go of control of the events and just believe that everything is happening for a reason. This helps us to release our fear and doubts. The same occurs when we trust ourselves; we begin to listen to our inner voice and follow our intuition.

"You have to trust your inner voice," the Subconscious always tells us.

Trust is a wonderful healer for the body. It creates a special peaceful energy inside that leaves no space for worry and hesitation. The energy in the body begins to flow better and become more harmonious. You can practise feeling trust in your body by just focusing on this energy and noticing how good it makes you feel.

Imagine that you trust yourself completely now. What will be the first thing that you do? What would you like to achieve knowing that you trust yourself?

FREEDOM

Freedom is a gift that we have on a soul level. We come to this life with a free will and an opportunity to choose to do whatever we wish. Then, as we grow up and learn about life, we begin to perceive our reality differently and sometimes forget about the freedom of our soul, adjusting to the circumstances around us. We build a certain image of ourselves and our abilities, which creates an illusion of a constraint that we have to follow.

The feeling of freedom comes from the inside and allows us to act according to our wishes, regardless of the restrictions that we perceive around us. When we are free, we realise that nothing is limiting us, either physically or energetically, and we can live our life following our soul desire.

Freedom has to be realised from within. Many times in life we are waiting for a permission to do something: from other people, from the circumstances and even from ourselves. These illusionary blocks give us a temporary feeling that we are not free. The way to overcome these traps is to listen to the heart and reconnect to the energy of freedom inside of us, which is our divine right.

Freedom is a beautiful feeling that turns us into a magical bird that can fly anywhere in life. We can imagine that we are free to create great things, explore our sacred gifts, be open and loving with people and spend time in a way that we enjoy. The feeling of freedom is healing as it makes the energy flow better in the body.

Imagine that you are a bird. What would you do? Where would you fly in your life?

Freedom releases us from the limitations of our mind and opens the doorways to fulfilling our dreams. When we listen to the feeling of freedom, we connect to our soul and align with our life purpose. This allows us to experience what we came here to do on Planet Earth without limiting ourselves.

Every day provides us with a chance to follow the feeling of freedom and express our creative gifts. For example, if you feel like painting a picture or writing an inspiring poem, this is your soul asking you to express your freedom. Once you listen to this feeling and do it, it will be easier for you to repeat it next time. Small acts of kindness to yourself will lead to bigger changes that will help you to develop the feeling of freedom in your life.

You can connect to the feeling of freedom through meditation and imagination. For example, you can visualise yourself as a soul travelling throughout the Universe and doing whatever you would like to do. Float, create and explore what you like. Feel completely free and enjoy having a free choice. Just this feeling of infinite possibilities and openness to the world will liberate your mind and help you to move forward in life.

What would you do if you were completely free? How would you change your life now?

MEDITATING ON POSITIVE FEELINGS

All of the beautiful feelings that we have discussed vibrate on a very high frequency and thus promote good health. The nature of these feelings is uplifting and harmonious and they create a flow of energy in our body that helps us to heal on the level of the vibration.

We can invite each one of these feelings into our body if we feel that our vibration is going down or is out of balance. We just have to listen to the body and understand what kind of a healing vibration it needs at this moment. Is it love? Is it joy? Is it peace? The more we pay attention to these tiny vibrations in the body, the more perceptive to energy we become and the more we can develop our healing powers.

We can heal on the level of frequency using our own energy.

For example, if your body feels constrained and limited in self-expression, perhaps you can work with the energy of freedom. You can focus on inviting liberating energy into your body and bathing your organs in this feeling. This will allow your body to remember the feeling of freedom again and release all the limitations. Or if you feel agitation and nervousness in your system, this could mean that your body is calling for the energy of peace. Then imagine the serene waves of peace entering your body and mentally shift your vibration to a new frequency.

A type of a vibration in your body will indicate what kind of positive energy you need to invite now. If you find a lower energy in your body, invite the opposite frequency of a healing nature.

All of these positive feelings can be invoked and worked with as energies. You can invite these feelings during a meditation. As soon as you ask for a particular feeling to come, it begins to enter your space just like magic. It is almost as though we are opening a portal to that feeling and a new frequency is being born. It is instant. For example, if you focus on the energy of gratitude and ask it to come to you, this vibration will immediately begin to be transmitted to you. Or if you invite love into your cells, it will start to work on them straight away and rearrange the energy inside of your body to recreate the balance. This is truly a majestic power!

The energy of love, peace and joy is alive. They are like little beings whom you can invite into your space every day. In the morning, you can imagine that the beautiful energy of love is entering your room and gently touching your aura. As you build up this feeling, the energy of love will get stronger and will allow you to bathe in it like the sea. You will notice that your mood elevates and your body feels better. You can carry the energy of love all day with you, like a special friend, and ask it to look after you in all situations. This is a very powerful practice that is very easy to do. Let us now enjoy this exercise to work with a positive feeling.

PRACTICE TIME
MEDITATING ON A POSITIVE FEELING
◊   Find a comfortable position in a quiet place, take several deep breaths going through your whole body and relax for a

moment. Keep your eyes open. Spend some time enjoying the peaceful setting around you and just breathe.

◊ Take a look at the energy around you and feel your space. Connect to the invisible air in your surroundings. What does it feel like? What vibration do you pick up from the space around you?

◊ Now let's feel what kind of energy will benefit you the most today. It can be the energy of love, joy, peace, freedom, gratitude or any other positive vibration. Just pick the one that comes to you first. Now imagine that this beautiful energy is coming to your space now, like a light breeze. Let it just appear around you. Imagine that it is filling the air, almost like a paintbrush, and creating this delightful frequency there. You may even start to see what it looks like.

◊ Play with this energy and imagine that it is getting stronger and stronger in your space. It is everywhere around you. Now close your eyes and let this feeling go inside of your body. Feel it with every breath, as it is coming to you more and more. Give yourself completely to this energy. How does it feel to you? How does your body respond to it?

◊ Explore how this feeling is travelling within you. You can direct it to the parts of yourself that need it the most. Just relax in this healing energy and imagine that you are becoming transparent. Let yourself become this feeling for a moment.

◊ Spend as long as you need bathing in this healing energy. When you are finished, send your gratitude to this feeling for coming and helping you today. Begin to take several deep breaths and bring the awareness back into the body. Slowly return your consciousness to the present time and space and completely awaken yourself.

◊ You can repeat this exercise with any of the positive energies that we have discussed. Every time you will find new inspiration coming to you from these delightful invisible energy helpers.

LOWER-VIBRATIONAL FEELINGS

While positive feelings fill us with light and high vibrations, low-vibrational feelings can have an opposite effect on our body. These feelings are made of denser, lower energies and can bring our emotional and physical state down. We experience these feelings when we feel angry, upset, frustrated, jealous, or go through any other kind of challenging emotions.

Lower-vibrational feelings can affect our energy and compromise our immunity.

Inevitably in our life we encounter lower-vibrational feelings and experience them as a part of our journey. Life brings us a variety of circumstances and people, producing different emotions inside of us. We often feel ashamed, confused, upset or annoyed when we react to challenging life situations. Nobody likes to feel sad or angry, but these feelings are helping us to learn about ourselves and choose the right frequencies on our journey.

Lower-vibrational feelings are important lessons that we choose to experience on Planet Earth. We come here to learn how to love, how to be kind to ourselves and other people, how to harness our emotions and how to see the light in dark times. Through experiencing lower-vibrational energies we understand eventually that we are made of light and we can move on to the higher frequencies as a part of our spiritual development.

Lower-vibrational feelings can act as a tool for spiritual growth.

Lower-vibrational feelings are not to be judged or criticised; rather, they are to be understood and accepted, because they help us to move forward to a higher level. These feelings have a powerful quality of teaching us to see the difference in the frequency and explore the range of the vibrations available on Earth. This is a skill that we learn as a part of the Earth experience – being able to operate in the lowest and the highest frequencies, and choosing the ones that benefit our spiritual development the most.

These feelings also help us to understand more about ourselves. As we enter lower-vibrational states, we delve into the story of our life experiences and look for the primary causes for these feelings. This exploration can help us to understand how different situations affect our emotions, and can teach us to step beyond them and learn forgiveness. It is almost as though we temporarily lose ourselves so we can find our true self again. As we evolve, we grow out of lower energies and develop high-frequency abilities such as love, kindness and gratitude. This is a journey that we are all going through and we are helping each other to graduate from this university of life.

In this section we will explore different lower-vibrational feelings and discover the effect that they have on our body and energy.

ANGER

Anger is a strong emotion that brings explosive energy into the body. It reflects our perceived inability to change a disagreeable situation and can often leave us feeling helpless. In an attempt to change things, we electrify the energy and can direct it to ourselves or to other people.

Because of its burning nature, anger can have a considerable effect on the energy of our body. It can literally make it boil. When we experience prolonged anger, especially if it is directed at ourselves, the energy can get trapped inside and make the body go out of balance. The atmosphere in the affected organ can get red, heated and inflamed. In the same way as we get inflammation on our skin and the area feels swollen, itchy or painful, anger stirs up the frequency and produces distorted waves of energy in our body. Before we know it, we become the victim of our own anger.

The energy of anger is a storm to our body and it distorts the natural state of harmony.

Anger could be a reason for many ailments that are developed in our bodies. The unexpressed and untreated elements of unbalanced energy can get stuck inside of us and form into physical ailments. In QHHT sessions, we often receive information that cancer is caused by anger that has been nurtured in the body for some time. For example, emotionally, cancer can be seen as a result of an old hurt towards somebody who treated us unkindly in the past or a situation that made us feel angry and we couldn't change it. Very often anger can be directed at ourselves, and this way it becomes even more destructive.

In one session, the Subconscious explained the reason for extreme psoriasis of the client as anger, which was being expressed through the skin as a reminder to deal with his emotions. The information came this way: "When he gets angry, the blood is boiling and it brings distortion to the energy in the body. This results in the inflammation of the skin. He has to change his reaction to challenging situations in life." In this case, the Subconscious was performing the healing during the session by calming the blood and balancing the energy in the body. It recommended to the person to react wisely in different life situations and to express his feelings honestly to people instead of keeping the anger inside.

Anger has to be expressed and let go.

This brings us back to the idea of how important it is to regularly check the emotional state of our body and release the energies that make us feel unbalanced. You can ask your body: "What emotion are you feeling now?", "Where is it hidden?", "How can I help you to release it?" The body will always give us a clue and provide us with suggestions of how to improve our wellbeing. We just need to listen.

In the case of anger, forgiveness and letting go are the key elements that can help us. Once we determine what is making us angry and understand the message of the situation, we can take time to meditate and balance the energy in the body. We can spend time releasing the anger from the body and speaking it out properly, so this energy can leave us. We can also retrain ourselves to react differently to various challenging situations and choose to follow peace and love, rather than the energy of anger.

The Subconscious always underlines the fact that healing has to take place from the inside and not from the outside, because it is a much healthier and natural way of balancing our energy. Healing from within may take a longer time and demand more persistent work, but in the end, it will produce a stronger result that will last.

When do you feel angry? Why do you feel angry? How does anger speak to you when it comes? How would you describe it? How does it interact with your body? If you could release the anger, how would you do it?

WORRY

Worry is a state of being nervous and anticipating the negative outcome of things. When we feel worry, we don't trust the natural flow of life and we think that something bad might happen.

Worry is our attempt to participate in what is happening, and to try to control the circumstances. This disturbing energy usually paints negative scenarios in our head and, if we listen to them, they grow bigger and can take charge of us. Worry has an ability to distort the illusion of our life experience and make things look scarier than they really are.

For example, we can worry for our own life and how things will turn out for us in the future. This happens when we doubt whether we are secure in many areas of life, such as health, material stability, care, love and emotional balance. We can also worry for other people and their safety, especially if they are not present with us and we can't help them at that moment. In an attempt to make things better for others, we can succumb to an overwhelming feeling of anxiety. Worry doesn't differentiate between big serious things or small insignificant problems; it is just an energy that takes us away from the now and makes us tremble with fear over something that may not actually happen.

Worry is an illusion that takes our mind away from the present moment.

This stressful energy can create an imbalance in the body. When we feel worry, the energy inside of us becomes disturbed and starts to vibrate like small electric charges. The body becomes tense and alert, which prevents it from naturally healing itself. Worry takes our attention away from relaxation and trust, the energies that are essential for self-healing.

In a state of worry, we almost punish ourselves with this unpleasant energy instead of giving our body peace and love. We think we need to worry because this way we can influence the situation; however, the majority of the time we are just giving our energy away to a disturbing idea that could be imaginary. We feed this idea with our thoughts and we can become trapped in it, which leaves us drained and powerless.

Worry is a sign that we need to relax and turn to self-love.

The problem with worry is that it can create a habit. This energy has quite a persisting quality and can become tempting to give in to. The more we subdue to worry, the easier it is for it to take us over next time. This constant anxious state can make us forget that worry is not natural and healthy for our system. The body has to learn to readjust to the peaceful state of being in order to heal. This process may take some time.

Meditation and energy healing exercises can help a great deal to release the worry. We only need to remember what peace feels like in order to start slowly coming back to our natural balanced state. With time, the energy of peace will begin to heal the tensions in our body. Any regular healing practice, which brings relaxation into your body, will encourage this transformational process.

The feelings of love and trust can help to let go of worry. Begin to notice how you are feeling at this moment and what kind of energy you really need more – for example, peace, love or joy. Then try to direct this positive energy towards yourself next time that you feel worry. Tell yourself calming words: "I love you. All will be fine". Do something that you enjoy to bring the energy of peace back into your life.

What does the energy of worry feel like? How does it interact with your body? What changes do you experience in your body when you feel worry? How would you like to feel instead? What can you do instead of worry?

SADNESS

Sadness is a feeling that we get when we see or experience something upsetting. It is usually an event that we cannot change but that we wish could be different. We can feel sadness for ourselves, for other people, for situations in our life, for unkindness in the world and so on.

Sadness goes directly to our heart and brings our energy down. It is like an invisible weight that hurts our heart and doesn't allow us to feel joy and happiness. We can experience short moments of sadness or prolonged times of sadness, some of them lasting for all our life.

We can feel sadness, for example, when we lose somebody or something precious in our life, or when our dreams haven't worked out yet. It is kind of a nostalgic feeling that makes us feel connected to something we used to have or something that we would like to have in our life. The misalignment of a desired scenario in our mind and the current situation in the reality can make us feel upset.

Sadness can become a habit because there are truly many occurrences in the world that can bring us this feeling. Life can be unfair, cruel and upsetting. Many times, we have to see other people suffering and we can't do anything about it. This can leave some sensitive people tormented, as they can intuitively absorb the pain of other people. Spiritual growth is the power that can help us to see the bigger picture in life and understand that many souls choose difficult lessons on Planet Earth in order to evolve as spirits. If we look at the bigger picture, we can raise above the sadness and learn to see the positive sides of challenging situations in life.

Sadness comes from a good intention; it is an inward attempt to make the world a better place. However, like any other lower-vibrational feeling, sadness can get us carried away. When we give it a lot of time, sadness can put an imaginary burden on us. Through the thick energy of sadness, it may be harder for us to allow ourselves to experience joy and happiness. This can create the blockage of universal energy that flows through us, and make us see the world in dark colours.

We choose the glasses that we put on our eyes.

Awareness can help us to find a balance between feeling sad and having a positive outlook on life. If we have a tendency to feel sad, we can give ourselves moments to express it; for example, spend some time crying, singing, writing or speaking about our feelings. This will help our sadness to be heard and released outwards. Then we can choose to consciously go back to noticing the wonderful things around us. When we look for the good things in our life, we are definitely going to find them, because our eyes will show us what we are looking for.

Look for sadness and you will find it, look for joy and it will be there.

A powerful exercise to work with sadness is to imagine yourself as a little child who feels upset about the world around. You can take the little child into your hands and cuddle them with a lot of warmth and love. Tell the child how much you care for them and reassure your little self that everything is going to be alright. When you do this visualisation, you are actually working with your inner sadness; you transform it and release it from your body with kindness.

Doing things that make you feel joyful is also a remarkable way of alchemising sadness. When you do something that makes you feel happy, you are healing your heart and tuning it to a lighter vibration. For example, a good solution would be a physical activity, maybe a fun active game, swimming in the water, yoga or relaxation exercises. We can find natural medicine in our body that can counteract the sad emotions and reconnect us to our joyful self.

What makes you feel sad? What kind of a feeling is it? How does sadness act in your body? What would help you to transform your sadness?

FEAR

Fear is a strong inner response to a situation that is perceived as dangerous. The overwhelming energy of fear can make us get stuck and freeze, being afraid to take a next step.

Fear is a natural reaction that comes when we want to protect ourselves and not step into situations that could be potentially harmful. While in some cases fear can be helpful and can indeed stop us from getting into trouble, in other cases it can become a habitual energy that prevents us from achieving our best potential in life. We can become fearful of small things, which can cast a doubt on the flow of our creative energy.

Some people find that they feel fear to move on, to start new projects and to express themselves. When working with fear, it is important to understand where this feeling comes from and what the real cause for it is. Perhaps it is an experience from the past that needs to be resolved and let go of in order to reach new avenues in life. Maybe the situation is not as scary as it seems but we are being deceived by our own distorted perception or a past experience of a negative nature. Once we step into our greater power and understand the limitlessness of our consciousness, we can release the fear and act from our heart.

In one QHHT session, a woman saw herself as an unusual being in a picturesque unearthly place, with beautiful green hills and majestic castles high up in the sky. She was wearing bright colourful clothes and was involved in working with magical liquids, alchemising and mixing them up. In one of the scenes, she was standing on a hill and wanted to go to another one, but didn't know how to do it. The hills appeared very high and separate from each other. She began to focus her intention on the other hill, and suddenly silver rails appeared in the sky from nowhere and took her to the destination. This proved to be a significant moment in that life, the reason for which was explained afterwards.

In the second part of the session, we asked the Subconscious what the meaning of that life was. They replied: "It was to show her that she has got nothing to be afraid of. She needs to step into the unknown. Even if it looks scary and you don't know how it is going to work, you can still do it. And as soon as you start walking, the ground will appear below your feet and will take you there."

It was a very powerful message that reminded that person about her power to create without fear. Being an artist in real life, she had many projects and plans that she wanted to accomplish. This session helped her to reconnect with her gifts and have more courage for her creative work. It is very soothing to know that there are higher powers that help us to achieve our dreams, even if we can't see them from the beginning. The Subconscious is very wise!

Fear is an illusion that can give invisible shackles to our creative mind.

The energy of fear itself can be very destructive for our body. As it is designed to make us freeze in dangerous situations, the vibration of fear can bring the effect of paralysis to our own energy body. Clenched by fear, our energy becomes trapped, stagnant and unable to move. In long-term situations, it can also affect the physical body, as subtle energy transforms into physical matter, making our organs unbalanced and blocked.

When we work with healing in QHHT sessions, we always ask for the cause of a certain illness. And very often the cause is explained as fear. They say that fear can be trapped in a particular organ and can create an imbalance there. When lower energy is found in the body, the Subconscious works on cleansing the organ with the white light and gives recommendations on how to release the fear from the body. They always say: "Just let it go. You don't have to hold it anymore. There is nothing to be afraid of. You are well looked after."

The awareness of our great consciousness can help us to release the fear of the mind. When we realise who we are on a soul level, we learn to trust the flow of events in our life and listen to our intuition. We also learn to observe ourselves and the energies around us, choosing the appropriate vibrations to interact with. Then, if we encounter fear in the space of high awareness, we can recognise it quicker and remember that we are larger than that and let it go.

Love is a beautiful healing remedy for fear. It is exactly the opposite vibration to it on the frequency range. Love dissipates fear, like the sun melts the snow, and has the power to transform our energy to a higher level. When fear comes in, we have a choice: do we listen to love or do we listen to fear? And every time that we make the choice to follow love, we get stronger and more connected to our courageous self.

> *What are you afraid of? Where does this fear come from? What does it feel like in your body? If you were to choose love instead of fear, what would you do?*

GUILT

Guilt is an unloving feeling that is directed towards oneself when we believe that we have done something wrong and continue to carry the blame for it. Guilt is a form of self-punishment that can erode us energetically from within.

Guilt reflects a judgmental assessment of our own behavior in different situations in life. It is like an inner marker that tells us that if we have done something wrong, we need to rectify the situation and act for the highest good of all. However, in many cases, guilt gets blown out of proportion as a result of a constant blame by ourselves and other people, and it can become a habitual reaction rather than an intuitive signal from within.

> *Constant blame can create a perpetual feeling of guilt that surfaces in everyday life situations.*

As guilt is usually a sign of a lack of love, it carries a very low energy for the body. It is like putting ourselves in a cage and treating ourselves badly for a very long time. All the cells in our body are constantly listening to our thoughts, so after a while of dealing with such energy, they can get used to being diminished and punished. This unfair treatment disturbs the balance in the body and doesn't allow us to breathe fully in life.

Carrying guilt is unhealthy for the body and the soul.

When we feel guilty, we decide that we are not worthy of good things and create a blockage that inhibits our growth, happiness and the enjoyment of life. We get into a pattern of self-punishment and think that it is necessary to be strict and unloving to ourselves. Guilt can become a habit and be triggered by smaller events bringing us back to the source of this feeling.

And very often the source of it is in our childhood. How many times we were told that we were not doing things right and that we were guilty of something! In the tender mind of a sensitive child, this belief can creep deep inside and can sometimes be carried throughout the whole life. It makes it worse if such accusations are accompanied by shame or, even worse, public shame. These situations then become an inner nightmare and the person will try to do anything to avoid this feeling again. This can create a cycle of repeated self-accusations and being unloving to oneself.

Did anybody tell you that you were wrong when you were a child?
Were these your own words or did somebody else put it into your head?

Unfortunately, the lack of self-love patterns formed in childhood often attract similar situations in a grown-up life. As we get used to being blamed and carrying guilt as a child, we find ourselves in similar vibrations again, this time coming from different people in our adult life. We can attract situations that trigger this inner feeling. These moments are given to us to understand that there is something that we need to change about the way we feel towards ourselves.

Sometimes the feeling of guilt can stem from a past life. A typical example would be a lifetime when a person is unfairly accused and punished for doing nothing wrong. This is a common scenario in a past life regression, when a person gets blamed for what was perceived as wrongdoing at the time and spends their whole life in prison, being treated unwell, without a chance to escape. The damage and suffering from such a past life can be carried by a soul for many centuries and can still cause an outbreak of unexplained guilt in this life. Lots of people experience this feeling and can't understand why they have it. A past life regression can help to get to the root cause of the problem and release it because it is no longer relevant in this life.

The good thing is that we are powerful enough to turn around this feeling through the practice of self-love and forgiveness. As we grow spiritually, we realise that we have needed to experience lower feelings in order to evolve and reach an awareness that we are ultimately made of light. We learn to forgive ourselves and other people and we understand that we did the best we could in all situations. The light of love and acceptance takes away the shackles of guilt and sets us free.

Self-love and forgiveness are the best healing remedies for releasing guilt.

Saying positive things to yourself is a very helpful way to heal the feelings of guilt. As guilt can sometimes become an unconscious habit, we need to reprogram our mind and teach it to react kindly and lovingly to ourselves. This transformation can sometimes take some time, but it will inevitably result in a more loving attitude, which will then lead to positive changes in our life.

You can start with a simple practice of repeating uplifting words to yourself daily in every moment in time. After some repetition, it will become a new healthy habit. For example, you can say to yourself "I love you", "Well done", "I think that you are wonderful" and any other phrases that are made of high energy. The loving feeling of these words will disperse the weight of guilt and will create a truthful mirror of your beautiful soul.

What makes you feel guilty? Is it your own feeling or did somebody else give it to you? How does guilt behave in your body? If you could say something loving to yourself instead, what would you say?

FRUSTRATION

Frustration is a low-vibrational feeling that can bring our energy down. This feeling appears when we want something to happen but it just doesn't work. The misalignment between our hopes and expectations and the physical reality creates a feeling of frustration.

Frustration can be related to ourselves and the way that we measure our progress and success. We may be trying hard to achieve a certain outcome but, no matter how much we try, the desired effect is not coming. This can leave us in the space of irritation and discontent. We may begin to lose self-belief and feel that we are not able to achieve further progress in life. Like any other low-vibrational feeling, frustration has the tendency to grow in power when we give it too much attention.

Frustration can also be related to people around us and the way that we see them. Perhaps we feel that something would benefit another person and we try hard to create this change for them, but it doesn't seem to happen. We may also be expecting something from another person, which feels right for us, but it doesn't come, so we begin to feel disappointed.

If you feel frustrated about something in your life, try to bring the attention back to your inner source of inspiration.

Energetically, frustration reminds us of a feeling of being scratched by a cat in our chest. When we feel frustration, the energy in the body drops down and creates a lack of harmony. Frustration can drain our creative powers and prevent us from believing that we can achieve our dreams.

Frustration is also a sort of self-punishment feeling. It stems from a lack of self-love and makes us focus on what we haven't achieved instead of the things that we are already doing very well. If we change our perspective and make a choice to nourish our positive qualities, we can return to self-appreciation and inner satisfaction.

Acceptance of the situation and knowing that you are doing your best at all times can heal the feeling of frustration. You can tell yourself "thank you" and appreciate the work that you do and your input in the situation. This feeling will change the vibration inside of you and will bring you a more positive outlook on life.

Turn the attention inwards and find positive qualities in yourself.

Observing the moments when frustration comes can help you to reverse your feelings and turn back to the inner creator, forming a healthy habit of self-empowerment. You are already doing wonderful things in your life and you deserve proper appreciation and respect from yourself. Gratitude can be perfect fuel for alchemising the energy of frustration into a positive healing vibration.

When do you feel frustration? Where is it located in your body? If you were to replace frustration with something else, like love, appreciation or gratitude, what would you choose?

WORKING WITH LOWER-VIBRATIONAL FEELINGS

As we can conclude from these observations, all lower-vibrational feelings have one common characteristic: they bring our energy down.

Metaphorically, we can imagine that lower-vibrational feelings can stick like glue to our energy field and take our power away. It is especially true when our own energy is feeling weak – for example, when we are tired, not well nourished and upset, or when we don't look after ourselves enough.

Once a lower-vibrational feeling gets hold of us and establishes its presence, it becomes more difficult to get rid of it. Residing in our energy field, the low feelings can get triggered easily by the outside world, sometimes without our conscious permission. Fighting these feelings can bring more of the same energy again, because we tend to feed lower-vibrational feelings when we think too much about them. We give them energy so they grow.

At the core of any ailment is the lack of love. If we look closely at every lower-vibrational feeling that we have discovered in this section, we will see that they all stem from a lack of self-love and they describe the feeling opposite to love. If we loved ourselves, would we succumb to the destructive energy of fear? If we cared about ourselves, would we upset our cells with worry? What energy would we choose that would actually nourish and enrich our body?

Love is the most beautiful and healing feeling on the planet. It is a high-frequency energy that powerfully counteracts the dispiriting effects of all lower-vibrational frequencies. Love is such a strong remedy that it can be used for virtually any physical ailment or any emotional imbalance.

We can find many different ways to work with lower-vibrational feelings in order to transform them. This path may vary for different people. Some will prefer to learn to let things go and cleanse themselves from lower energies. Other people would choose to focus on the energy of love and uplift their vibrations as much as possible. There is also an option to combine several techniques because they all represent important stages for self-discovery and healing. Every way is effective and will become a valuable chapter for the exploration of your healing gifts.

Choose the way that resonates with you.

Experiencing lower-vibrational feelings is an important part of our journey. Without them, we wouldn't grow so much and we wouldn't get the chance to go deeper within ourselves. These darker feelings evoke self-understanding and allow us to get to the core of who we really are. Let us approach them with kindness and see how they can help us to transform ourselves in a positive way.

LETTING GO

Our life is a constant process of receiving and giving. This natural exchange is a part of our experience: we receive a feeling and we give it back to the Universe. Nothing stays forever and everything gets transformed in its essence as life goes by. Letting go is a principle of life that we can see everywhere around us.

When it's time to let go, don't hold on to it.

We hold on to the railing of a staircase when we go up and then we release it. We eat a fruit until we reach the stone and then we throw it away. We turn a movie on, we watch it and then we turn it off. Everything that we get to hold in our hands, we release it after we finish our experience. Something else is coming to us.

Releasing gives space for new things to come into our life.

In the same way, when we receive a feeling, we can go through it, learn a lesson from it and afterwards release it. It has served its purpose and now it can go. However, sometimes it can be hard for us to let go of a feeling because we become very connected to it and see it as a part of ourselves. We begin to associate with a certain vibration and may even think that we need to carry this burden, not being worthy of liberation.

Can you live without the feelings that are bothering you? What would it be like to be free from them?

Learning to let go is very connected to the feelings of self-love and forgiveness. The act of letting go itself symbolises our wish to nourish ourselves with the highest possible frequency. We feel so much love for ourselves that we want to liberate our body and mind from lower-vibrational feelings and surround ourselves with only beneficial energy.

If you could forgive and release this feeling now, how would you do it?

You can imagine that you are breathing out your negative feeling into a colourful balloon and seeing it going up into the sky. Release all the energy of this feeling into the balloon and watch it going away until it completely disappears. This visualisation practice will help you to let go of the lower feelings and vibrationally separate from them. You can practise it in a meditation with your eyes closed, while taking deep breaths, working with each feeling in turn.

See the balloons with your sad feelings flying up into the sky and disappearing.

You can also experiment with the practice of letting go of a feeling the moment it comes to you. It can take the form of a game where you observe yourself and notice what kind of energy comes to you. As soon as an unpleasant energy comes, acknowledge it and release it immediately from your body. Even if the mind tells you to entertain this feeling and go deeper into it, release it. Let it be your simple practice to learn to let go. You may find that this small exercise will help to bring bigger changes into your life.

Allow yourself to move on.

NOT REACTING

Every time a particular energy is trying to enter our body, be it fear, worry or any other downward frequency, it resembles a telephone call. We can sense that this energy is coming. At this point, being in a state of awareness, we have a choice of whether to accept this energy into our being or not.

If we choose to accept it and give it more thought and attention, this energy can start to grow and take a vivid shape. It enters our body through an easy gateway, usually a weak spot, and finds a place to settle down. From there it can interact with us and control us. At this point, it becomes more difficult to work with this energy because it has already acquired a substantial presence in our cells.

Now imagine that your energy field is strong and powerful. You feel very connected to who you are and you know exactly what is good for you. You emanate light and positive energy. Then any external lower energies that come to you will bounce back from your energy field. They won't find any comfortable place inside of you and will feel unwelcome in the light of your energy. Your strong presence and awareness will counteract a lower feeling that won't match your vibration anymore.

Don't play the game of the lower-vibrational feelings and they will soon lose interest in you.

So, before you start dwelling on any sort of a lower-vibrational feeling, you can try to simply ignore this energy and not let it into your energy field. Do not respond. Don't pick up the phone. Imagine that this feeling has no power to touch you and pretend that you are not interested. If you do it for long enough, the energy of lower frequencies will lose interest and leave you. Every time that you do it, you are building your strength and saying to these energies: "You have no power over me. Go back to where you belong."

There is nothing wrong with releasing the lower energies from the body. There is a space somewhere in the Universe for them. We don't have to interact with them or carry them as a burden. The Universe will recycle them with love and maybe send them to a place where they are needed and can be worked with. You decide what kind of vibration you want to be included in your energy field.

EXPLORING

Sometimes it is worth exploring lower-vibrational feelings as they can provide some insight into our life and reveal to us the patterns that we have formed. Many of these feelings have a repetitive nature and can be triggered by certain life experiences. We can observe the way our feelings come up and, depending on the situation when they come, trace their origin.

Why am I feeling this way?

Perhaps you are experiencing a feeling of anger that is provoked by the people around you, who are being careless and self-centred. Why does it make you angry? Have you had an experience like this in the past? Is there anything that you could shift in yourself in order to feel better about the situation? Understanding more about our feelings and being observant helps us to grow beyond the situation and take control of it.

It is worth understanding why we react in a certain way to a situation.

Some feelings that we commonly attract may have originated in the past. When we find the root cause of such an experience, we can heal it and release this pattern. For example, imagine a little girl had an unpleasant encounter with a big dog that barked at her and frightened her. As she grew up, she kept this unconscious memory and developed a fear of all dogs, even if they are small and harmless. What scared her as a child stayed in her subconscious mind and can be triggered by a similar occurrence in adult life, even though there is no obvious danger to her safety now.

In a hypnotherapy session, we can go back to that very first instance when she experienced the fear of a dog. As soon as she becomes aware of the root cause of the problem, she will begin to heal. When the lady sees the scene from the point of view of an adult, she can understand that she is safe now and can leave this episode in the past. With the help of the therapist, it is possible to talk to the little girl and tell her that she is protected now. Healing the primary cause of an issue brings healing to the current moment in life.

When was the first time that you had this feeling?

You can also explore a lower-vibrational feeling by just communicating with it. In a meditative state, you can ask the energy of fear or worry where it comes from and what message it carries for you. This practice will provide an insight into the cause of your feeling and also give a chance for it to be expressed fully. Sometimes feelings just need to be spoken about. When you turn to it with kindness and ask for help, it might give you an intuitive explanation and guidance about how to transform it.

"What are you teaching me, fear?"

An alternative exercise would be to write about your feelings and express them on paper. Sometimes feelings get suppressed because they can't find a way out. We may be afraid to mention it to other people or even admit it to ourselves. When we express our feelings honestly on paper, we give them a chance to be released from our energy field into the open space. We will also begin to perceive them separately from us, which will give us a much clearer picture about their qualities and origin.

Imagine that you are absolutely free and nobody is watching or judging you. Release your hand completely and allow the writing to just flow as a river; this will help your Subconscious to take over and show you many interesting revelations. Give your writing some time and patience and you will see that at the end you will reach the core of the issue.

Give freedom to your feeling so it can be released.

Drawing is another wonderful way of working with your feelings. If you don't want to write about it and put it into words, just draw it. It doesn't have to be a perfect drawing that makes sense; you can just draw an intuitive abstract image to express yourself and give freedom to your feeling. This therapeutic process will help you to release the energy of the feeling and connect to it as an observer. Feel the symbology of your picture and ask yourself: "What does this expression mean to me?"

LOVING THEM

When lower-vibrational feelings visit us, they want our attention as they are provoking us to make a change. They are almost saying: "Maybe you can learn to react differently this time. See what you can do." If we approach these feelings with love and accept them, then we can listen to their message properly and respond in a positive way.

Love is the best healing remedy for transforming lower-vibrational feelings.

If we respond to a lower-vibrational feeling with anger and frustration, we might be feeding it with more negative energy. As like attracts like, when we get upset about a feeling, we are entangling ourselves more into it. What we want is to surround ourselves with as much warmth, kindness and understanding as possible. Then the high energy of love can start to melt the lower feelings down and transform them into positive energy.

When we give love to a person, a feeling or a situation, we give them magical energy that takes away lower vibrations.

Love is the most powerful remedy that we can give to ourselves in moments of need. It is a natural healing energy that surrounds our feelings in a sea of loving light, a presence that we can generate ourselves. It is almost like we take fear, worry or loss into our hands and we let it know that everything is okay. These feelings need our love and warmth to become free again.

"It's okay. I love you. I understand you," say to your feeling.

You can try to react with love to any feelings that come to you and see what happens. Imagine that you are placing your feeling in warm hands, surrounding it from all sides and making it feel very loved. You will sense how the feeling of love smooths the sharp edges of the feeling, calms it down and gives it the energy of acceptance and peace. These energies are healing and will shift the vibration of your feeling back to alignment.

Your feeling needs love. It has been suffering for too long; let love heal it.

We often hear during QHHT sessions the Subconscious saying the words "Only with love". This sometimes happens when the person asks how they should deal with a certain situation or a person in their life. The Subconscious recommends to approach everything with love, whether you need to stay in certain circumstances for longer or leave them. It feels like love is the essential remedy that we can always use in life, be it in healing, relationships or finding our life purpose.

Turn to love in any situation and let it transform the energy to balance.

You can connect to your energy and feel what aspects of your life may not be receiving enough love at the moment. Are there any situations, personal qualities or life experiences that need more love from you? Imagine them in your hands and direct your loving energy to them. Let the warmth of your heart bathe them in love and tell them how precious and special they are for you. This will start the healing process and soothe these feelings naturally.

TURNING TO HIGHER VIBRATIONS INSTEAD

A very effective way to deal with lower vibrations is to surround ourselves with higher frequencies and let them dissolve the dense energies. When we turn to a happy vibration, we can release lower frequencies and refocus our mind to the positive side of the situation.

Change the focus of your feeling and concentrate on the positive.

When a little child is crying and feeling upset, his parents show him a toy to distract his attention and make him feel happy again. In this example, we are diverting the focus to a higher energy and helping the person to look at the positive side of life. We can use the same technique with ourselves when we remember about our positive feelings and focus on them purposefully to replace lower energies.

Remember about something that makes you feel happy.

Lower feelings have an ability to have a hold on us and manipulate us energetically. The more we focus on an upsetting feeling, the more serious and alive it appears to be. We can shift our mind by turning to higher vibrations and tuning in to their frequency. When the energy of high vibrations becomes strong enough, we can look back at the initial feeling and notice that it is not as big and powerful as it used to be in the beginning. It simply dissolves in the light of positive energy.

Higher vibrations can diminish the power of lower frequencies.

Our world is so full of illusions that we can focus on one feeling and it will have an effect on our life experiences just because we strongly believe in it. For example, if we constantly worry that things can go wrong, we are putting an energetic pressure on our reality and this affects our experiences on the level of frequency. In reality there may be absolutely nothing to worry about, but we create this illusion with the mind, and thus it starts to gain power.

We have a choice of which vibration to focus on.

If we change this filter and focus instead on the energy of joy, imagining that we give it to all our life situations, then joy becomes the prominent energy in our life and starts to influence our experiences. The situations that we encounter will become easier and we will flow from one success to another. You can imagine it like wearing glasses with different shades, each shade representing a certain predominant feeling in your reality. You can experiment with these shades and see which one of them brings you the best possible result in your reality.

A good way to let go of old habits is to turn to higher frequencies and raise our vibration. Rather than fighting an old feeling, we can choose to experience a higher energy so the old habit simply won't cling to us again. For example, when giving up smoking, resisting cigarettes and focusing on their negative effect doesn't always work. A more effective way would be to start to do something of a higher vibration – for example, go to a health club, mix with people who are interested in wellness, surround ourselves with nature, practise meditation. Then we will naturally release the frequency of cigarettes from our energy field and it will be easier for us to let them go physically.

Look for the opposite of your habit. What would help you to shift this vibration?

It is important to surround ourselves with the energies that make us feel good. Our environment affects the way that we feel so much! Friendly, kind people; relaxing, peaceful spaces; an uplifting energy at home – all this opens the doorway to healing. When we focus on the joys of life and on laughter, we instantly raise our frequency and disperse lower vibrations. Always look for positive energy to offer you a helping hand.

There is a little trick that you can use if you feel that lower energies are coming to you. You can begin to affirm to yourself that everything is fine and that the Universe is working in your favour. Then take a piece of paper and write a list of affirmations that state the opposite to the lower feeling that you are experiencing. For example, if you feel a lack of self-confidence and need help with achieving your goal, you can write: "Things work out for me perfectly. The Universe loves and supports me at all times. I am the favourite person of the Universe."

This exercise will help to shift the energy from low to high, even if you feel reluctant to believe it in the beginning. It is recommended to read these affirmations several times per day with a strong feeling, imagining that you are uniting with these words energetically. This will change your perspective and invite more high-vibrational energy into your life.

PRACTICE TIME
WORKING WITH A LOWER-VIBRATIONAL FEELING

◊ Take a comfortable position, close your eyes and take several deep breaths. Turn your attention inwards and connect to your energy. Think of a feeling that you would like to work on today. It may be a feeling from the past or something that you are experiencing at the moment.

◊ As you listen to your energy, ask your body to show you where this feeling is located inside of you. Observe the way that it behaves in your body and how it interacts energetically with you. Tune into the feeling and ask it where it comes from. Describe this feeling to yourself. What is it like? Say things that you feel; let the feeling express itself. Keep breathing deeply while you are doing it.

◊ Now let's go back in time in your life to the moment when this feeling first started. Just allow your memory to take you back to the right time and place to show you where this feeling originated from. Look at the scene. Feel it. What happened there? What were you feeling? Who was there in the scene and how did they act? Look at the scene with love and explore the origin of your feeling.

◊ Connect to your intuition and ask yourself if you can do anything to change your feeling. How can you transform this pattern in your life? Can you change the vibration of this feeling with your own energy? Let your inner guidance give you some messages. Perhaps it is time to let this feeling go. If that's the case, you can say to yourself: "I can now let go of this feeling. It doesn't have to bother me anymore."

◊ As you do it, begin to breathe deeply again and start to release the feeling from your body. Make a firm intention to let it go and believe that it is happening at this moment. Feel it. You can even imagine that the feeling is leaving your body through a portal, drifting away with the white light. Just let it go. What would it be like to be free from it?

◊ Enjoy the feeling of being renewed. Affirm to yourself that you are free now and you are ready to step into a new life. Smile to yourself and enjoy this beautiful state of being.

◊ When you are ready, start breathing deeply and begin to return the awareness back into the body. Take your time to connect to the present moment and space. Bring back your full consciousness and start moving your body gently to return to the full awakening. How are you feeling?

FEELING THE ENERGY OF OTHER PEOPLE

The gift of feeling guides us to choose the right vibration in our surroundings. The inner radar determines whether we need to interact with a certain vibration or stay away from it. This is the beauty of the wonder of feeling – it always knows what is good for us.

Within this gift we find the talent of sensing the energy of other people. We are all very intuitive beings who are able to pick up the energy of everybody who we encounter on our way. Sometimes the energy of others is so strong that we can sense it from a distance, even before we see them. This is a part of a natural process of recognising each other's energy through extrasensory perception.

When we interact with other people, something remarkable happens. Our energies connect and begin to communicate with each other. Without knowing it, we are exchanging subtle telepathic messages on a deep spiritual level. We share our feelings, our past experiences, our intentions, our sacred gifts and the intricate patterns of our aura. This information travels between our energy fields and, if we open our hearts and listen to the energy, we can decode the messages and understand each other in a more genuine way. We are telepathic by nature.

Feeling the energy of other people helps to improve our connection and understand each other in a deeper way.

It is not difficult to feel each other's energy. While staying grounded and connected to yourself, you can begin to sense what energy waves are coming to you from another person. If you let go of appearances, words and thoughts, and just connect to what you feel, you will be able to perceive the vibration that the person emanates. Is it light? Is it uplifting? Is it mysterious? How does it make you feel? Trust what comes to you first. It is like the language of the soul; the feeling in your aura will tell you an incredible story about this person.

When you talk to another person, feel them energetically. What energy do you pick up?

Feeling the energy of other people is not born from a space of judgement. It is a way to get to know each other better and reach a deeper understanding about our connection. Even if the energy of another person is very different from ours, it doesn't mean that it is better or worse – it is just a different vibration. We all go through various experiences in life and our unique energy is formed this way. Energy communication gives us a wonderful opportunity to express love and compassion to each other because we connect to the true nature of our soul.

There will be people who feel very close to your energy and their presence makes you want to fly and do wonderful things. These are the souls that are very similar to yours and that help you to bring out the best qualities in you. In the presence of these people, you feel comfortable, loved, inspired and very creative. You suddenly realise that your soul is waking up and wants to do great things for yourself and others. These people are very precious in our life as they guide us in the right direction of our soul growth.

If the energy of another person doesn't resonate with you or makes you feel uncomfortable, you may be experiencing an energy that has a different vibration to yours. The unique combination of your energy fractals may not be in alignment with this energy. Without judging this energy, you can strengthen your energy field and learn more about this vibration by observing it. If you sense that this energy is not right for you, perhaps you could leave and join other vibrations that are closer to your frequency range. It is a choice. In any case, it is important to be respectful and kind. Sometimes, if you feel that a person is going through a difficult time, you can even send them light and love; this will help them to access higher compassion and healing.

Deep inside, on the level of the soul, we are all made of light. We came here as light beings and decided to learn what it is like to be in a physical body and experience emotions. Many of us have gone through challenges in this life and experienced fear, sadness, anger, helplessness and many other upsetting feelings. All of these energies can leave an imprint on our energy field and create the vibrations that we pick up in each other when we meet.

When we connect to other people on the level of energy and the spirit, we get to the core of our being. We then see through the fears and lower vibrations and we connect to the true essence of who we are. This practice really helps forgiveness and understanding because, by focusing on our inner light, we remind each other of that higher aspect inside of us. When you meet people, you can look them deep in the eyes with love and see their soul there. Observe the beauty of their soul and reflect their divine light by looking at them with kindness.

Approach people as beings made of light. This will transform the way that you both feel and improve your communication.

Sometimes very special people enter our life. They are like angels or messengers and they carry a very light energy. These people may appear in our life just once or step into our path at a very important moment to help us by bringing a message. You will always recognise these people by a special feeling that appears inside of you when you see them. You just know that this is somebody very important to you and you have to listen to this person. The message may come through words, or bring you an awareness just through their magical presence.

Every person that you meet can bring you a new energy and a new feeling. It is almost like you enter a different portal every time you see them. People in our life offer us a sea of opportunities for learning about energy. It all depends on your path at the moment. What would you like to explore? What frequency would you prefer to be with now? Who helps you to grow and elevate your energy? Ask these questions and follow your heart when you choose your companions.

PRACTICE TIME
SHARING A LOVING FEELING WITH ANOTHER PERSON

◊ This is an exercise that you can perform with somebody you love or somebody you would like to explore a deeper connection with. It is an exchange of energy with an intention of making another person feel better, and also of receiving this energy yourself. This is a truly beautiful practice that can heal relationships, encourage the feeling of love and help us to understand each other better.

◊ Find a quiet space where there are no distractions and you can both relax and delve into the energy world. Take a comfortable position, sitting opposite each other, and begin to breathe deeply to enter a meditative state. Allow the breath to release the tensions and worries and enjoy a peaceful moment of relaxation.

◊ First let's connect to the energy of your heart. Imagine that your heart is opening up and spreading the energy of love through your whole body. Feel that you are bathing in your own energy and enjoying the warmth and kindness of your heart. Spend several moments encouraging the flow of love inside of you.

◊ Now look at each other and start feeling the love for each other. Imagine that you are transferring the energy of love with your eyes and with your heart to the other person. Feel how the energy of your heart is getting bigger and is opening for giving and receiving.

◊ There is a channel of love between you two now. Focus on this energy and let it nourish you and bring the best in both of you. Imagine that you are healing the other person with your love. It is the most beautiful remedy in the Universe. You are being transformed right now.

◊ Feel how much you love and appreciate this person. Even if you are not very close, the warmth of the heart will bring the connection between you. Somewhere deep inside, you know them very well. Feel the flower of love opening in your heart and transfer the petals of kindness to each other.

◊ Enjoy exchanging the loving feeling in this telepathic way. You are both receiving so much love in your hearts. You are connecting to who you are. In the end, say thank you to each other, direct the love inwards and meditate for some time in your own energy. Become aware of your own aura and maintain this positive frequency for yourself. After you have finished, come back to your space and slowly return to the full awareness in the here and now. Thank you for doing this beautiful work!

SIX

THE 5TH WONDER OF THE SELF: WE CAN LOVE

Love is the most beautiful feeling that we have on our planet. It is a precious energy that unites us all and helps us to see the good in each other.

Love starts in the heart and grows like a flower inside of us. It touches our body, our emotions, our experiences and people around us. Love is like a magic wand that can heal, transform and bring the light into our life.

When we feel love, we look at the bigger picture of every situation and we develop acceptance and trust. We choose to love the person and the circumstances, regardless of the temporary hurdles and challenging lessons that they provide to us. Love helps us to forgive and release our emotions.

Love can bring us back to ourselves. When we forget who we are, we become confined to the illusionary aspect of ourselves – the limited self. This is when we listen to our mind and doubts. When we are feeling love towards ourselves, we embrace the great sacred spirit that we are and we unite together with it. We can do so much more when we feel love.

Love helps us to connect to ourselves.

There is much more love in the world than it seems. Love is in everything around us: in people, in nature, in the works of art, in the moments of divine connection. When we focus on the beauty of life and begin to see love in everything, we bring this energy back to us. Love responds to us and shows itself in its full expression.

Love begins life. We connect to the person who we want to share love with and we create life together by starting a family. Love creates projects and brings enlightment to our activities. Love is the energy that makes every moment look beautiful. With love, we see the best in others and help them to manifest their highest potential through our kindness.

Love is a special ingredient that makes everything that it touches shine. It makes food taste delicious and emanate bright energy. It makes a piece of art stand out and attract our attention. It makes the touch so pleasant and healing. Love is transforming.

Love is the most sacred gift that we can give to ourselves. With love, we empower ourselves so much that we can have the courage and strength to go forward in life and achieve the goals that we planned. Love is like a healing nectar for people who need more care and attention. When we receive love, we blossom, open, grow and express ourselves freely.

Love is healing.

We can help each other to activate this feeling in our hearts and connect to the energy of love. It is very easy to do when we just remember about love in every moment; we can send it to ourselves, send it to other people and the world around. Love can transmute the old feelings of hurt and perform healing miracles.

The answer is always in our heart. Let us follow the steps of love and rejoice in this energy.

LOVE IS ALL THERE IS

Love is what permeates everything around us in the world. Every tree, every flower, every person is vibrating with the energy of love in their heart. Love is a beautiful light frequency that unites us all in one.

When we look at the world with the eyes of love, we see the truth around us. We go beyond our fear and the illusion of limitation and we delve into the only dimension that is real. And this is love.

Love is the only real thing that exists.

Let's imagine that we are walking in a dark forest with big, gnarled trees casting shadows around us and not allowing us to see the sunlight. We feel fear and doubts as we are walking through the menacing forest, and the more we focus on the scary trees, the more darkness emanates from them. At the same time, if we look up, there is a beam of light in the sky that is travelling throughout every living thing in the forest. This beam of light is love.

As soon as we begin to focus on that light, the forest magically transforms. The darkness goes away, the light permeates everything and creates a beautiful glow everywhere around us. The moment we connect to the light, we begin to see it more. And then the trees become very friendly and kind; they open their branches to show us the way. This makes our pathway clear and enjoyable. We look around and notice magical butterflies and colourful birds everywhere in the forest. And the most fascinating truth is that the forest has always been that beautiful. It is just that we were not looking at it through the eyes of love.

Imagine that you are putting on love glasses and seeing the world through them.

Our life is a forest. There are all kinds of beings around who are teaching us something important about life and showing us different kinds of energy. We are walking the path and taking the steps to learn about ourselves and explore the divinity of it all. We can experience fear, confusion, sadness, loss. We can also experience joy, happiness, love and peace. The more we begin to see the light inside and outside, the more radiance starts to appear around us. We can transform the forest of life ourselves, by letting the light in. Love helps us to see the good in all around us and act from the space of the heart.

INVITE LOVE INTO YOUR LIFE

We invite friends into our house and have a cup of tea together. This brings us a new happy vibration, the energy of joy, understanding and mutual expression. We get enriched from the presence of loving people in our life and we take a step forward to invite them into our space.

In the same way, we can invite the energy of love into our life. Imagine that love is a person who you can welcome into your house and have a cup of tea together. Love can visit you just like your best friend and make your day very special.

Love is energy. We can invite it into our life.

You can start the day by inviting the feeling of love into your room and your body. You can literally say the words: "I am asking the energy of love to come into my life and bring me happiness and joy." Then imagine it appearing in the air and filling all the space around you. As soon as you focus on the vibration of love, it will begin to permeate your room. It creates an instant magical effect – all we have to do is just ask this energy to come.

Focus on the energy of love and imagine it all around you.

You will start feeling a very warm sensation in your heart and your body. Your thoughts will soften, and worries will give space to understanding and love. Simple daily activities will be filled with a special feeling of kindness. Love truly transforms our experiences like a magic wand!

Sometimes love will knock on our door by itself. Then we are blessed with this feeling and we need to recognise it at this very moment. Love can come in so many different ways: through the person that we meet, through a cuddly animal, through the rays of the sun in our window, through the petals of the flowers that we grow. Sometimes a simple moment is so filled with love that we can feel the divine presence all around us. It is a perfect opportunity to connect to this feeling and receive its healing energy.

Our hearts are naturally tuned into the vibration of love.

See love around you as much as you can. Find it in every object and every situation. Underneath every leaf that you pass by there is a wonderful berry that shines with the energy of love; we just need to look beyond the veil and see the truth. Look for the energy of love in all and it will show itself to you like a beautiful diamond.

YOU ARE LOVE

The main person who needs love in your life is yourself. Nobody will be able to give you as much love as you can give yourself, as people in our life only reflect our own consciousness.

The amount of love we see in our reality reflects the amount of love we have for ourselves.

You are a courageous soul who has gone through many life experiences and done your best in different life situations. You worked so hard to understand this reality and be kind to yourself and other people. You have chosen one of the most difficult planets in the Universe to experience physical life in and you are on the journey of healing and spiritual transformation. You did so well.

You deserve to receive love and be grateful to yourself. Being the main character on the stage of your life, you need to receive a lot of love to continue and carry out your life purpose. Imagine that you are the hero of a beautiful movie and you would like to support the main character in the best possible way. How would you show love to yourself? How would you give yourself strength?

When love for ourselves is flowing well, we can give it beautifully to others.

You are a flower that was seeded in the soil of the Universe. You were watered with the love of the planet and were given the ground to walk on. As you were growing up, you were admiring other flowers and seeing love in them, which was beautiful. Now it is time to also look at your own wonderful flower and encourage yourself as much as possible on your journey.

There is no end to the love feeling. There can never be enough of love. You can keep giving it, and giving it to yourself, and more will come. You are filling a beautiful vessel with pure radiant water, which is eternal. Every time you pour water in the vessel, it starts to shine and sparkle with powerful light.

You are giving a gift to yourself by pouring love into you.

If you begin to feel love for yourself, don't think that you need to stop. It is not selfish to focus on yourself. On the contrary, it is the most natural thing in the world. This is the feeling that will help you to grow and expand and will also help others to do the same by following your example.

If you were to focus only on loving yourself now, what would you do?

Every time love for yourself comes to you, say "More". Don't stop, don't limit yourself only because you may have been limited in the past. Now it is the time to become unlimited. How many gifts would you like to receive? What would make you feel happy? What wonderful things can you do for yourself now? These are all the expressions of love.

When you vibrate on the level of love, you emanate the most beautiful frequency in the world. Everybody is going to feel it when they meet you. The people, the flowers, the animals, the birds, the trees; even the water, the air and the sun will feel it and become happy. They will catch your loving vibration and experience the same feeling.

Spread the music of your love into the world and healing will come to many others.

Love creates a special music that is playing in your energy field. People can hear this music and enjoy it. The right souls will be attracted to your energy and will prove to you even more how cherished you are. You will enter a higher dimension of being and step into a flow of miracles when you allow love into your life.

YOUR BODY NEEDS LOVE

Your body is like a child who is pure, innocent and very loving. It really trusts you and looks after you; this is why it is working day and night to provide you with the best experiences possible in the physical world. Just think how many functions our body performs at the same time! Thousands…

The special energy of our body is listening constantly to us. It is open to our guidance and is digesting the emotions that we go through. It does its best to release the energy of fear, suppressed feelings and stress from our body. The body is working all the time to cleanse any lower energies and purify us from toxins. We can only feel gratitude to our body for its service.

Thank you, dear body!

Imagine that all of these millions of cells were created especially for you! What a beautiful gift it is for us. Each one of your cells represents the unique portrait of you and works incessantly to make you feel good. Our body is here to bring us comfort, the ability to move and interact with others. Without its faithful work, we wouldn't be able to experience the physical world in all its diversity.

We have the power to feed our cells with any energy that we choose. We can give them love, healing, gratitude, joy, courage. Because the cells are constantly listening to us, they will soak in the energy that we are giving them and begin to adapt to the new frequency.

Ask your body what kind of energy would benefit it the most now.

Just like any living being, be it a person, an animal or a plant, our body needs a lot of love. It deserves our appreciation for all the work that it is doing for us. When we give our body love, it is like taking a small baby into our hands and embracing them warmly so they feel very loved and cherished. In the energy of love, the body doesn't need to hold on to pain or old hurt anymore; it can let it go and be free again.

When we completely love and accept our body, it doesn't need to create illness anymore.

Love is the highest frequency that our body can receive. It is a pure divine energy that helps the body to bring back harmony and peace.

When we feel love, our cells are happy and can resume their proper function. Love is a magic remedy that gives us the permission to heal. We can use this beautiful opportunity to remind ourselves of our inner power.

HOW TO GIVE LOVE TO THE BODY?

Daily, hourly, every moment…

The body needs love like breath and there is no limit to the kindness that you can share with yourself. You can find hundreds of ways of showing appreciation to your body. Touching, talking, exercising, bathing, meditating – these are only a few paths to choose from to heal and replenish your physical self.

First and foremost, listening to your body is an important way of showing love. The simple act of paying attention to your body will comfort your system and increase the healing effect. You can agree on what time you are going to meet your body and how you are going to show appreciation to it. For example: "Today I am going to be kind to my body and we are going to relax in the garden and listen to each other."

Arrange a healing date with your body.

The way that you prepare for spending time with your body is also a way of showing love. You can create a healing atmosphere with candles, colourful objects, aromatic herbs and relaxing music. Everything that you do for your body with love counts and contributes to the healing effect for your physical self. The body is so wise that it realises your intentions and plans before you even know it yourself. It will cooperate with you.

Some parts of your body, especially if they have been neglected for years, may need extra time to get used to your love and kindness. Make sure that you give them special attention and keep saying nice things to them, for example: "I love you", "You are so good",

"You make me feel very happy". You can literally feel how the energy changes in the body as you say these words of love.

And then, of course, there is action. The listening and preparation naturally lead to the actual time devoted to helping your body and looking after it. You are saying: "I have listened to you and I am going to do everything that I can to make you feel good." The body will smile and reflect back your kindness and positivity. Going to the gym, doing yoga, walking in the park, changing your diet and meditating are practical ways of showing appreciation to your body. Every little act counts.

Create your own recipe of showing love to your body.

There is no one right way of giving love to your body; you can find your own perfect recipe according to your needs and intuition. Enjoy finding the ways to make your body happy and set this as your priority – this way all the energy will flow into a healing direction. Just remember, there is never enough of love! We can show it to ourselves every moment of our life.

LOVING YOUR BODY WITH TOUCH

We are born into this world as physical beings and touch is an essential part of our life. Through touch we can express our feelings, connect to the energy around us and interact with each other. When we touch, we charge our hands with a feeling from the palette of different energies and we transmit it to ourselves or another person. This feeling can be love, tenderness, excitement, encouragement and so on. If we don't put enough love and respect into our touch, it can also become disturbing and unpleasant. The energy of the touch carries the true intention of the person and the receiver intuitively picks up this feeling.

Touch is how we express our feelings to ourselves and other people.

Touch carries a wonderful opportunity to help ourselves and others. It is like a magic power that can charge the body with special energy and transform the cells. We can direct kindness, love, compassion or any kind of a healing vibration with our hands. This creates an instant uplifting effect that we feel in our body and soul. Most communication between people happens non-verbally, so we can use this gift to help each other to heal and recharge.

When the touch is accompanied by a warm loving energy, it becomes healing.

Many times, when a certain part of our body is feeling unwell, we subconsciously bring our hands there and touch it. This is our first instinct to use our hands to heal this part of us. The truth is that our hands already know how to help our body and they are naturally tuned in to the healing energy. We just need to listen to this wise power and let it show us the way.

People who practise Reiki and other forms of energy healing are very aware of the power in their hands. They know that they can heal, uplift, release and transform the energy with the power of their hands. This healing technique is available to everyone and is a wonderful way to learn about your natural gifts to balance your body.

Even if you haven't yet learnt a certain healing practice, you can simply use your hands by following your intuition. You can caress, embrace and massage your body gently and show it love this way. We are all energy healers by nature, we only need to realise it. There is a lot of healing energy in our palms; this power comes straight from the heart. Every time we touch our body, we are giving this love to ourselves, and in this way we activate our healing gifts.

There is a lot of power in a loving touch and it can bring miraculous transformation to the body.

Our body is a beautiful temple and should be treated like a god or a goddess. Indeed, what can be more wonderful than the body that we chose to have our experiences in? It is a true miracle that we have a physical form that helps us to explore the world and perform myriads of functions at the same time. It is something to celebrate!

Think about energy. Everything that we give love to expands, grows and blossoms. If we give love to a small child, it makes them happy. If we give love to a plant, it grows better. It works the same way with our body. We can watch miraculous transformation happening in our body when we shower it with love and appreciation.

Touching your body can become a beautiful ritual that you can perform for yourself. You can create a relaxing atmosphere to prepare for this healing practice, maybe light some candles, play soft music or use aromatherapy. Create an intention to show that you want to give love and healing to your body. The body will feel it and the healing process will start instantly. Make sure that you are not in a hurry and that you really enjoy this practice; this experience can bring a state of inner bliss.

PRACTICE TIME
LOVING YOUR BODY WITH TOUCH

◊ Spend a moment just breathing deeply and connecting to your inner self. Look at your hands and feel them. Imagine that your hands are becoming warm and loving as though they are being filled with beautiful light energy. Your hands are emanating pure light and love. Connect to this energy and enjoy the relaxing sensation.

◊ Think for a moment how much you love yourself regardless of anything, unconditionally. Connect to the feeling of love and appreciation inside of you. Then start gently giving yourself loving caresses all over your body, imagining that you are placing the best gifts into yourself: love, joy, gratitude, appreciation, care, kindness. Touch your body softly, taking a loving care of your head, your hair, your chest, your stomach, your arms, your legs. Really go with this feeling as though at this moment nothing else exists in the whole Universe – just you and your body.

◊ Caress yourself in a way that feels right, knowing that you have got enough time to express your true love and appreciation. Enjoy every moment of touching yourself and explore every part of your body like the rooms of the healing temple. Every organ has got its own language and its own energy. When you touch it, imagine that you enter a sacred space and listen to its messages. Then respond with deep love and respect to your body. You will get higher knowledge about yourself at this point.

◊ You can choose any way of touching that you like. You can just hold your hands on your body to bring the feeling of safety to yourself. You can move your hands in gentle circular motions to open the channels in your body and balance the energy. You can caress yourself like a little child and shower yourself with love and appreciation. Listen to your body and your intuition. Let your hands lead this healing process. Your heart will guide you in the right way.

◊ You can even add a little element of talking and say nice things to yourself when you practise loving touch. For example, you can say: "I love you", "You are beautiful", "You are absolutely wonderful", "You are a joy to be with", "I respect you so much". Bring your feelings while you are saying these words and they will have a powerful effect on your healing process.

◊ When you are finished, say thank you to yourself and your body for doing this exercise. Stay for some time in the healing energy that you have generated and enjoy this loving frequency. It is a deeply transformational practice that you can do as many times as you like.

LOVE IN EVERYDAY LIFE

Once you begin focusing on the bigger loving aspect within you, all the rest of your life will fall into place. Your relationships will become more harmonious and you will feel better about yourself. You will realise that difficult situations are just experiences and you don't have to spend so much energy thinking about them. Instead, you can give all this beautiful energy to yourself and expand even more from it.

The world around us has plenty of opportunities to express love to ourselves. Every moment gives us a chance to smile to ourselves and to experience joy. Maybe a walk in the park makes you feel happy. Maybe you enjoy being in the company of the people that you love. Maybe you like going to a comedy show and having fun. Feeling love towards ourselves stretches further than meditation and can be found in everyday life. How can you show love to yourself daily?

Every moment is an opportunity to express love.

When you start aligning your actions in life with the love for yourself, your inner power will shine even more. It is almost like you are mirroring the way that you feel inside to the outside world and these two powers join together and become even stronger. Now they can align in one and bring you the best experiences that you can have on this planet.

Before you do something, ask yourself: "Is it loving for me to do it?" "What would I really like to do now?" These questions will instantly bring you on the right path of inner guidance.

We might need some time to break away from old habits. Sometimes we give too much time to distracting activities and we don't treat our bodies with respect. It takes time to realise what actions don't serve the energy of self-love anymore. But as soon as we begin to listen to this energy, it will start showing us a new, loving way of being. Then every moment will give us a choice to make the right decision for ourselves and grow stronger from it.

LOVING YOURSELF IN THE MIRROR

Mirrors were created in our reality for a reason. They are a wonderful opportunity to see ourselves both in a visual and a spiritual way. Mirrors give us a chance to look into our eyes and connect to our spirit, exploring who we really are on a deep level.

Mirrors are wonderful opportunities for self-exploration.

There is a much deeper dimension in the mirror than the one we see just on the surface. In addition to the physical reflection, it also shows the energy that appears to be predominant in us at that moment. We can see this energy through the subtle vibration in the mirror. The mirror points out exactly what is happening energetically in our life and shows us a particular aspect of our multidimensional self that we need to see now. This is why we sometimes appear different in the mirror – the energy changes according to the way we feel and what aspect of us stands out the most at this moment.

Look deeper in the mirror and you will see the truth inside of you.

Not only does a mirror give us a chance to know ourselves better, it also opens the doorway for self-love and acceptance. When we see our reflection in the mirror, we have an opportunity to nourish ourselves with the energy that we mostly need at the time. We can literally send love to our reflection and this energy will replenish ourselves and make us feel stronger. Mirrors offer a unique chance to uplift, encourage and appreciate our inner self.

Everything that you give to the mirror, you receive back multiplied.

Never miss a chance to give yourself love in the mirror. Stop, relax, look yourself in the eyes and say how much you love yourself. Give the energy of courage and support to your reflection – it needs it so much during the day! Mirrors are very powerful. They give us an opportunity to heal the body and watch the miraculous transformation in front of our eyes. The energy in the reflection will change according to the energy that we send to ourselves. For example, if we say: "You look wonderful today, I love you!", the mirror will take in this energy and bring it back to us in double.

What would you really like to say to the person in the mirror?

Everything is energy and whatever we send to a particular destination always reaches it, whether it is a word, a thought or a feeling. A mirror is one of the most powerful ways to work with ourselves on many levels. It provides physical, energetic, emotional and mental comfort. You can spend ten minutes a day sending good energy to your reflection and you will create a positive portrait of yourself. Make the mirror your best friend.

TALKING LOVE TO YOURSELF

Our voice is the song that we sing to ourselves every day. We choose the lyrics and the music for the song and, with the right intention, we can make the most wonderful melody that will bring us an abundance of positive energy.

The word 'love' itself has a very high frequency. Throughout the years, people have been using this word with the intention of expressing their beautiful feelings, so now it is charged with powerful healing energy. When we say the word 'love', our heart opens up naturally and allows kindness and warmth to flow freely in the body.

Saying "I love you" to yourself is a miraculous incantation that can bring wonderful changes to the energy of your body. You can literally feel how your energy is starting to transform and blossom inside when you hear these words. You can even close your eyes and say these words slowly, feeling how they are coming directly from the heart and bathing your whole body with blissful energy. With each word, breathe and open your heart even more to your loving self.

I love you very much!

Of course, you can express love to yourself with any words of praise, appreciation and positive energy. For example, you can say: "You are a very good person", "Everything that you do is perfect", "I support you in all situations", "You are my favourite being", "I understand you very well." The way that you say these words is also important – say them slowly and kindly, because your manner, voice and tone of speech carries energy too.

Express your loving feelings tenderly and softly, as if you are giving yourself a gift.

All these words are the elements that build the powerful foundation of self-love. Even if at the beginning you may feel hesitant to say them, just start. Just begin. And like magic, the energy of love will start to take over and feel stronger, as though you suddenly remember what it is like to be the real you. You are Love.

Notice how your cells positively respond to the energy of love when you are kind to yourself. They open up to you and bring their invisible hands to embrace you in joy and gratitude. Healing and release happen naturally when we are in tune with the energy of love.

You do not need a reason to love yourself. Love yourself for being here and now.

You have incarnated on Planet Earth with a powerful mission. You have taken a step to enter a physical body and experience this life. Only strong beings can do that. This step alone deserves a lot of love for the courageous person that you are.

You are unique. Let yourself know about it.

There is no need anymore for self-punishment. You can safely release the habit of criticising and judging yourself because you simply don't need it. You are much bigger than that. You are a beautiful, shiny being, so expressive, delightful and full of loving energy. I can see your light right now. Even if you do something that you think is wrong, it is only a step of learning; you can forgive yourself and move on to your magnificent self.

PRACTICE TIME
LOVING YOURSELF
◊ You are already filled with the energy of love just from reading about it. Now we are going to bathe in this healing frequency even more. Relax, close your eyes and get ready for a very pleasant inner journey.

◊ Every breath is taking you deeper and deeper. You notice how your whole body is beginning to get very relaxed and comfortable. Focus on your heart. Feel the love in your heart. Imagine how your heart is opening more and more and allowing the love to flow through it. Visualise that your love is like colourful birds that are flying out of your heart now. Observe them with admiration.

◊ Your heart is projecting an image right now. All the love that is coming from your heart is forming a screen in front of you and you can see yourself on this screen. Imagine what you look like and trust the first sensations that you receive. What do you see? Describe it to yourself. You may appear as a person or just as an energy being.

◊ What do you feel from yourself on the screen? What kind of energy do you have? Connect to the image of you. Feel the love towards yourself and project it from your heart into the screen. You will receive this energy instantly.

◊ What would you like to tell yourself? What do you really need to hear now? Say it to yourself aloud or telepathically; the message will be received in any way. Imagine that the words are coming from your heart and are being projected into the screen. Pour more love into you.

◊ Ask yourself about your gifts. What are you really good at? What talents did you bring with you to Planet Earth? Let your intuitive feeling tell you about it.

◊ Now express gratitude to yourself for all the wonderful things that you did in this life. And also praise yourself for all the challenges that you went through on your journey. Embrace every moment and every step of your life with deep love and appreciation. You did so well!

◊ Imagine now that you are giving yourself a very warm hug from the heart. Tell yourself how much you love and support yourself in everything. Stay in the warm embrace as long as you feel like to fully replenish yourself. You can say: "I am with you!"

◊ In the end, tell yourself that you can always come back to the same screen and send even more love to yourself. Let the screen slowly disappear and flow into your heart, where it belongs. Feel complete. Breathe deeply to start to awaken your body again and bring all your senses back. Your heart is bigger now and you know how much support you have. Orientate yourself back into the room and bring your awareness fully into physical reality by moving your body and opening your eyes.

LOVE YOUR DARKNESS

You are perfect as you are. You are unique and beautiful. You came to this world with your gifts and you are shining them to the Universe and the people around you.

You also sometimes have challenges. These are the lessons that you chose to go through in this life on a spiritual level. These lessons can be difficult and painful. At times you may experience lower vibrations and may not be at peace with yourself. You may encounter other aspects of yourself, like anger, dark thoughts, damaging habits or repeated patterns, and you may not be comfortable with some of them.

In the moment when we are experiencing a challenging part of ourselves, we can find it difficult to deal with. It may seem so dark and sticky that we don't know how to get out of this situation. We may even feel angry with ourselves for doing the same thing again and again, thus creating a cycle of self-punishment and criticism.

What our lower aspects actually want to show us is the opposite. They want us to recognise the self-love within us again and pay attention to our big, beautiful spirit rather than our small, limited aspects. They point us in the right direction by misleading us. We temporarily take on a masquerade costume of a dark beast in order to experience it and understand that underneath it there is still a beautiful prince or a princess. We have never been otherwise. We just chose to experience the darkness to learn from it and grow spiritually.

Our dark sides give us an opportunity to grow and develop.

The lower aspects ask us to look at ourselves and remember light again. They are actually reminders of what we are not and they serve us as faithful friends to help us rediscover love, purity and kindness within ourselves. They came here to help us to remember who we are; without them we wouldn't have recognised the magnificence of our spirit.

So, what is the best way to deal with our dark aspects?

Love them.

All they want us to do is to look at them with love and understand them. Our anger, sadness, frustration and pain just need love to be directed at them so they can be released. When we send love to our challenging aspects, we give them the power to change quicker. We almost grant them peace and freedom so they can have a permission to transform and disappear. We no longer get annoyed at ourselves for repeating the same cycle and not listening. Instead, we bathe ourselves in love and understanding and this is what sets us free.

Our lower aspects are like little children asking for help. They don't want to be criticised, they want to be loved and accepted.

Like magic, love transforms everything. If we were looking at a black screen and began to bring the light of love into it, the screen would start to change. There would first appear some white patches on it, then they would start to grow and play with each other to unite and merge. Then they would form bigger white patterns and cover most of the screen. And then the light would get so strong that there would be no more space for darkness. This is how our spirit grows.

Your challenging aspects are your beauty. As a spirit, you so courageously chose your difficult aspects to bring into this life and work on. You came here to learn patience, forgiveness, self-belief, strength. It is your assignment, your spiritual dissertation, and you were very brave to agree to this complicated program. Imagine the strength of your spirit, which chose to have such an important assignment here. This deserves appraisal.

You can spend as much time as you need to learn a lesson. There is no time. You are a good student.

Going through our lessons, we are growing and expanding more as a spirit. It is like going up the stairs, where the lower stairs are the basic emotions that we are learning in this life and the higher stairs are the enlightening states of being: love, peace and acceptance. We need to master our foundation and handle the emotions first in order to step to a higher level of our spiritual development.

Your power comes from every aspect that you are.

During one QHHT session, the Subconscious gave some beautiful advice to the client. The lady was struggling with self-belief and the power to move forward in life. Her Subconscious said: "She has to accept everything about herself and love herself no matter what she does. Even if she does the craziest thing, she still needs to love herself for that. This will heal her." These powerful words apply to many of us, as we often find it difficult to accept ourselves in challenging situations. When we embrace all our actions in love, we help ourselves to move on and release any limitations that are holding us back.

It is an act of kindness to accept yourself in everything that you do.

You can practise a small exercise of saying a loving thing to yourself even if you think that you have done something wrong or not to your level of expectation. Instead of turning to criticism, you can remember to show understanding and kindness to yourself. This will melt down the feeling of guilt and help you to embrace yourself in love, empowering your future actions.

FORGIVENESS

Forgiveness is one of the gifts that we learn in this life and a wonderful opportunity for personal transformation. A lot of physical discomfort and emotional baggage comes from us being unable to forgive and release our negative feelings about somebody else or ourselves. Old emotions and grudges tend to stay in the body and produce a damaging effect, even if the situation happened a long time ago.

Sometimes we cannot understand why a certain person acted in a way that made us feel hurt, upset, humiliated or unloved. We see the situation from our own perspective as we know where we stood at the time. But why did they do what they did? It can be difficult to see and understand – and even more so, accept – that the other person had to act in a way that upset us. It takes some courage of spirit and the loving expansion of consciousness to see beyond their actions.

When we put ourselves in the body of another person and try to understand how they feel in their position, taking into account their background and their emotions, we can go outside of our own vision and see the situation from a different perspective. We can literally detach from ourselves and watch the scene as an observer, making our conclusions based on the feelings of each participant.

Why did you act this way? How did you feel at the time?

Once we see the situation from aside, the truth comes to us more clearly and we are not dependent only on our own emotions. We can see the scene as a theatre stage where the actors are playing their roles. Then we can connect to the energy of each actor and understand why they had to play the part that they chose and how they felt about the situation themselves. This can give us solace and comfort.

It doesn't mean that there is a need to justify somebody's behaviour. The idea is to set ourselves free by understanding why the person acted the way that they did. Perhaps they didn't know how to behave in that situation; they did the best they could according to their knowledge and experience at the time. Maybe they didn't want to hurt us but their emotions took over and they lost control. They could have been feeling unsafe and unloved themselves at that moment and not able to give enough love to anybody else. They could have been suffering too. Perhaps it was the only way they were taught to behave in the past as they have been mistreated themselves. Could this be related to your story? All of these connections can help us to understand other people and forgive them.

The truth is that we all came here to learn. We put on different costumes and take on various roles to come to this planet and act out our story and learn something from each other. We learn love, patience, self-belief and trust as we go through our life experiences. Sometimes the roles that we choose can be quite difficult. A person close to you may choose a role to upset you deliberately so you can experience a temporary limitation and rediscover yourself through finding self-worth and inner strength.

The numerous stories of past life regressions teach us about the roles that we take in life. The souls plan their lives long before they come to live on Planet Earth. We often see how members of the same soul group sit at a big table on the spirit side and plan a lifetime together. They have a discussion about what kind of life they want to choose, what will serve their soul advancement the most and what lessons will help them to evolve. In accordance to that, they choose their body, their country, their family, their purpose and the roles that they want to play for each other. Some of them decide to be a husband and a wife, some a parent and a child, some best friends or enemies. We know our most important people on a soul level long before we meet them in the physical life.

Then we incarnate in the physical realm to enact our roles and have the real-life experience. We forget what we have planned in the spirit realm. There is a phenomenon similar to amnesia – a deliberate temporary memory loss about the spirit life so we can go forward in our incarnation and learn our lessons. If we knew all the answers in advance, it wouldn't be a test, they say. So here we are – on the stage with the members of our soul group, learning lessons together and figuring out how to be happy and at peace.

According to information from QHHT sessions, Earth is one of the most difficult planets for learning as it offers a challenging program for the souls who wish to incarnate here. It is a much denser planet than others and many souls find it hard to adapt to the heavy frequencies that exist on this planet. Many people feel lonely and not belonging here, because deep inside they remember that they come from somewhere else, a place where the energies are lighter and more pleasant.

On Earth we can learn about human emotions and physical limitations, and many times this is done through difficult life situations and challenging puzzles that we have to solve. It is like a school that we sign up for in order to grow spiritually. We are all students and teachers at the same time. Knowing that, perhaps we can raise beyond the limited perception of our life and grant forgiveness to the people who are playing this courageous incarnation now.

An interesting example of how these connections work was shown in one regression experience. A lady came to the session wanting to find out why she had been abused by her ex-husband in this lifetime. During the session she went to the other side and met the abuser in the spirit form. They talked about it and found out that they had planned this situation together long before this life. They agreed to play the role of the abuser and the victim so they could raise beyond the feelings of hurt and anger and learn to love each other. The most incredible thing was that it was this lady's soul who asked the soul of her husband to play this difficult role so she could learn love and kindness this way.

Her husband's soul didn't want to do this hurtful act, but she convinced him in the end. This is the dialogue that went on between the two souls:

"I really don't want to do it to you."

"Please, I need to learn my lessons. I am asking you to do it."

"Okay, I will do it but only because I love you. And it will be very hard for me."

This information can be difficult to accept for some people as we often can't understand why we have to experience violence and ill treatment in this life. From our perspective, as people living our life on Earth, it may feel outrageous and unfair. But perhaps there is another layer of knowledge beyond it, in the spirit realm, another reason for this happening, which can help us to receive higher understanding about our spirit growth. This is what regression work can help with. As a result of that session, the lady was able to forgive her ex-husband and let go of the past feeling of hurt from her body.

When we meet the higher aspect of another person, we can understand and forgive them.

The Subconscious always talks about the importance of forgiveness. They say: "You have to forgive each other while you are living your life. You have to do your best before this life is over and you go to the spirit side." Forgiveness is essential for several reasons. First of all, it provides the liberation of the spirit and heals relationships with other people. Secondly, it helps our soul to grow and step beyond the feelings of resentment and bitterness. It also helps to heal our physical and emotional body from blocked energy. Forgiveness is a healing tool that can improve the way that we feel and open our hearts for new, good things in life.

Forgiveness is the healing of the soul.

Forgiveness is sometimes easier than we imagine it to be. It is like a bird that we hold in our hands and we can let it fly into the sky and enjoy the beautiful sunlight. As soon as we have the intention to forgive, this process is already happening and we are becoming free in a natural way. Forgiveness is about letting go of the situation, releasing it from our heart and our body.

Forgiveness can take a form of a simple yet profound exercise where we connect to the spirit of another person and release the sad feelings about each other. It doesn't necessarily require the presence of another person; we can just close our eyes, connect to our heart and imagine their energy. A lot of powerful healing is happening in the etheric realm the moment that we tune into forgiveness. Both parties receive liberation and soothing as they release each other energetically. These exercises are usually very emotional and can bring a beautiful transformation to the participants.

As soon as you decide to forgive, the process will start happening on the energy level.

Asking for forgiveness is healing as well. Sometimes we feel that we have done something wrong, perhaps unintentionally, and we would like to let the other person know that we didn't mean to hurt them. Simply asking for forgiveness from the heart is a key that opens the doors for love. It is a beautiful, liberating act that connects us to the energy of truth and kindness.

Forgiveness helps us to evolve and to grow. Our spirit goes to a new level when we are ready to release our negative feelings. It may seem daunting in the beginning, but as soon as we start sending the energy in the direction of forgiveness, it begins to work. We feel a lot of joy from this process. Our soul recognises that we want to become free and it will help us in all possible ways to reach inner liberation. Just our intention to forgive plays a major role in this breakthrough.

When we meditate on forgiveness, we release a lot of energy from our body and mind. In such meditations we can imagine that we interact with the higher aspect of another person and connect to their pure light. This way, we can reach the level of soul communication and achieve deep healing and understanding.

Forgiveness is a loving gift that we give to our soul.

PRACTICE TIME
FORGIVING OTHER PEOPLE

◊ Close your eyes and take several deep breaths to relax. Keep breathing deeply for some time until you feel a pleasant state of tranquility coming to your body.

◊ Connect to your heart and feel which situation and which person in your life need forgiveness right now. Let it be the first image or feeling that comes to you; your heart will guide you.

◊ Imagine this person in front of you now. Feel their presence and ask the higher aspect of their soul to come and meet you now. If you like, ask for the permission to meet their Higher Self.

◊ Connect to the energy of their Higher Self. What do you feel from them? What is this person like on a soul level? Feel their true essence. Ask the Higher Self what this person is going through in their life now. Do you sense any difficulties or challenges? Connect to them lovingly with your higher understanding. You can ask their Higher Self for a message for you.

◊ Now let us feel the relationship between the two of you. What do you sense about your connection? Imagine that there is a ray of light between your auras which represents your link in this life. What is this light like? Now connect to your heart and tell the person how you feel about them. Ask them to forgive you for what you have done, even if it was something small. Let your heart help you to find the right words. Even if you haven't done anything wrong, you can still ask for forgiveness to open the process of healing between the two of you.

◊ Now it's time to forgive them. Open your heart, connect to your kindest aspect and say to the person: "I forgive you." Tell them what you forgive them for and affirm that you release any bad feelings about the situation. Truthfully mean every word that you say; let it come from the depth of your soul. Take time. At this moment your intuition will guide you; you will understand exactly what has happened between you two. A feeling of relief is coming to you now. Say everything that you need to say. And then release. You are free.

◊ If you feel like, you can wish the person well and send a beautiful light to them. Imagine that their presence is beaming with a glowing light and they are receiving healing energy. If you don't wish to stay connected to this person, you can say: "I now release you with love and gratitude. Thank you and goodbye." Feel a sense of liberation and freedom between the two of you. You can repeat this exercise again if you feel that more forgiveness work is needed.

◊ When you are finished, leave the scene and return to the current time and space. Take several deep breaths to bring the awareness back into the body. Move your body gently and come fully back to the present moment.

FORGIVING YOURSELF

Perhaps an even more precious gift that we can give to our soul is to forgive ourselves completely.

We have all done things that we may be sorry about or feel that we could have done better. At the time we made a choice to act this way from the level of awareness and soul development that we had. We chose to experience this situation in order to learn from it and, even if we made a mistake, we did the best that we could in those circumstances.

We do our best in all situations.

Every moment is an opportunity to grow and, if we look from a higher perspective, there are no mistakes, there are just experiences. Things were supposed to happen this way; you were supposed to learn what you learnt and teach others around you. Acceptance of the situation and love to yourself will help you to release the lower feelings about it. Your experience on Planet Earth is the one to be celebrated, uplifted and encouraged by your spirit.

Healing happens when we accept ourselves as we are and we forgive ourselves for everything that we did.

Sometimes it might feel difficult to forgive ourselves. We could have been carrying a bad feeling for a long time and we might think that we don't deserve forgiveness, or we need to work a lot to repay our 'debt'. But is this weight really serving us in the best way? Perhaps releasing us from a prison of our feeling would be a much more loving act than self-punishment, and it will benefit ourselves and people around us.

Forgiveness is the key. You deserve forgiveness.

Sometimes you might feel that you have done nothing wrong at all and there is nothing to forgive yourself for. This may also be true. But at the same time, once you start this practice, you might find the hidden feelings inside of you that you have been carrying unknowingly. Once you start to speak from the heart, truth will surface and you will get a clearer picture of your life. Forgiveness will help you to understand yourself more and release the unnecessary feelings from within. Being humble will bring you to another level of spiritual growth.

Forgiveness heals the heart.

The most beautiful gift we can give to ourselves is to treat ourselves with love and understanding. No matter what happened in the past, you are the person that you are now and you did very well. Focus on the positive aspects of your personality and let them grow and expand.

You are a powerful being who has stepped on a courageous path of being yourself and going through your lifetime experiences. Some of these experiences were tough but you did very well to pass them, and you became stronger and learnt valuable lessons from them. You are absolutely unique on this planet; nobody else has the same set of experiences and the same aspects of the soul. You are a star!

Treat yourself like a special being and let the light beams shine on all the darker sides that you would like to heal inside yourself. This altogether is your power and, without the challenges, you wouldn't know the light. Enjoy every aspect of yourself. You are so special.

PRACTICE TIME
MEETING YOUR HIGHER SELF

◊   Close your eyes, take several deep breaths and relax completely. Let your breath take you deeper and deeper so you can begin to feel your inner self.

◊   Connect to your heart and start feeling love within yourself. Imagine that with every breath you are filling your heart with love more and more. Remember what love feels like. Let it grow in your heart and make it glow with light beams.

◊   Imagine that love is spreading from your heart to all your body like streams of water. They are nourishing every part of your body and making you feel loved and appreciated. Observe how every part of your body is touched with kindness and gentleness. Focus on the parts of you that may feel lonely and cold.

◊ Now ask for your Higher Self to appear to you. Take a moment to connect from your heart. Visualise your Higher Self standing in front of you in full light and glory. This is your higher aspect that knows all the truth about you and holds your best intentions. Allow the first image or feeling to come naturally to you. Look at this beautiful being. What do you see? What do you feel from your Higher Self? Describe it to yourself.

◊ Start directing the love towards that being and feel how wonderful and unique you are. Ask your Higher Self if there is anything that they would like to tell you today. What path are you on at this moment? What can help you the best way to achieve your purpose? What support are you receiving from your Higher Self? Just feel the messages in your heart; it will be the first words that come to you.

◊ Ask your Higher Self if there is anything that you need to release or forgive yourself for. If there is something, then join with your Higher Self to bring love to that situation and release it from your energy field. Let your Higher Self be your guide in this process, as they know you very well. Just follow the guidance that comes to you naturally.

◊ Now you can say these words to yourself: "I am sorry for not seeing who you truly are. I promise to see your beautiful, magnificent self. I promise to be your best friend and look after you. I promise to trust you and follow what your soul wants to do. I promise to stay in touch with your heart." Feel every word that you are saying and notice the healing effect that it has on your expanding spirit. Feel free to change the words in a way that feels right to you.

◊ Say thank you to your Higher Self for all the love and guidance they have given to you. Remember the image that you saw and keep it in your heart so it always stays with you. You can repeat this practice as many times as you like and it will benefit you again and again.

◊ Now breathe deeper and start bringing your awareness back into the body. Start feeling your body and moving it gently. Reconnect with the current moment and place. Orientate yourself completely in the body and, when you are ready, open your eyes. Well done! Your Higher Self is very grateful to you for this experience.

DIRECT LOVE TO ALL SITUATIONS

Love is like a magic wand that we can direct to different situations in our life. Love changes the energy of a situation immediately and transforms our perception to a higher vibrational energy.

Sometimes, when we are in a difficult moment in life, we forget about love. We can get distracted by other feelings, like fear, worry, concern and limited thoughts. We then forget that the greatest power that we have inside of us is the power of love. We hold the key in our hearts for changing the reality of our lives. With love comes understanding, acceptance, new solutions and a change in a positive direction.

As soon as we start to focus on love, the energy in our body changes. We feel a warm rise within, as though a beautiful river starts to flow in a green valley. This feeling suddenly becomes very familiar and very dear, as though we have always known it so well. We come back to who we really are.

And then the veil drops. The old troops and dark forces decide that there is not much to do here anymore and they leave. Worry subsides, fear disappears, concern gives place to acceptance and peace. In the space of love there is only joy, there is only courage, there is only the real you.

Love changes the energy of situations and brings kindness into our lives.

If a challenging moment comes to your life, direct your love to it. Reconnect with the all-encompassing feeling of love in your heart and send it to this situation. For example, if there is a difficult relationship, imagine that you are pouring love from your heart into your connection with the other person and soften it with your warmth and kindness. Let love disperse all the negative feelings in your relationship and show you only what is real there.

If you are going through a situation in life that needs a solution, let it bathe in the healing power of love. Surround yourself with a lot of love energy and imagine that it cocoons you and relieves the situation. Release your feeling of control and let love put everything into place. It is almost like we invite the higher power to deal with our situation while we can just relax and observe it happening.

Love your situation and it will start changing.

Love is the best cure that we can find for ourselves and our life. Not only does it transform the way that we feel about a situation and release the negative feelings, it really changes the frequency of the situation so it can be solved in an easy and positive way. This is a magical trick that we all have access to in our hearts.

THE RADIO OF LOVE

The radio of love is the channel that you can tune into in order to receive only words of love in your head.

Imagine that there are many radio stations all around you in the Universe. They are like wavelengths of energy and you can connect to them and listen to them. Each one of these radio stations has its own subject and favourite tunes. You can choose to listen to any radio station and select the frequency that appeals to you the most.

Turn on your favourite radio station in the Universe.

Today we are going to tune into the radio station of love. Yes, there is such a radio station and it is playing right now in your space.

Look around. Imagine that you can hear a subtle voice of the radio presenter and listen to the invisible music in the air. All of the energies around you are doing one thing right now. They are telling you how much they love you.

What would your personal love radio station be like?

Let us tune into it now and imagine that we can hear it. You are listening to a song of love that was created especially for you. What would your love song be like? Would it be an orchestra or a piano instrumental music? Imagine that you can hear a song that represents a hymn of how wonderful you are. Play and enjoy this song on your radio.

Now imagine that there are some voices on your personal radio station that can only speak about their loving feelings to you. They are the hosts on your radio station. You can almost see them in your space as you focus on their energy. These radio hosts know everything about your special gifts and your power in this lifetime. All that they want to do is encourage you and tell you how good you are. What are they saying now?

Maybe you can hear them telling you how unique you are and how much they are grateful to you for being yourself. Maybe they admire you for what you do and wish you well in your future projects. Let their words come naturally to you, on the spur of the moment, and you will be surprised how much love there is for you on your special love radio station!

Listen to your personal radio station saying: "We love you very much! Thank you for being here!"

You can even go further and imagine that the hosts on the radio are applauding you and congratulating you for your achievements. This will give you a boost of confidence and significantly increase the amount of love that you feel for yourself.

This exercise is great fun and it helps to create a beautiful flow of love and appreciation in our life. The best time to practise it is in the morning when you are feeling fresh, so you can start your day with positivity and playfulness. If your mind begins to doubt this exercise, just quiet it down for a moment, say that it is only a game, and continue listening to the most loving things that you can hear about yourself.

You are your own radio station!

THE SHOWER OF LOVE

Like we take a shower every day to wash our body, we can wash ourselves with the most powerful source of energy – love. The energy of love is available to us in abundance whenever we want to connect to it and we can take this healing shower as many times as we want daily.

To begin this exercise, you can imagine that there is a shower of love just above your head in the form of energy. Start feeling the love flowing into your body from the top of your head down, filling every part of yourself. Imagine that there is an ongoing source of love that keeps nourishing you with this beautiful energy. Feel how this invisible healing shower is washing and replenishing all of your cells. Give in to this flow of love and let it take you over for a moment.

You can carry the shower of love with you everywhere you go.

Imagine that there are only loving thoughts in this flow of light. Anything that doesn't respond to your loving thoughts disappears in the shower of love. Feel that there is only love that surrounds you at this moment. Focus on the limitless source of love that is always within you.

It is recommended to do this exercise twice a day – in the morning, when you first start your day and you are ready for new experiences to come, and in the evening, before you go to bed, so you can praise and congratulate yourself on the day and prepare for a restful sleep.

LOVE TO OTHERS

We are walking on Earth with a beautiful energy in our hearts and a healing frequency in our hands. This energy is available to us all the time if we just become aware of it and use it. We have a wonderful chance to share this energy with each other and uplift people around us with love.

Visualise for a moment a different version of a street that we see every day. Imagine that everybody in the street is smiling, looking at each other with love and feeling connected in the heart. People are holding hands, laughing and saying beautiful words to each other, even if they only just met. Let us assume that it is possible, at least in our minds. When we imagine this, we are one step closer to this dimension of our reality.

Let's imagine that everyone has a beautiful energy field made of different colours: green, blue, purple, yellow, orange, pink. As we interact with each other, we are sharing some of this light with one another and helping our collective positive energy to grow. Then, as we look at each other with love, our eyes emanate a magnificent sparkling light that fills everybody with purity and kindness. Can you picture it?

Now let's imagine that our hands are full of glitter and colourful light and, as we direct our energy with our palms, we share this magic with one another. Everybody is sharing and receiving uplifting energy at the same time: the people, trees, plants, houses, rocks, birds, water. We are dancing and bathing in each other's love from the heart. Would you like to be in a place like that? It sounds good, doesn't it?

We can create the world made of love. It starts with ourselves.

When you connect to somebody, remember that they are made of love. Imagine that you see love in another person while you are talking to them, as though you are communicating with love itself. See love in their eyes. You invoke it by seeing it. Respond to people with love and it will help them to remember their own love and feel happier. You are the awakener of love in other people. You can make them feel better about themselves just by the way that you approach them.

We just need to remember that we are love.

It is very simple to start creating love around us. It starts from within. It starts with a feeling – a willingness to spread kindness around us. It is that invisible source of energy we have all been looking for.

Start small. Begin with little acts of kindness to other people as you are going through your day. These actions will be the building bricks that will make the whole world a beautiful place. Little acts of love are simple: a pleasant look, a kind smile, a nice compliment. It is very simple! But within a second the energy will go up and the feeling of magic will envelop both of you. It is an act of generosity that you are giving to the world – allowing people to see their magnificent light again.

I enjoy walking the streets and smiling at people even if I see them for the first time. I enjoy taking people by the hand and sharing the energy of love with them. There is something magical that happens when we talk to strangers and open our hearts to them. We become one for that little moment and our worlds unite. It may be just one second of connection but it opens a beautiful space of kindness for each other. And we can all do it.

SEVEN

THE 6TH WONDER OF THE SELF: WE CAN CREATE

Creativity is a gift that every person has from birth. We are all part of the creation process ourselves as we are manifested by the Source as an integral element of this beautiful world. The power to create is passed on to each of us from the Source, which carries the essence of this creative energy.

We create as we breathe, we create as we walk, we create as we live our life. Everything that we do is an act of creation and, knowingly or unknowingly, we are constantly shaping our reality.

Each one of us is a creator and we can use this energy to manifest our reality.

Some of us have been told as children that we can't create; that to create we need to be distinguished, have special gifts or talents that we might not have. This is not true. We all have a talent. Each one of us is gifted. And we create all the time.

Every living being is connected to divine inspiration and can channel this energy with ease. All that we need to do is follow our inner joy and do what feels right in the moment. Creativity is about inner freedom and being true to our feelings. When we create, we are expressing our soul, whether it means to create a beautiful work of art or simply enjoy the moment and be who we are.

When we direct our thoughts and energy into purposeful creation, we become masters of shaping our reality. We no longer live in an unaware state; instead, we use our energy to create our life and experiences. Just like we create a painting made of beautiful colours, we create our life based on the energies that we choose. The Universe always prepares us gifts when we cooperate with it!

We can feel intuitively what we want in life and surround ourselves with these energies. We can play, connect, interact, sing, dance – do everything that we want with these energies until they become a part of our vibration and start to manifest on the physical plane. This is a part of the creation.

The process of creation is a joy. It is not an effort. It is as simple as a smile, as jolly as laughter and as flowy as a river. We are creation; every cell of our body creates incessantly: it reproduces, it processes, it grows! We are that cell but in a bigger version. We are the Creator.

Creativity makes our soul happy.

If we take our mind away from the idea that creativity is only for selected people, we return to ourselves. We accept that we have always been creators. We have created our life, we have created our circumstances, we even created our own body and our talents when we were on the other side, planning our life on Earth. How creative is that!

Our gifts are inevitably coming back to us now. People are remembering again that they have the power to create freely and this is what brings them happiness. Imagine that each person is holding a beautiful crystal ball of light in their hands and this ball is showing them their creative powers.

Give yourself permission to create.

Creation is in every moment – look around and see it. See how the clouds are moving in the sky and changing their shape – this is creation. See how the birds in the trees are singing a song together – they are creating. See how children are running in the streets and laughing just because they are happy – they are creating. Now see yourself as a part of this and realise that you are a part of the creation. You are here for a reason and the Universe rejoices when you are expressing yourself.

BEGIN WITH YOURSELF

What would you like to create? If you were to connect to the happy feeling inside of you and focus on what you want, what would you like to bring more into your life now?

Let us close our eyes and relax for a moment. Let go of your worries and concerns. Allow an open mind to be with you. Feel with your heart what you truly deserve in this moment. Take whatever comes to you first and believe it.

Imagine it in your mind. What would it look like if you were to have it? Allow the energy of your wish to come to you. What does it feel like?

Now ask yourself: "What can I do to create this in my life? Is there anything that I can do, think or focus on to bring these energies into my life?"

You will get an answer. Perhaps you could do more things that make you feel happy within yourself. Maybe you could spend more time with like-minded people who will give you ideas and positive energy. Or perhaps you just need to trust yourself more and follow your intuition.

A lot of energy that comes into your life depends on you. You are the source of creation, the generator that produces a certain type of energy and then finds a similar vibration in the physical space. Whatever you think, feel or do takes an energy shape, travels in the Universe and connects you to other energies of a similar frequency.

Generate the energy that you would like to have more of in your life.

You create every day by being who you are and focusing on your chosen energy. You can use the first part of the day to celebrate and invite the energy that you would like to attract on that day. For example, you can ask the energy of freedom to come into your life and imagine how it enters your space and aura. You can bathe for some time in this high-frequency energy and let it be your guide for the day. This will bring the energy of your choice into your physical reality.

THE BEAUTY OF CREATION

Creation is so vast! It is in our breath and imagination but it's also in our hands, our voice and our heart. There is no end to creation as the energy can take any form in our reality.

When we want to create, we first receive an inspiration in our minds. It is a sparkle, an idea, something that is magnetising us. Then we focus on the inspiration and manifest it in the physical realm with the help of our action and creative powers. Some people create beautifully through art, some can sing and perform, others write stories and poems. Everybody has got a special talent of their own.

You just need to ask your creation how it would like to be manifested in the physical realm.

The beauty of energy is that once you start working with it, you will find a way to become more creative. Your inner flow of inspiration will guide you. Deep inside of you, you are already creating something spectacular. Your project already exists in the subtle energy dimension. You only need to listen to this energy, connect to it and bring it into the physical world. And trust it completely! The energy already knows how it wants to be manifested.

When you receive a sparkle of inspiration to create something, don't put it off. Embrace this energy and welcome it into your reality. Do it at that moment, exactly when it comes. It is so important to catch the moment and respond to the invitation in that fraction of time. It is like a portal that is opening and asking for your attention. If you respond to it, you are showing respect to your creativity and the energy of inspiration will reward you in return.

For example, if you feel that you want to write something and this energy is calling you, don't hesitate. Take a piece of paper and a pen and start writing. Just express everything that comes to you at this moment in a flow. Don't think about it, don't judge it. Accept it. Give it some support and love from yourself. This is the freedom of creation.

Many times, inspiration will catch you in most awkward moments, for example, when you are on a train, talking to somebody or being in a hurry somewhere. It is like a tiny knock on the door of your heart that says: "I am here. Can you please listen to me?" And then it wants you to stop whatever you are doing and channel the energy that is coming through. At this moment it is important to give inspiration a chance to be born. You can take a piece of paper and scribble your idea quickly before it evaporates in the energy of the space around you.

Sometimes the Universe wants you to pause what you are doing and start creating.

And once you start, just let it be. Let it flow through your body like a river. Your creation may not seem perfect to you in the beginning.

259

But it is only an illusion. Everything happens exactly the way that it should. Every child is beautiful when they are born and so is your creation. Inspiration needs to find its way into the world and you can give it a chance by trusting its loving whisper.

TALK TO YOUR CREATION

Imagine that your creation is coming in. It is an inspiration that wants you to create something new, to breathe this energy into your life. It may be a project, a short story, a poem or a painting. It appears there, as a feeling, and is calling for your attention. What does your creation want you to do?

Initially creation wants you to respond. It is trying to wake you up at this moment and tell you: "I am here. Please look at me." Creation appears in you for a reason and it always does so at the right time as it knows how to reach your heart.

The first thing that we can do with our creation is listen to it. We connect to its essence and allow it to take us on a journey. For example, if you had a glimpse of inspiration to write a short story, you can connect to this feeling and explore it further. Meditate for some time on what you want to create, visualise it, then write it down. Your inspiration has a very special vibration, almost like a radio station, and it will become more vivid when you listen to it.

Listen to the music of your creation and turn the volume up.

Then you can show how much you respect your creation by actually trusting it and following it through. You can give it valuable time during the day and allow yourself to focus entirely on your project. This way your creation will feel that you are responding to it and will supply you with even more ideas. Creation doesn't understand that you might have other plans or duties to perform; it wants you to follow it here and now.

You will find creativity flowing easier if you respond to it at the moment when it is calling you.

Once you are in the process, it is a flow. Your hands are forming a figure made of clay, your mind is creating a fantastic story, your fingers are playing a musical instrument. Creation is flowing through you like water and it knows how to find its perfect way into the physical world. We only need to trust it and enjoy this process.

So, the idea is to interact with our creativity like a living being. We open the door for the project to come and we are dancing together and having a beautiful time. Creativity is a channel that is full of ideas, images, inspiration and knowledge. We can tap into this channel and receive guidance from it.

For example, it is helpful to visualise our dream projects and imagine how they come true. We can write down our ideas and send support and encouragement to them. We can even ask creativity some questions and feel what comes back to us. Anything that makes our relationship stronger with our inner channel will bring more creative energy into our life.

Engage with your creativity like with a dear friend.

Imagine that you have been chosen by beautiful beings of light on the other side to channel this project on your planet. There is a reason they have selected you and they trust that you have the gifts to render this energy into the physical world. You have to trust yourself and the process of creation and believe that you are capable of doing it. We can do so much more than we can ever imagine.

LOVE YOUR CREATION

Your baby has just been born. You are holding your baby in your hands and you can see their beautiful soul in the trusting eyes. All the baby wants from you is love and acceptance. This baby is your creation.

As soon as we produce something into the world, it begins its own life. Like a baby who needs nourishment and care, our new creation needs our support. We can do it by showing our love and encouragement to our creative projects.

Your creation needs your love and acceptance to grow into a beautiful being.

Your project wants you to admire it, to see the best in it, to look at it with loving eyes. Don't we all want that? Then it will have much more confidence to shine to the world. It will grow from your love and support and will respond to you with the same positive energy.

It would be hard to imagine looking at a newborn baby with criticism or a desire to change them. This would go against our nature. We love our babies as we feel the divine energy in them. The same energy exists in our creation. No child likes being scolded or feeling unloved. And so doesn't our creation. We need to give a lot of love and support to everything that we do.

Love your creation. Give it strength by expressing your gratitude and admiration.

The more we love our creation and the more we believe in it, the more other people will love it too. It is almost like we bless our creation with love and we set it on a path of recognition. We enchant it with beautiful energy and people will feel the same when they come in touch with it.

Imagine that you are writing a book. You are looking at a piece of paper, which has just been produced by your inspiration. What do you feel? How is your creation talking to you? Allow yourself to connect to the pure energy of your writing. Feel what is emanating from the paper and begin to direct your love into it.

Look at your creation and just breathe it in and accept that it is a part of your soul. Imagine that you can't judge such a beautiful part of you. Feel pure love coming from your heart and adorning your creation. You will feel the same love coming back to you.

When a child is born, they need more time to develop and grow mature. This is a part of their journey. In the same way, our creation may need some time to take the right shape. When we accept it and love it at every moment, our creation feels more confident to continue its journey and grow into a strong being.

Perfection is only an illusion in our eyes. It is how we choose to see the world and what we believe in at this moment. Sometimes things that may not look perfect on the outside are full of loving energy inside and that makes them wonderful. What really matters is the energy of your creation.

Things become perfect when we love and accept them.

Your creation is beautiful, pure and unique. It is the energy that came from you and it carries your divine essence into this world. Showing love to your creation will help you to manifest it in the most delightful way.

SOURCES OF CREATIVE ENERGY

Sometimes we may find ourselves in periods of time when we don't feel any creative energy. It is possible to get stuck in our everyday life routine and forget about our creative essence. Fortunately, there are little doorways that can take us back to our source of inspiration very quickly.

Essentially, everything that we see around us is a part of creation. It comes directly from the Source and is looking at us to remind us of our own creative self. We can find creativity in nature, in the people that we meet, in our own feelings and emotions, in life circumstances. When we look at things that make us feel happy or remind us of the meaning of life, we get one step closer to our creative energy.

To start with, nature has already provided us with beautiful masterpieces, which we can find anywhere that we look. Every day we see stunning trees, colourful birds, charming animals, perfect geometric shapes of flowers and leaves. When we go to the park, we are already stepping into the art zone where we can get a lot of natural inspiration. Nature has the power to calm our mind and connect us to our heart and soul. It balances our energy and wakes up our inner child, who is a powerful creator. You can spend time in nature and write down your thoughts, just feeling what energy comes to you in the moments of stillness.

Nature brings us closer to our Inner Creator.

Another source of creative energy can be found in the works of art already made by other people. Throughout our history talented people have given life to beautiful paintings, architectural wonders, impressive sculptures, profound scripts, which we still study and admire. These souls were drawn by a strong power inside of them that guided them to produce these works of art. They often spent their lifetime creating this treasure for us. Now we are left with this incredible legacy that we can see in museums, art galleries, streets and even our own homes. All these masterpieces remind us of our own creative nature. You can spend some time connecting to the established works of art and channeling this energy to yourself.

It is also true that when we spend time in the company of people who engage with their own creativity, we get the same vibration ourselves. Like attracts like, and people who enjoy expressing themselves in a creative way naturally bring up this power inside us. These souls are light beams on our path and they help us to reach new wonderful destinations. If you would like to have more creativity in your life, support your inspiration by finding those who share your interests.

We help each other by sharing our creative energy.

Creative energy is an alive power that shows itself to us all the time. We just need to notice it and let it take us on a journey. It helps to observe the energy at different times of the day. When do you feel creative? What sparks your inspiration? What would you like to create today? You can write down the things that make you feel inspired and then follow your intuitive steps. Let the energy be your guide.

We can also listen to the energy of creation and perceive what it is like. Creation resembles a dance, a flow, a free expression of our spirit. Anything that represents a free flow of energy will connect us to our creativity again. For example, dancing, singing and moving will make us feel freer and enrich our spirit with inspiration.

Energy of movement opens the channel of creativity.

Creativity is about forgetting the mind and tuning into the heart. It is a moment of divine inspiration, connection to the Source. Our own body can help us to let go of the mind and become free in our expression. We can practice activities that involve the use of our hands, like pottery, painting, decoration, cooking. These hobbies are great for releasing the limitations of the mind, as the energy of our hands will activate our creative powers and align us with our deeper purpose in life.

And finally: just do it. Taking a moment now and doing something that your heart is calling you to do – this is the most powerful recipe for bringing in creative energy. The simple act of expressing yourself in the present moment. So, let's not wait and let's start now!

PRACTICE TIME
CONNECTING TO YOUR INNER CREATOR

◊ Close your eyes, take several deep breaths and relax. Allow the breath to travel through your body and bring you peace and comfort. Spend some moments connecting to your breath.

◊ Now bring your awareness to your heart and feel it. Breathe deeply into the heart and allow it to grow more and more. Imagine that your heart is expanding in your chest and is bringing you a pleasant feeling of warmth in the body.

◊ Imagine that you are no longer confined in your body and that you are growing beyond it. Every breath creates more space for you and makes you expand. Feel your spirit growing and becoming limitless as a pure vast consciousness.

◊ Now feel that you are becoming bigger than your room. Your energy is expanding and expanding. There is no limit to you. You are becoming bigger than your house, bigger than your street, now you are as big as the whole city. You are embracing all that there is: the people, the trees, the birds, the houses. Feel that you connect to all that there is at once. Become endless.

◊ Feel this limitless spirit of yours and ask it: "What would you like to create now?" You have the power to create anything that you want in this world. Feel the first thing that your spirit is telling you. This is the right answer. Connect to this feeling and let it embrace you.

◊ Now see how your dream is being created. Watch it happening. Imagine all the details, the scenes, the colours, the feelings. Imagine how you and other people interact with your creation. Visualise your project in this world. This is all YOU. It is happening right now, at this moment. Enjoy your powerful creation!

◊ Let the joy of your creation stay with you. Breathe freely and happily because you are now connected to your dream. Feel the vibration of your creation in your body. You are free to create as much as you wish. Keep this feeling in your heart.

◊   After you have finished, begin breathing deeply and connecting to your physical body. Slowly return your awareness to the present moment and start to move your body gently. When you are ready, come fully back and open your eyes.

CREATING THE ENERGY FOR YOUR FUTURE

Creative energy can be used not just for the projects that we bring into the world. It also is the power that governs the whole Universe. We can align our creative energy with the flow of the Universe and shape our reality this way.

Every moment we are sending something new into the Universe. This is a very important process to be conscious about. We give the Universe a chance to hear us by thinking, talking, feeling, imagining and acting. We are, in fact, in constant contact with the Universe and we are whispering messages to it all the time, whether we are aware of this communication or not.

The Universe is listening to us all the time.

Everything that we produce by feeling, talking, interacting and visualising is creative energy. And this is the energy that the Universe takes from us as clay and shapes it into our reality according to its vibrational pattern. It is a simple process of reality creation.

We can learn to direct our creative energy to the Universe, helping it to manifest our reality on the basis of positive energies that we would like to invite into our life. We can imagine that we are the artists of our lives and we are holding colourful pens that represent our thoughts, feelings and dreams. In front of us, there is a white canvas where we will paint our future life. What colours would we choose to create our drawing?

We are the creators of our life.

Your heart and soul will help you to decide where you would like to direct your creative energy. If you close your eyes and go a little bit deeper into yourself, you will reach the right level of your consciousness where you will see your true dreams. Your soul visions are much bigger than your daily goals; you just need to connect to your heart to feel them.

Let us decide what we want to plant in our garden of life and choose our seeds with care. Every seed will send the messages of our wishes to the Universe. We can make the process of creation really joyful and pleasant if we choose our seeds consciously. And, like magic, this will allow the Universe to bring even more positive energy to us.

PRACTICE TIME
THE CANVAS OF YOUR FUTURE

◊ Close your eyes, take several deep breaths and relax completely. Allow the breath to travel through the body and release any tensions and thoughts. Turn your awareness inwards.

◊ Imagine that you are standing in a beautiful room that has a lot of light. It is a pleasant and relaxing place. Spend some time exploring it. How does the room appear to you? What do you see around you? Notice that you are holding a white canvas in front of you. Feel the energy that emanates from it. This is the canvas of your future. You can create anything that you like there. Spend a moment to connect with the energy of the white canvas.

◊ Now imagine that you are holding beautiful paints of different colours in your hands. What colours do you see? How do they feel? Explore them slowly with curiosity and joy.

◊ Let's begin to fill the white canvas with your wonderful colours. What colours would appear there first? What energy would you like to give to your future? Watch the colours painting your white canvas, almost of their own accord. Let the Universe point you in the right direction and show you what you really need in your life. Allow the colours to be very free and just observe this magical process of creation.

◊ Expand your painting. Imagine that you are adding several dimensions to it and that your painting is almost becoming alive. You are now holding a canvas that is a moving picture and shows you different images of your beautiful life.

◊ Look at your painting and feel its energy. It is emanating a powerful frequency into your magical room. What do you feel from the painting? What is the future holding for you? Imagine that you are breathing this energy in and being nurtured with your creation. Spend some moments just connecting to it.

◊ You and your creation are one now. You are completely merged together and you are enjoying feeling uplifted and being confident about your powers. Observe your wonderful room and see how it has changed since we started. You are a miracle!

◊ You can repeat this exercise any time that you like. Each time it may acquire a new perspective and will give you more details about what your soul is dreaming about. Doing this exercise regularly will also help to strengthen the energy of your dreams and enable you to have a clearer picture in your mind about your creation.

◊ When you are ready, say thank you to the Universe for receiving your dream and know that it is being worked on now. Begin to breathe deeper and allow your body to slowly awaken to the present moment and space. Move your hands and feet gently and return fully back to your consciousness.

CREATE THE ENERGY IN YOUR AURA

Creative energy expands to all aspects of our life. It enriches our hands so we can create beautiful objects, it enters our minds so we can write fascinating stories, it resides in our hearts so we can feel happy and inspired. Creative energy also exists in our aura and can be reprogrammed for our success.

We can use creative energy to transform our aura.

Our aura is the energy space that we carry around us day and night. It is a sphere of light that is made of our feelings, experiences and memories. Everything that is happening to us has an effect on our aura. If we feel down and upset, these vibrations lower our energy and the aura can lose some of its strength and colour. When we feel delighted, high energies reflect in our aura and make it shine bright with light. So, in a way, we are the creators of our own aura.

We have the power to change our energy field and nourish it with uplifting vibrations every day. If we choose to think more positively and direct a beautiful sparkling light into our aura, we can make it pure and strong. Energy Creation offers a meditative visualisation, where you can imagine new colourful energy in your aura and create visual objects of light around you. This way you can improve the energy flow in your body and invite a miraculous vibration into your life. Your energy will shift and you will feel lighter and more balanced, both physically and emotionally.

Let us create your aura based on the energy that you choose. Feel what you would like to bring into your life now to feel good. Perhaps it is a loving energy that is beaming with pink and yellow colours? Or maybe you would like to invite the energy of peace, which soothes you with purple and green? Let us imagine how this energy is appearing now around your body. Focus on your heart and direct these beautiful colours into the space around you. Feel how your aura is transforming, becoming clearer and brighter. It is almost like you are carrying a sphere of love around your body.

Now let's play with the energy of joy. Imagine how the vibration of joy would feel in your aura. It is almost like you are dressing yourself in a special outfit made of positive energy. Send the sensation of laughter into your energy field and imagine that you are bathing in a very high uplifting frequency.

Choose to emanate love, happiness and laughter into your aura.

This is how you can create any type of energy that you need just with your imagination and a positive feeling. You can start your day by imagining beautiful sparkling stars in your aura. Let them cover all your body and elevate your energy, making you feel like a star yourself. On another day, you might choose to visualise blossoming flowers and divine rainbows enveloping your body with colourful light. Every time that you add a new energy to your aura, it becomes a part of you and begins to positively influence your body and your life. Everything that you imagine becomes true, first on the energy level, and then on the physical. Feel free to experiment with Energy Creation, it will make you feel wonderful.

By creating your aura, you are creating your future self.

There are so many ways how you can transform your aura – it is really limitless! The more you are going to connect with energy, the more you will realise what exactly you need to do at this moment and the right information will come to you, like a channel.

Working with energy is truly magical and helps you to open a new chapter in your life. Explore the energy the way your imagination is telling you to, because by doing that, you are giving yourself a chance to find your own path.

CREATE THE ENERGY IN YOUR HANDS

Our hands carry beautiful energy. It is like an invisible flow of light that we turn on every time that we connect our palms. This light can be directed into the Universe and bring healing energy to the whole world around us, including ourselves.

Our hands also carry wisdom. They are the guardians of knowledge about our soul and our powers. Each hand has a special vibration that can tell us more about ourselves just by the frequency of energy. We can read information about each other by touching our hands and feeling their unique vibration. The energy of the palms gives us a story about our character, our gifts, our life path and the challenges that we go through. This energy is absolutely genuine and can be trusted because our hands reflect the frequency of our soul.

The hands are books about us that we can read.

When we focus on the energy of our hands, our inner world starts to change. Suddenly we begin to feel more peaceful and balanced. It is almost as though we touch a magical button in our body – everything starts to come back to a healthy function. Our inner energy becomes stronger, aligning the vibrations in our body and bringing us back to who we are. The subtle voice of our hands is telling us that everything is going to be alright.

If you want to start working with energy, you can follow these very simple steps. In the beginning just bring the two palms close to each other and feel the energy between them. You will notice that something begins to change and the energy is getting warmer. You might feel small tingles or a magnetic sensation. Keep your hands together and connect deeper to your own energy. Ask yourself how your hands feel and focus on the first sensations that you receive. The energy will soon expand and will appear much stronger in your palms. The key in this practice is to trust your feelings.

The energy in your hands is the voice of your soul.

272

When we hold our palms together, we create new energy. It is a simple act of manifestation, performed with our own hands. The infinite source of energies in the Universe gives us a choice of subtle vibrations to generate. We can focus on a feeling that we would like to bring into this world, for example, love, friendship, beauty, joy, peace. As soon as we begin to focus on a chosen frequency, the same energy appears between our hands and starts the healing process. It works like magic.

The more we concentrate on this energy, the more it begins to grow. Our whole body starts to change and adapt to the new frequency of light that we have just invited into our aura. It benefits not only us but also the world around us, as everything begins to transform listening to this very familiar vibration. This beautiful practice is called Energy Creation.

Our hands bring us back to our essence.

As a result of this process, we create the light. It appears between our hands and is shared with our body and the world around. This light carries a very high frequency and can perform miracles. It touches and goes into everything that it comes in contact with, connecting people to their divine power. Our hands can heal physical illness, restore the harmony in the body, balance the mind, inspire the soul and make us all connected again. The light transforms low energy into high energy, and we can create this magical power with our own hands.

Every time you create energy with your hands, you add something wonderful to the world. A part of your soul comes forward and generously reminds others of the light that they have inside. You create a positive impression in the world and others will join you as soon as they recognise their own power to create energy.

Creative energy is everywhere. But mostly it is in ourselves. Like a divine river, it travels from our soul to our heart and from our heart to our hands. Let us find the creative power inside of us and play with energy.

PRACTICE TIME
CREATING AN ENERGY BALL

◊ Place your hands together so the palms are facing each other with a little distance between them. You can do this exercise either with your eyes open or your eyes closed; both ways will benefit your practice.

◊ Take several deep breaths and focus on the energy of your hands. Imagine that it is appearing in the middle of your palms, like a stream of water. Connect to the warmth between your hands and allow this energy to become stronger. Feel that the power is growing and becoming more vibrant with every breath that you take.

◊ Let us focus on this feeling. What is the energy of your hands like? Does it feel warm or tingling? Is it strong or gentle? What does this energy remind you of? Allow the first sensations to come to you and trust them. Your energy is unique and will show itself in the right way to you.

◊ As you focus on the energy of your palms, your inner flow is increasing. Now you can begin to move your hands in the space slowly, as though you are playing with energy. You can move the energy to different sides, you can expand it and then make it smaller again, you can just play spontaneously with your hands. Follow your feelings and give in to this intuitive dance for a moment. Listen to the voice of your own palms.

◊ Now let's begin to shape this energy into an energy ball. Imagine that you are creating a sphere of light with your hands and it is growing more and more in front of your eyes. Follow your intuition and play with the energy, forming a beautiful ball of light. Just listen to your hands and let them create the energy intuitively. The ball is in your hands now.

◊   This is the most magical moment. We are holding the ball of light in our hands and we are going to charge it with energy. Feel what you would like to create in your life now: love, happiness, joy, success or health. Let this feeling come to you naturally – your energy already knows what you need. Now imagine that you are breathing this energy into your ball and it expands, like a balloon with air. Charge your ball of light with the energy of your chosen vibration.

◊   Now we need to choose where we are going to place our ball of light. Focus on your body and feel where you need this energy the most. There will be a part of you that is calling for this energy, for example, your head, your heart or your stomach. Move your hands and bring the energy physically to that part of yourself. Your instinct will guide you in a perfect way.

◊   Hold your hands there for a while and transmit the energy of your ball into your body. Imagine that the energy is flowing from your hands, like water from a jug, and it is filling your body with peace and love. You are connecting to the part of you that needs your attention the most at the moment. Feel the magic happening in your body and know that healing is taking place. Keep your hands there for as long as the energy is flowing – allow plenty of time to recharge yourself.

◊   When you are finished, relax your hands and place them on your knees. You created a beautiful ball of light! Now it is time to integrate the energy and let it soak into your body. Just sit quietly for some time to allow the energy to find its space in your body. You are absorbing the goodness of your creation now.

◊   Take deep breaths again and begin to feel your physical body. Every breath is bringing you more and more to the current time and place. Start to orientate yourself in your space and your body. Take as much time as you need to bring your awareness fully back into this moment. This is a wonderful

275

Energy Creation practice that you can repeat as regularly as you like. Every time you will generate more healing energy and receive helpful guidance from your own hands.

CREATIVITY IS EVERYWHERE

The Universe gives us an opportunity to be creative every moment of our life. There is so much that we can do around every activity to encourage the creative flow.

Creativity is a way of being.

Creativity starts early in the morning when we wake up and decide how to begin our day. We choose our first thoughts, plans, movements and actions. All of this can be filled with a new creative power and acquire a pleasant flavour of our own expression and freedom. We can invite a beautiful energy of our choice into our house and ask it to stay with us for the day.

I invite the energy of love into my space now!

The way we dress is also a form of creation. We can experiment with different colours and combine various elements together so they can complement the energy of our day. Every piece of clothing carries its special vibration and when we put it on our body, we connect to this energy and emanate it to the world around us. For example, wearing shoes of bright colours will help you to clear the energy of your path and add playfulness to it. In the same way, putting on your favourite shirt will bring you the energy of luck and help you to attract positive things during the day. We can create an incredible energy flow just with our choice of clothes.

The way we prepare our food is another form of art. There is such a beautiful variety of colours and shapes that exist in the food; we can create a real feast for our bodies when we cook. Every fruit and vegetable has its own special frequency and, when we listen to its language, we can understand what our body needs the most at this moment. You can just ask yourself what kind of food is calling you now and create a meal based solely on your intuition. Combining cooking with a loving song or uplifting words will enrich the food with even more flavour and bring healing energy into your body.

The list goes on with every activity that we can think of. You can brush your hair in a creative manner, enrich your bath with new delightful scents and colours, decorate the room in a way that looks harmonious and vibrant. Creativity lives in every step of our life.

Playfulness is a friend of creativity. Instead of following the usual routine during the day, you can imagine that you are starting a brand new way of life, just trusting the first sensations that come to you. It is almost like an invisible energy comes to you and is inviting you to be free and spontaneous.

Experiment with new things and let every moment of your life be magical.

Creativity continues throughout the day as we go to work, meet people and interact with the world. We can make our experiences special by visualising uplifting images and inviting positive energy to our thoughts. If we add love and playfulness to our thoughts and feelings, we can metaphorically decorate our routine day and make it brighter. *"I am enjoying this moment so much, thank you, Universe!"*

Creativity is an important aspect in our communication with other people. We can allow more self-expression when we talk to people, going beyond the small talk and turning to meaningful subjects instead. We can shine our soul in a conversation just by sharing what really matters to us and speaking from our heart, choosing kind and loving words. The more we use our own energy of expression, the more other people will feel drawn to us.

Creativity is about being who you really are.

Even taking a simple walk can be creative. Instead of using the same route and the same thoughts of the day, we can embark on a new adventure of a random walk. Stepping out of the house, we can allow ourselves to move in a spontaneous direction, following the voice of our intuition. We can choose to explore the small elements that we see on our way: trees, houses, sky, clouds, colours. It is almost like we are painting a new picture with our own eyes. This is creativity!

Creativity is about allowing ourselves to be who we are. It is the expression of our soul, being like a child and listening to the energy of the moment. Creativity responds to our willingness to be creative and gives us more as we step into this realm. And then life becomes truly multidimensional and so much more enjoyable.

EIGHT

THE 7TH WONDER OF THE SELF: WE CAN SHINE

We are beings of light. We are shiny, beautiful souls who came to Earth to experience life together. Each one of us came from the light and is made of pure light.

Before we came here, we used to live together in a big space full of radiant energy. It is a magnificent place where we were all connected as one. This place felt like home and there was no separation between us. We were a part of one consciousness that is pure divine light. We knew each other so well in this light and kept this memory deep inside of us.

On Earth we decided to take a separate journey and experience what it is like to be in a physical form. We chose to come as people, animals, trees, clouds, water and stones. Each one of us has chosen a part, a story and a purpose in life. We have all agreed to come here and to share this experience together.

When we interact with each other in this reality, we sometimes forget that we came from the light. Home feels so far away, like a distant memory, and we often think that it never existed before. We get distracted by the illusions of life and get entangled in our emotions, thoughts and concepts. People have given everything a name, a description, an opinion, and we tend to see the world through the strict frames that were created by our own minds.

But if we look beyond the veil of concepts, what do we see?

When we choose to focus on the energy of everything, we see a stunning picture. There is light travelling around us like currents of energy, interconnecting and uniting all of us. We see that every living being carries this light inside of them and it shines bright when they emanate love. More so, we see that the big consciousness of light is still here with us, guiding us in life and sharing its abundant love with everybody. Our home is still with us.

Every living being is made of light.

If we all remembered that we were light, there would be no more pain and suffering. Our problems would disappear in the light and we would focus on the positive energy and goodness in each other. Light is what brings us back to who we are and heals us.

Your light is unique and wonderful. It is like a mysterious book of knowledge – it contains the records of your soul journey and your great talents. Your light is also very kind and loving; it can help other people to remember their true self. The light is your guiding power and your source of energy in this life.

Your light is always with you. Wherever you go, whatever you do. It keeps shining inside of you. You cannot lose your light. When you remember your light, you feel warm and peaceful because you come back to who you are. You also feel powerful as you know that you can perform miracles in your life. You have the greatest gift on this planet – your light.

People around you can sense your light. They begin to feel better and more comfortable when they are in the presence of your light. They begin to remember their own light more and empower themselves through it. This brings them back to their essence.

You were invited to come to this planet to bring your light in and share it with this world.

Shine your light.

WHAT IS YOUR LIGHT?

What is your light like?

Let us get to know your light...

Breathe deeply and relax. Focus on the beautiful energy inside of you. What do you feel?

Now imagine your light. What is it like? Is it colourful? Is it sparkly? Is it strong? What does it bring into this world?

Become your light for a moment. Trust that it is there. It is simple.

Just remember your light and feel it. Know that it is always there and you can shift your consciousness to connect with it. Your light opens the gateway for your spiritual growth. Love your light and just be it.

Your light is with you every moment, every instant of your life. It is like an old friend, somebody who knows you very well and takes wonderful care of you. Your light brings you the best experiences in life through its loving guidance.

Listen to your own light; it is one of the most beautiful voices that you have.

Your light is your power and your unique fingerprint. It carries beautiful information about you and it makes you who you are. Your light cannot be replaced or taken away – it is a gift from the Universe that helps you to serve yourself and others. Thank you for bringing your light into this world.

Every time you think of your light, you connect more to it and it begins to respond to you. When we give our attention to the beautiful aspects inside of us, they start to expand. Your light is the same – it will get stronger as you think about it.

Let us open the path of your light.

THE BEAUTY OF LIGHT

Light is a pure healing frequency of a high-vibrational level. It resides in the subtle energy world and can enter our physical space when we focus on it and invite it into our life. Light has special powers that can bring magical changes and healing to our planet and to the life of every individual.

Light is our gateway into the positive future.

When we vibrate on the frequency of light, we feel more connected to who we are and we emanate our soul energy. This is the most genuine way of communicating with others as light comes directly from our heart and shares its true vibration with the world around.

We have nothing to hide and nothing to be afraid of when we are in the light. The light is taking care of everything. It dissolves any feelings of pain, sadness, guilt and self-punishment and it brings us back to our natural selves. Light reminds the dark energy of its natural light and, just like magic, the dark clouds in our body begin to transform into white flowers.

The natural quality of light is healing and balancing and it can work with our physical, emotional and mental aspects. The high energy of light appears instantly when we ask for it to come and it goes to the place that needs assistance the most. The light works eagerly and precisely and it knows exactly how to help us. It can heal an organ in the body, release heavy emotions from the mind, bring harmony and peace to our life. We can send light to our friends and family, create high energy in our living spaces and even direct it to the past and future. It is a truly miraculous power.

Light also helps us to resolve situations in life. If we have an issue that we would like to work on, be it a relationship, a conflict or an important decision, we can simply imagine a big ball of sparkly light enveloping this situation. We can surround it lovingly with the white light and imagine that it is dissolving the lower vibrations and filling them with a lot of radiant energy. The healing vibration of the light will transform the situation and bring us a positive change quickly.

Light is very happy to assist you in healing.

Light brings us closer together. It is as though we remember again who we are and we can interact with other people without the need to prove ourselves. We accept each other in the light and we can be compassionate about our challenging aspects. Light brings us simplicity and understanding.

It is curious that we are naturally drawn to light. During the day we enjoy sitting in the sun and bathing in its shiny rays, and at night we are invited to observe the glitter of the stars and the moon. Light makes us feel comfortable and pleasant. People who emanate light become our beacons in life and guide us towards our best decisions. In the light, we are all one and we intuitively know which way we should follow.

LIGHT GUIDES US INTO THE SPACE BETWEEN THE LIVES

When souls leave the Earth plane, they usually see the white light coming to them and calling them. It feels very pleasant and familiar and they just know that they need to follow it. This is how the souls are guided to pass on to the next level. The light comes as a helpful hand and guides us gently from this life into the space between the lives.

There we are greeted by our guides and the soul family in a warm and kind environment and we are invited to review our lifetime. We watch our life on a big screen made of light and we make our own assessment of our experiences. Shall we come back and learn more? Or are we happy with the way we lived it? What have we achieved and what lessons have we learnt? This review helps us to understand our spiritual progress and make decisions for the next lifetime.

There is a lot of light exchange that is happening on the other side. The beings there are made of light and they understand each other instantly through telepathic connection. You know immediately who is who and what they are saying to you when you look at them. For example, you can recognise a member of your family just by the unique vibration that they emanate. This gift is coming back to Earth now. We are beginning to remember the ability to read energy and communicate through light again. The other side is teaching us this knowledge and we can receive it in a meditation or a regression session.

In QHHT sessions, people usually describe the life between the lives as a beautiful place where everything is made of light. It often looks like an energy version of our planet, operating on a very high frequency. This place also has nature, fountains, castles, libraries, healing sanctuaries and wonderful locations, which are all made of light energy. It is a divine place to be in! When clients regress to this space, they often experience deep emotions, such as love, peace, joy and they feel the connection to important knowledge. It is important to realise that we can all communicate with this place and gain information from it.

Often souls receive beautiful healing on the other side. They are bathed in a colourful light made of a healing vibration which helps them to release the lower energies from their body. Especially the souls who have had difficult lives need to have a good rest before they continue their journey, so they are invited to the healing sanctuary to bathe in the light. This takes away the pain and clears the heavy memories from the previous incarnation. They can spend as much time as they like on the other side and then choose to incarnate again to learn more lessons and grow spiritually.

PRACTICE TIME
CONNECTING TO YOUR INNER LIGHT

◊   Close your eyes, take a couple of deep breaths and relax. Breathe slowly and deeply for some time until your body and your mind begin to feel comfortable and at peace.

◊   Focus on your heart and imagine that there is a little light shining in there. Connect to it for a moment. It is your own flame. Feel this light and let it appear more and more in your imagination. What is your light like? How does it feel to have it in your heart? Explore it with your sensations.

◊   Allow your light to grow now. The more you breathe into it, the bigger it gets, like a beautiful glow spreading in your body. Let your light be free and show you who you are deep within. Feel how it is expanding in your body. Reconnect with the power of your own light now.

◊   Imagine that your light is like a flame and the more you look at it, the stronger it becomes. Feel that there is no limit to your light and you are bathing in its beauty right now. Place the light around your body like a shiny aura and relax completely into it. Enjoy being surrounded by your own light. Spend as much time as you like in your light until it begins to feel perfectly natural.

◊   Your light has a message for you; listen to it. Let it express itself and tell you something important. The message may come as a word, as an image or as inner knowing. Trust it. Become aware of the higher wisdom within you.

◊ Carry your light with you wherever you go. You can ask it to stay with you and to guide you in life. And every time that you need to listen to it, just remember about the beautiful glow inside of you and connect to it again.

◊ Spend a moment feeling grateful to your light. You can now begin to come back to your body and to the current time and space. Bring your awareness back into the room and to your physical self. Start moving your body gently and return to the full awakening.

THE HEALING POWER OF LIGHT

Light brings us back to who we are. It connects us to the highest frequency of energy, which is healing in its essence. When we think of light, we heal naturally.

Being the purest high frequency, light naturally brings the same healing frequency within us. When we communicate with light, we cleanse our energy and raise our vibration. This brings healing to our body and shifts us to the new level of being.

Light can help us with any problem or situation, both on a physical and emotional level. It can help us to heal our body, to purify and strengthen our aura, to clear our path, to heal our relationships. Light can do so many things and can be applied to literally anything that needs healing in our life.

Light is like a magical solution that can bring positive changes to our wellbeing. It is capable of the impossible, healing us from old wounds and restructuring our physical body back to balance. When we cooperate with light, we work with the highest divine power and it grants us healing.

Many spiritual healing practices are based on the power of light – for example, Reiki, energy healing, light meditation and more. People have recognised the healing power of light and they use it abundantly in their practices. Light appears naturally in meditation when we connect to the higher aspect of ourselves and receive guidance for healing.

In a way, light has its own consciousness and it comes at the right time to help us. Light appears when people suffer, when they need support, when they are ill – there are orbs of light circulating around the person's body and healing them, sometimes even without their conscious awareness. Imagine that light is like an old friend and when it sees that we are in trouble, it rushes in and dissolves lower energies to bring us peace and balance.

Light also appears naturally when we experience high energies like love, joy and happiness. It comes to people during special gatherings: at weddings, birthdays, celebrations, parties. Light comes here to support us and encourage the flow of love between us. It almost says: "I am here! Look at me and feel me. I am always with you."

Light has consciousness that communicates with us.

When we want to purposefully connect with the light, meditation is one of the best ways to do it. During meditation, we close our eyes, relax our mind and let the natural light energy come in and heal us. We can visualise light in any way that we like – for example, like a shower of glowing energy going through our body or like the radiant sun spreading its healing golden rays. Light has the power to appear when we call it and it comes to us naturally through intention.

Light comes instantly when we call it.

QHHT sessions provide a beautiful example of how light works. We collaborate with the Subconscious in order to find out what kind of energies are affecting a person's life. The Subconscious scans the body and detects the areas that need healing, explaining why they are experiencing a certain issue. In most cases, there is a connection between an ailment and the person's emotions, either from the present or from the past.

Then the Subconscious decides how they want to help the person. They may agree to heal the organ instantly during the session using the white light. Sometimes they may choose to do it gradually and ask the person to work on it themselves so they can learn a lesson from it. This happens because some ailments are messages from the person's soul that they need to understand in order to grow spiritually. For example, in one session, a lady asked about a small red mark on her hand that she couldn't heal. The Subconscious gave an interesting explanation and said that it was a 'reminder' about her life purpose. They explained that if they removed it, she could forget what she needed to do in this life. But once she stepped on her life path, the mark would disappear.

When the Subconscious heals the body, they always use the light and high-frequency energy. They summon the white light into the body and begin to clear the dark places, bringing the balance into the organs. This helps to release the pain and negative feelings from that area. Very often, the person will actually feel the light and say that it is going through their body and healing them. It comes as a warm and pleasant sensation that they often describe as tingling.

Light can restore the energy flow in the body and release the toxins. It balances the body and cleanses it from the energies that don't serve it anymore. On many occasions, minutes after working with the body, the Subconscious will say: "It is done." This means that they have finished working with the organ and brought it to complete health and harmony.

It is truly beautiful to watch the Subconscious healing the person. One can feel the higher wisdom coming through and giving us genuine guidance and help. The Subconscious is capable of removing the physical pain from the body, clearing emotional blockages and bringing new rejuvenated energy. It can even dissolve the harmful substances from the body and create new healthy cells. Light only works for the person's highest good and will do the healing in the most natural and safe way.

Light can create new cells in the body and perform miraculous healing.

Now is the time when we can bring our healing gifts back. We no longer have to rely only on external help to heal our body. We have the unique power inside of us. There is an incredible source of healing that supports us all the time and brings the harmony back into our life. This is the power of the Light.

PRACTICE TIME
WHITE LIGHT HEALING MEDITATION

◊ Close your eyes, relax and connect to your inner self. Begin to breathe deeply and allow your body to feel calm and peaceful. Direct the breath through your body and release any tension or heaviness that may be there.

◊ Imagine that you are walking in a beautiful place of your choice. It can be a green forest, a sunny meadow or a wonderful beach where you can relax and enjoy some time. What is it like there? What do you see around you? Spend a moment connecting to your beautiful place and visualise it in every detail. Feel the calming energy of nature as you relax deeper and deeper into it.

◊ Look up into the sky and imagine that there is a beautiful white light coming to you from above. It is bright, sparkly and glistening. This light comes directly from the Source and feels warm and inviting. Connect to the light and feel its presence. What is it like?

◊ Now the light is coming down and is gently touching the top of your head. Imagine that the light is like the gentle caress of somebody who loves you and cares about you. It is kind and pleasant and it is touching your head softly. Allow any sensations that come to you at this moment.

◊ The light is entering your head and spreading inside like a shower of bright light. Feel how it is washing every part of your head like crystal water that has healing powers. It touches the front, the back, the sides of the head. Relax and release any tensions from your head as they dissolve in the healing light. Your mind is getting clearer and your thoughts are disappearing.

◊ Now allow the light to travel to your eyes and begin to heal them. Imagine that warm waves of healing energy are bathing your eyes from all sides. You are cleaning your eyes with the white light and allowing them to be peaceful and relaxed. Release any impurities or tensions from your eyes and let them breathe freely.

◊ The light is travelling to your nose and washing all the organs in your breathing system. Allow the light to balance your breathing through the nose and cleanse the passages. Feel how the light is also travelling to your ears and washing them with its healing power. Notice that your hearing is improving as the light is working with your ears. You will know exactly which parts to touch and how to work with them if you listen to your intuition. Relax into the light.

◊ Feel that the light is healing your mouth now. It is filling this space like a white glow made of energy. Allow the light to gently treat your gums and give them vitality and strength. The light is clearing any lower emotions and stress from your jaw. Imagine that the light is touching every one of your teeth and enveloping them in a clean, sparkly energy. The light is cleansing and healing your teeth and is travelling all the way from the roots to the enamel, making your teeth strong and powerful.

◊ Now the light flows down your throat, creating a tunnel of light there. It shines on any impurities or tensions and releases them gently as they disappear in the light. You can even open your mouth slightly to feel more of this healing power entering your body. Feel how the light balances your throat and allows it to function perfectly. It is helping you to express your truth more freely and gives you the power to formulate your words in a beautiful way.

◊ From the throat, the light travels down to your bronchi and your lungs. Breathe deeper to invite as much light as you can into your chest. Feel how the light is entering every cell in these organs and cleansing them so they can function perfectly. Imagine that your respiratory system is a tree and the light is entering every branch and every leaf on that tree. All the impurities are being cleansed and you can breathe deeply and fully.

◊ Now there is so much light in your body that everything appears to be shimmering bright. Allow the healing energy to travel to your heart. All the light is concentrating in your heart now, forming a beautiful ball of white light. Your heart is a treasure box that needs a lot of love. Let us give it to it right now. Feel all the old pain and hurt dissipate in the power of the white light. Release and forgive everything from your heart now. You deserve to carry this light in you and enjoy your pure divine energy.

◊ From your heart, the light is growing even more. Visualise how beautiful shiny wings are opening up and expanding from your back and your shoulders. What are your wings like? How do they feel on your body? Imagine that they are moving gently now. How would you move them? Allow the wings to take away any pressure or heaviness from your shoulders and upper back. You are light, you are weightless. Enjoy the wings giving you freedom and the energy of love.

◊ Now the light is washing the energy down your arms, like a beautiful sparkling shower. It is taking away any pains from the joints and the bones and it is helping your arms to be strong. Allow the light to go all the way down to your hands and feel how they are vibrating with shimmering bright light. There is so much healing power in your hands now. Hold this pleasant sensation for some time and enjoy feeling the light in your palms.

◊ Now let us work with your spine. It deserves a lot of healing as it is helping to hold your body. Imagine a pillar of radiant white energy enveloping your back and giving it strength. Fill every vertebra with the white light and let it become clean and balanced. Wash your spine several times up and down with the white light. Visualise that your back is becoming straight and sturdy. Work on the areas that need your help the most and support them with the light.

◊ From here we move to the stomach and the digestive system. Allow the light to enter your solar plexus, a very important part of the body that needs love and care. Feel how a big ball of shiny light is appearing in your stomach and giving healing to all the organs in your digestive system. Envelop that part of your body in the bright light, washing and purifying any organs that need healing: stomach, liver, pancreas, gall bladder, colon. Let the light direct you in the right way as it knows exactly what needs to be healed.

◊ Now let's move to your sacral area, the reproductive organs. All the light is gathering there now. Feel how the light is transforming the energy in your reproductive system, cleansing it and filling it with love. Imagine that the light is liberating your sacral chakra and raising its frequency. Every organ is beaming with shiny bright light. You are free to flow and to create whatever you like.

◊ Finally, the light is moving down the legs, through your knees to your feet. Feel how your legs are getting stronger and more balanced as the healing energy is bathing them with powerful light. Release all the weight from your legs into the ground and liberate yourself from any heaviness or attachments that you might be carrying. Feel the freedom in your legs and allow yourself to walk confidently in the direction of your path.

◊ Now all your body is shimmering bright and you can feel a shiny sphere of white light surrounding you. It is protecting and guiding you in life. Feel how the light is vibrating in every organ, in every cell, making your body emanate the pure frequency. Feel gratitude to the white light for doing the healing and bringing you the perfect balance. You are one with the light now.

◊ Start breathing deeply and begin to slowly return to your full awareness. Feel your body and orientate yourself physically in this time and place. Feel that the white light is still with you and you are carrying this beautiful frequency day and night. Enjoy the healing light!

DISTANT HEALING

Light travels through time and space. Like a shining star, it spreads its unique healing vibration across the Universe, touching different places and times.

While living in a physical reality, we don't always realise the power of the light. It is truly incredible and can perform miracles beyond our imagination. Light can travel with the power of our intention and bring healing to distant places and people who are far away.

Light heals through time and space.

When we think about somebody in our life, we tend to believe that true communication only happens when we are in physical contact with each other. While it is true that we connect well in the actual presence of each other, there are other powers that connect us deeply through distance too. Such are our thoughts, feelings and currents of subtle energy that constantly travel between us in time and space.

If we spread the light through these invisible currents of energy that connect us, we will send healing energy to each other. It is like communicating on the phone but using healing energy instead of the signal. Imagine how the light is travelling through a tunnel and reaching the other side with a cosmic speed. This is what happens when we send healing to another person.

We can heal each other by thought, imagination and energy.

The beauty of light is that it travels instantly and we can send it to any corner of the world, regardless of where the receiving person is. You may be in one country and your loved one may be travelling on the other side of the world and you can imagine that the light is reaching their body and their aura. They will receive it immediately.

One of the ways to send distant healing energy to somebody is to visualise them surrounded by the white light. You can imagine the person as they are, or as they appear to you at that moment, and then begin the healing work, in a similar way as we did in the white light meditation. You can visualise the light touching their head, their heart, their solar plexus and their aura. Imagine that the light is working especially strongly in the areas where the person needs help the most. Usually, the light will just guide you in the right direction and you can go through the whole process intuitively.

As the light has a consciousness of its own, you can communicate with it while doing the healing. For example, you can ask the light for a message about the person – perhaps they can tell you something that can benefit their wellbeing or empower your healing work. You can also ask the light to keep working on the person and stay in their energy field for as long as the healing is needed. This will help to continue the healing process even when you are not meditating on it consciously.

Your intuition will be your guide in the process of distant healing. Sometimes you will feel inevitably drawn to helping somebody and the feeling will be just right. Then you know that you have to follow your inner guidance and work on healing. Other times, you may feel that you should not interfere in the healing process of the person and a word of prayer will be enough. In this case, the energy may be telling you that it is better to leave the situation to develop in its own way.

Listen to your inner healer and let intuition be your guide.

Interestingly, healing energy can travel not only through our physical realm, but it can reach other realms too, such as the life between lives. Even if the person whom you would like to help has already left this plane, you can still send them light and healing. They may need it on a spiritual level and it could help to improve the soul connection between you two. In this case, you can visualise the person just in the same way as you do with distant healing and envelop them in the healing glow of light.

Not only space but also time is a vehicle for the travelling of the light. Time is an illusionary concept that we developed in order to function in the physical realm of this dimension. Outside of this realm, time doesn't exist as such. On numerous occasions in QHHT sessions, clients have reported being in a timeless zone when they leave the body in a past life and travel between dimensions freely.

Time is an illusion; thus, we can send healing energy through it.

Light is a magical solution that we can send to our past, present and future. You can imagine how the light is entering a scene from your life and dissolving any lower energy that may be there. Visualise the scene being transformed and becoming brighter and clearer. As you are doing it, the light will work on your current energy and bring healing to the present moment as well. All the times are connected and you can direct the light to any part of your life that you like.

As we heal the past, we heal the present and the future at the same time. All is one.

Working with the light to heal people in your life will significantly help to ascend your spirit. As you cooperate with the light and spread it for the highest good of others, light will come through you and touch you with its divine power too. You get healed as you heal.

Your spiritual growth is accelerated when you are on the path of helping others.

More and more inner guidance will come to you as you begin the process of healing work. You will intuitively know what you need to do in order to help somebody and heal them. The energy understands a good intention and will respond to you with a helping hand.

PRACTICE TIME
HEALING THE PAST, THE PRESENT AND THE FUTURE

◊ Close your eyes, take several deep breaths and relax. Allow the breath to travel gently through your body and relax every part of yourself. Imagine that your thoughts and tensions drift away with deep slow breaths.

◊ In your imagination, see yourself as you are right now in your life. Imagine what you look like, where you are, what you do. See the details of your current moment in life as much as you can. Notice what you feel about yourself as you are looking at this image as an observer. How does this person feel? What would you like to tell this person? Interact with them gently and lovingly. Feel how much you appreciate yourself and how grateful you feel for who you are.

◊ Now this energy is becoming bigger and is taking us into the past. Imagine that your past is like a timeline, with all your experiences, happy and sad moments, all the people that you have met in your life and all the places where you have been. Let us now collect a lot of light and send it into the past to all the situations that you have ever had in this life. It is like a powerful wave of light rushing into the past and cleansing and healing all the scenes that happened there. Let the light do the work, just visualise it. Feel if there were any blockages in any parts of your life; let them be dissolved with your love. Do it going back in time up until the moment when you were born. Empower yourself as a newborn with the white light. Feel how you are becoming free. Your intuition will guide you perfectly.

◊ Feel the love in your heart. Now allow this love and light to travel into the future, to all the experiences that you are going to have. Open your heart completely and let the energy of light shine into the future. Feel how you are blessing every moment of your future and giving love to yourself in every scene of it. Ask the light to look after you and to give you the best experiences according to your life purpose. Feel this sparkling light empowering every moment of your future life. You are creating miracles in your life right now.

◊ Now all your lifelines are shining bright and sparkly. Feel how the light is travelling everywhere in your life and is bringing you success and healing. You are blessed. Return all this power to the present moment in your life and see yourself again as you are now. Imagine how the strength of your past and the brightness of your future are coming together in this moment now and shining their power on you. Feel that there is nothing that can stop you from doing what you want and becoming the person who you want to be. Stand proud, full of white light and sparkling energy now. You deserve to receive all this

297

power. Your aura is becoming shinier and shinier; you are beaming your light into the Universe. You are a Master now.

◊ Breathe deeply again to start bringing your awareness back into the body. Enjoy the peaceful relaxing state that you have created for yourself and bathe in it, feeling how your body is gently returning to the present moment. Rejoice in this moment here and now, and return your full awareness to this time and place. Thank you!

ENJOY EXPLORING YOUR LIGHT

Your light is your very special friend. It loves you and cooperates with you whenever you invite it. It enjoys smiling, laughing and having a good time with you. At the same time, your light is a strong power that can transform your body and bring you perfect balance and harmony. Light is here for all of us to share with each other and benefit from.

Light gives people the mirror of their own healthy selves.

If you take the light in your hands and show it to other people, they will shine. A part of them deep inside will recognise that light and will want to know more about it. You will gently remind people of how beautiful they are and how miraculous their energy is. They become their own healers.

By giving light to another person, you are helping them to heal.

Light is limitless and can help you in so many ways. If you nourish your body and soul with the light, it will begin to work for you. You can bathe every cell of your body with light and imagine that your aura is expanding. The body will start to heal and the energy will take care of itself. Light is the most natural and beautiful healing power that exists in the Universe.

Be patient and gentle with the light. Trust it. It works the way it is supposed to work and knows exactly how to help you. Believe in the power of the light and let it come into your life and bring you a positive change. By doing this, you are giving respect to the light and it will respond to you with the same.

Deep inside you know, and deep inside you trust. Don't question.

The light will show you the ways you can heal yourself. It will connect you to the right people, it will shine on the paths that you can take and explore, it will select the right books in the bookstore and make you pay attention to them. Imagine that you are just sitting on the wave of light and it is taking you through life effortlessly and bringing you the right experiences. And so it is.

YOUR LIFE PURPOSE

Everybody who comes to this planet has a life purpose. It may be to help other people, it may be to learn how to love yourself, it may be to bring a positive change to this planet or even just to enjoy your time here. Your life purpose is written in your life plan, which you choose before incarnating on Planet Earth.

In the plan there are several selected options for your stay here: you chose your body, your family, your country, your life lessons and your purpose. All this planning is done in the space between the lives, where we decide with the members of our soul family and our guides what life we are going to choose next. We base our decisions on the lessons that we want to learn in order to grow spiritually. People often get very emotional when they find themselves in the space between lives as they remember about their bigger purpose on this planet.

When we are on the other side, we just know what is good for our soul development and further education in the physical realm. We choose life experiences according to the aspects of our soul that we want to improve. For example, souls sign up to learn love, compassion, patience, acceptance, kindness. These lessons often look simple from the other side but when we come here it becomes more complicated, because the Earth is full of different energies and we can get distracted from our essence and forget who we are.

The fact that we forget our past lives is for a reason, because if we remembered everything it wouldn't have been a test for us. Imagine going to school when you know all the answers already – it doesn't make much sense. We need to learn the lessons step by step, through our own experience, and this is one of the reasons why we come here.

Also, if we remembered all the information about our soul journey, it would be too overwhelming for our conscious mind. Some people may have had hundreds of past lives – it would be very difficult to have all this information and still function well in the physical reality. We are not at the high level of consciousness yet to remember everything about our soul experiences. But we do have a feeling and this feeling is telling us that we are bigger than the human body and that we have been travelling through time and space before.

I have always had a feeling that I don't belong to this planet and that this is just a temporary experience. Only when I was twenty-six did I find out that I chose this experience for a reason – because I wanted to learn to help myself and other people. Then my life began to make more sense and I started connecting to my purpose. I believe that exploring your life purpose is an ongoing process, because as you develop and grow, more and more aspects of your life journey are being shown to you. You may start with one journey but then shift to a different path, depending on how your intuition is guiding you.

Listen to your inner voice to connect to your life purpose.

This is what we are all looking for deep inside – our life purpose. Everybody – every plant, every tree, every animal and every person – has a life purpose. This is why we have decided to come here and this is what ultimately makes our soul happy. Without it, we feel as though we are not doing what we are supposed to be doing or we are wasting our time in life.

In QHHT sessions, we connect to the Subconscious and ask them about the life purpose of a person. This is one of the most common questions that clients bring to the session – they want to know why they are here.

The number one answer that comes up is that we are here to help each other. The Subconscious often says that we have chosen this experience in order to bring light to this planet and help other people to heal. There are souls on this planet now of a very high vibration and their life purpose is to bring light to the planet. Some of them are meant to be spiritual healers, some to look after the animals, some to help nature; some are here just to spread the light by simply being here. You may be one of them.

When connecting to your life purpose, you can ask the light to show you the answer. This can be done in meditation, when you listen to the energy of your heart and intuition. Your life purpose is usually connected to the things that make you feel happy and make your heart sing. What would you really love to do if you didn't have to worry about the material aspect and the social reaction? What brings you joy? What kind of energy resonates with you? What feels right for you? Asking these questions and feeling the answer will begin to connect you to your life purpose. Then step by step, you will be getting closer to it, just by sensing it and introducing this energy into your life.

Sometimes in a session people receive a very surprising answer. For example, they may be pursuing a successful career in a bank or a corporate environment, but they realise that they want to be healers and help other people. I have had many clients like this. It is always a very touching moment when people connect to their life purpose because they remember who they are.

Trust your instincts. You already know what you are here to do. Let your soul sing you this song.

PRACTICE TIME
CONNECTING TO YOUR LIFE PURPOSE

◊ Close your eyes, take several deep breaths and relax. Feel how the breath is going through your body and helping you to relax. Every breath is calming you down and making you feel more and more at peace.

◊ Imagine that the breath is taking you back in time, into the past. We are going through your life backwards to an earlier time, when you were younger. See yourself in a scene of the past that comes to you first. Watch it like a movie. What do you feel from that scene? What was happening? Describe to yourself vividly what you see and relive it in your mind. Now go back in time even more, to the time when you were even younger. What did it feel like? Let your Subconscious choose the right episode from your past so you can remember it. Connect to it. What were your thoughts at the time? What were you experiencing? Now let's go back once more to the time when you were a child. Go back as far as you can and remember an episode from your early life. How did it feel?

◊ Now let us go back even further to the time before you were born, when you were just a soul. Let it come to you as the first sensation. What do you feel? Where are you? What is happening there? Describe to yourself what you see. Trust any sensations that come to you at this point.

◊ Connect to your soul. What kind of a soul are you? What does your soul appear like? Does it have a colour or a special vibration? Let's feel what your soul is good at. Ask yourself what your gifts are. What does your soul like to do? Feel it with your heart and energy and just trust all that comes to you naturally. This will help you to discover your inner calling.

◊ Feel that you are uniting with your soul at this moment. Imagine that you become one and that your soul is healing you. Feel that it is giving you comfort, love, support. It is surrounding you with pure light and reminding you how good you are. It accepts you fully the way you are and it looks forward to being together with you. Ask your soul: what is your life purpose? What did you come here to do? Trust the first sensation that comes to you.

◊ Feel the connection with your life purpose as your soul energy is coming to you now and enveloping you in its light. Give in to the feeling of your purpose, let it surround you everywhere. Breathe the essence of your spirit and enjoy being who you are.

◊ When you are finished, take this feeling with you and begin to come back to the physical reality. Say thank you to your soul for this special connection. Start taking deep breaths and becoming aware of your physical body. Slowly move your body and become orientated in this time and place. When you are ready, open your eyes and come fully back.

SHINE AS YOU WALK

You are a beautiful being of light who has strong powers inside. You were born like a star on this planet and you bring so much joy to other people and the world around.

The Universe would love to see your light shining bright and see you happy walking the earth. When you recognise your light and carry it with grace, the higher powers will respond to you with kindness.

You are so talented. It is inscribed in your soul and in your life path. You already have all the gifts you ever wanted to have. Just look inside and find them there. You are so beautiful.

People around you will be delighted to meet your light, and they are looking forward to getting to know you and sharing the beautiful energy with you.

Your light is your strongest power. It signifies your presence and lets others know about you. In your light people can bathe and find happiness. Let them see it.

As you are walking in the street, imagine that you are surrounded by a magnificent light. Visualise it carrying you like a child in its hands and leading you to the places where you are supposed to go.

Feel the light in everything that you see and believe. Let the light pass through every person who comes in touch with you and every event in your life. Imagine that you are wearing special glasses that make everything sparkling with light in any situation.

You can even imagine that your breath becomes full of light and every word that you say comes out like a colourful bird and makes someone happy. You are the guardian of knowledge and enlightenment.

Your hands are full of light too and everything you touch becomes brilliant. It starts to wake up, to shimmer bright, to feel love and spread it to the world.

As you are passing the trees in the street, imagine that they are full of light too, as though the trunks and the leaves have a glistening aura around them and the trees are talking to you through the light.

And if you see that the light is calling you, follow this feeling and trust this pure energy. It will lead you to new lands and discoveries and open a new chapter in your life.

In other words, enjoy your light! You are special and you deserve to be on this planet and shine your beauty. Every time you do it, the Universe rejoices and supports you even more.

Be your light.

EMBRACE THE SEVEN WONDERS OF YOURSELF

Thank you for taking this beautiful journey with me! It has been an honour to know you, even though telepathically, through the pages of the book.

I can feel your energy and your dedication in exploring your wonderful self. I know that there are precious treasures within you and they make you a very special being.

I would like to know more about your Wonders of the Self! Can you share them with me? You can send them to me with the energy of your hands through distance, or with the light of your heart. I will receive them, for sure, and I will feel delighted to know how much you have embraced your beautiful self.

Don't stop at just seven Wonders of the Self. Find more wonders! Find ten, twenty, one hundred wonders within your magical self and rejoice in them. There are so many more miracles inside you. They are waiting to come out and start talking to you. Let us invite them here now.

Every now and again you can come back to this book and read again about your wonders. They may open a different aspect of you and teach you more about your divinity. Each exercise in the practice section is made to be used several times and it will serve you later in life again. Treat this book as your friend who wants to help you and sees the best in you. As so it is.

My heart is with you and I wish you a beautiful journey ahead! Let all your dreams come true and let the intuition be the guide on your path.

Afterword

You are sitting in your light now – you are shiny and bright. How do you feel now? Did you enjoy your journey? There is more, more to come; this is only a start. I am looking at you and I admire you – you are so beautiful. You have grown, you have expanded, you have taught me so much. I am your student. You teach other people a lot, too. By being who you are, by enjoying life, by showing your gifts.

Do not be afraid of your gifts. They are here to serve yourself and others. Shine them with love and let them open up like flowers. I really, really admire you. I admire your courage for coming to this planet and having these experiences. I admire your strength as you go through life situations and you become so wise and knowledgeable. I admire the love that you give so abundantly to other people. You deserve the best! And I would like you to receive the best. You are just so beautiful.

I hope one day to read your book. I think that you can make a very special creation that the whole world would appreciate. I can see the love in your book and the care that you have for everybody else. I can also see the love that you have for yourself and your creation. Whatever you choose it to be, it will be a gift for this world.

I thank you for being with me on this journey and for connecting to me through this book. Let the light stay with you and your own intuitive power guide you through life.

With love,
Maria Zhuravleva